Masters of
OLD TRAFFORD

Masters of OLD TRAFFORD

From Busby to Ferguson, The Inside Story of the Great Managers

PETER KEELING

ROBSON
BOOKS

First published in Great Britain in 2002 by Robson Books, 64 Brewery Road, London, N7 9NT

A member of **Chrysalis** Books plc

Photographs are courtesy of the *Manchester Evening News*.

British Library Cataloguing in Publication Data
A catalogue record for this title is available from the British Library.

ISBN 1 86105 533 1

Printed by Mackays of Chatham plc, Chatham, Kent

Contents

Acknowledgements

This book is based on interviews I conducted during 2001 and 2002 with key personalities whose lives have been touched by contact with Manchester United and its managers, from Sir Matt Busby to Sir Alex Ferguson.

I would like to thank Wilf McGuinness, Frank O'Farrell, Tommy Docherty, Ron Atkinson, Martin Edwards, Sir Bobby Charlton, Lou Macari, Martin Buchan, Nobby Stiles, Sandy Busby, Archie Knox, Peter Robinson, Lawrie Brown, Ian Greaves, Francis Lee, Tommy Banks, Tony Collins, Eric Harrison, Bryan Robson, Henning Berg, Ian Donald, Alex Morrison, Don Howe, Doug Ellis, Annie Kaye, Jim Barker, Jim Smith, Chris Muir, John Maddock, Len Noad, John Bean, Bill Foulkes, Roy Hartle, Selwyn Demmy, Bernard Manning and club statistician Cliff Butler: for their cooperation and for allowing me to interview them extensively, and giving me as much of their valuable time as I needed.

Masters of Old Trafford also contains material gathered during my forty years' association with Manchester United, taken from my own archives of press conferences and interviews, and comments in the public domain relating to the world of Old Trafford during this period.

Finally, my thanks to my son Ric for unravelling the mysteries of the computer. Without him the text of this book would still be lurking somewhere within the confines of the machine. Oh for the glorious days of the typewriter!

Preface

Preparing to write a book about Manchester United can be an awesome experience. When you look on the bookshelves at the mass of literature about the Old Trafford club, you wonder how anybody can write something new about Manchester United when it appears that every possible aspect of the club, and its history, has appeared in print a hundred times, written in a hundred different ways.

Nevertheless, I have persisted, and here is the result. The story of the men who, more than anyone else, have made Manchester United probably the most famous sporting institution in the world. The men whose influence can do so much to make or break a football team – the managers. And Manchester United, since the end of the Second World War, have had in Sir Matt Busby and Sir Alex Ferguson not one but two of the greatest managers in the world game.

This is not a blow-by-blow history of the club; rather a collection of portraits painted from various angles, the story of United's post-war supremos told through the recollections of those who played for them, worked in the background, or were simply friends and followers.

Over the period since 1945 Manchester United Football Club has enjoyed extraordinary success but also faced disappointment, personal conflict and – a word much over-used in sporting contexts but, in the case of the Munich disaster, utterly justified – tragedy. These events are recalled through the pages of this book by those who celebrated the triumphs, experienced the bitterness and endured the sadness. And along the way we will seek, though not altogether seriously, an answer to the question: Who was the greatest manager of Manchester United? Is there a true Master of Old Trafford?

I hope that the story will entertain, tell my readers something new about the many-splendoured club, and underline that those heroes out there on the hallowed turf are human beings too. Perhaps we can even have a chuckle about the fearsome Sir Alex. I must emphasise that one thing this story is not is an exposé or an attempt at politicking; but I hope to have provided enough untold stories to satisfy the most avid fan, while adding a light enough touch to give you a few giggles, perhaps even draw a tear or two, with an insight into the real mood behind the scenes, the joy and the heartbreak.

It was great travelling around the country, meeting old friends again while I researched this book, recalling past times. The careers of many of them were spread over eras involving three or four of the seven managers featured in this book, so although the story is roughly chronological, there are numerous diversions and byways and we will occasionally retrace our steps. Nevertheless it has been a delight to me to take a step or two back in sequence as a different person sits by the side of the storyteller, and eventually we have got through the roll call.

Incidentally, don't miss the final chapter just because you think you know all about what was supposed to be the last season of Sir Alex Ferguson's Manchester United career. You will find there plenty of stories you did not know or that you had forgotten about.

Louis Armstrong had it just right: 'What a Wonderful World' is a life in football. Tough as it sometimes is as a sports writer following the superstars and the nearly men, and fraught as following your team can be for the supporters, there really is nothing quite like it. I've been privileged to spend all my life in sport – as a performer, coach or manager as well as a writer. When asked what work I do I like to say that I've never worked in my life, but that I've been paid all my life for my recreation and my pleasure. So please try to remember that sport is competitive, but above all it is about comradeship *and* enjoyment.

Peter Keeling

It's Matt Busby, Peter!

Masters of Old Trafford. From Matt Busby, in and beyond the time when the ground was a blitzed shell after the Second World War, to Alex Ferguson, commanding all he could see before him in his kingdom, the Theatre of Dreams.

Both men proud Scots, both at the height of their profession throughout their managerial lives. How totally different in their place and profile in the game from a man such as Jock, the trainer of Mossley, a non-league club in the Greater Manchester area – yet Jock was just as fiercely committed to a life in football as the two giants of Manchester.

Jock was a wonderful old guy who, when I was player-manager of the International All Stars, volunteered to be 'sponge man' for our Sunday afternoon charity games that raised over £100,000 in a decade bridging the sixties and seventies. Malcolm Allison, Francis Lee, George Best, Nobby Stiles, Ken Barnes, Alan Ball senior and Johnny Morris (the great Manchester United star who played in the 1948 FA Cup final defeat of Blackpool) were just a few of the names who played alongside such showbiz stars as Freddie Garrity, Freddie Starr, Stuart Hall and regulars from *Coronation Street*.

And it was with affection, allied to stereotypically disrespectful dressing-room humour, that I greeted the familiar Scottish burr one Thursday night at the hour when Jock would usually ring me, asking what the arrangements were for Sunday's charity match.

'Is that you, Peter?' came rasping down the phone.

In the time-honoured manner of football, I replied: 'What do you want now, you old Scottish pillock?'

There was a silence, and then came the words that sent a chill down my spine: 'It's Matt Busby, Peter. I'm ringing to tell you that I've decided to retire completely, and would like you to send it round to the papers that I'm calling it a day.'

There is no need to ask me what was my most embarrassing moment in a lifetime of sport!

But Matt, so deservedly honoured when dubbed Sir Matt Busby, was quick to make me feel at ease when I explained my faux pas, and we had a laugh before going on to fill in the story with his thoughts on his headline-making decision. Afterwards, to make sure I knew there were no hard feelings, he would occasionally introduce himself on the phone to me with: 'It's the old Scottish pillock.'

That was during the summer of 1971, two years after he had stepped into the background to allow Wilf McGuinness to take over the team in a partnership which in later times would have been termed manager and coach. But Wilf's tenure in the hot seat at Old Trafford was brief – only from June 1969 to December 1970, when Sir Matt returned to take full charge until his final retirement seven months later.

It was a virtually impossible act to follow for Wilf, who was, is, and always will be totally devoted to Manchester United. Nothing sticks in my mind more vividly than his enthusiasm at the press conference held to announce that he was taking control of team matters. Chairman Louis Edwards introduced him, revealing that the club had received 65 applications for the job. Quick as lightning, with the repartee that has since earned him more money as an after-dinner speaker than he ever earned in football, Wilf added: 'That's right, and they all came from me.'

The great 1968 European Champions' Cup winning side was growing old together, and selective pruning and strengthening had been neglected. But Wilf McGuinness, who was younger than some of his players, was not the man to do it in his first managerial job. And the presence of players who were icons in football history did not make it any easier for him. After all, there are few players who would cut short their careers, even to help a friend.

So Wilf, a member of the backroom staff with Alf Ramsey's World Cup winners in 1966, joined the club of those managers who instead of a turkey have been given the sack just before Christmas. Directors through football history do seem to have a finesse in these things, don't they?

Yet few of those directors thought in their wildest dreams that they were embarking on a period during which United would fail for 26 years to follow up their English championship win of 1967, that they would not win the coveted title again until the first Premiership League season of 1992–93.

Frank O'Farrell, who followed Busby's second spell, was next to fail; but he was only given from June 1971 to December 1972 when promised three years to turn things around. More patience was shown to the ebullient Tommy Docherty, who lasted from Christmas 1972 to July 1977 and would probably have won the title back but for the directors' wives getting upset about his affair with the wife of physiotherapist Lawrie Brown.

The fans loved the Doc, but he had to go. Tommy left under a cloud, and the wise-cracking manner that had endeared him to everybody at the club suddenly took on a different aspect, chairman Louis Edwards pointedly saying at the induction of Dave Sexton as his replacement: 'It will be nice to have a gentleman as a manager.'

Introvert Dave certainly was, but a great coach. Not unexpectedly, there was no slick repartee from him at the top table as the world's press waited for his words of wisdom. Perhaps it wouldn't have gone down well in any case if he had cracked the joke that was to be told a thousand times by comedians at dinners and shows where the Doc was a guest of honour: 'Tommy, I wouldn't have sacked you. I'd have paid you to run off with my wife.'

Sexton was a soccer purist, who thrived on organisation and planning, and he inherited a team that his controversial predecessor had steered to the 1977 FA Cup final and a superb Wembley defeat of Liverpool. But success like that was not to be repeated in the Sexton era; there were no trophies for Dave. He left, however, with a unique record: the only Manchester United manager to be sacked after winning his last seven games.

The end came in April 1981, and there followed many spectacular performances under the extrovert Ron Atkinson, who reigned from June '81 to November 1986. The sacking broke his heart but not his spirit; on the night he was given his cards he called his players together for a massive party at his house. Chairman Martin Edwards was not invited.

In any case the much-maligned Old Trafford executive was busy planning his trip to Scotland to make the signing of Alex Ferguson that was to change the course of Manchester United's history. At last Sir Matt Busby's achievements were to be matched, and, in terms of League championships, surpassed.

The Nightmare Years were soon to be over. The day was dawning when the Theatre of Dreams would produce spectacular success that in modern times only Liverpool, with their Champions' Cup feats, have surpassed.

Even then there was heartache for Alex Ferguson before he set Manchester United on the road to glory. But things never were easy for the club, even in their greatest days.

In 1902 Newton Heath football club, on the verge of bankruptcy, had been renamed Manchester United. Within seven years United were winning their first League championship title, by nine points from Aston Villa and Manchester City. The next year they beat Bristol City in the FA Cup final at Crystal Palace, only to have their top players suspended by the Football Association after the game for supporting the Players' Union.

United moved to Old Trafford in 1910, and there has never been a dull moment since. They won the Championship again in 1911, relegating Aston Villa and Sunderland to second and third place. In the opening year of the First World War three players were banned for life over a bribes case, the shock waves from which carried over to the 21st century. There were stories that burly centre-forward Enoch 'Knocker' West had been wrongly banned, a campaign that took my mind back to the early sixties when I interviewed Knocker. He didn't seem in any doubt then that he was one of several guilty players.

After the war a major blow came when the famous Billy

Meredith, who had starred in that 1909 FA Cup final, crossed the city to play for Manchester City.

Secretary-manager John Chapman was suspended from October 1926 to the end of the 1926–27 season by the FA 'for improper conduct', a verdict that was never explained or contested. Sufficient to say that former player Lal Hilditch took over as manager for seven months, to be followed into the job by a former referee, Bert Bamlett, who had little success and eventually took United down into the Second Division in 1931.

It took over a year to appoint a new manager, but Scott Duncan was probably Manchester United's highest profile pre-war boss, lasting five years. Perhaps he was unlucky to be in charge in a decade when Manchester City were winning the English championship in 1937 from Charlton Athletic and the FA Cup in 1934 from Portsmouth, while Herbert Chapman was taking Arsenal to three successive First Division championships, thus repeating his feat with Huddersfield Town between 1924 and 1926.

Apart from two promotion seasons from the Second Division the thirties were devoid of real success, but in the background scout Louis Rocca was setting the stage for the Busby era, and Jimmy Porter seemed to be running the team as the Second World War approached.

The whole situation of the knowledgeable and likeable Scotsman who went on to manage nearby Rochdale seems shrouded in mystery. Nobody at Manchester United admits that Mr Porter was ever manager of United, and as far as the records go he is the invisible man of the club. However, respected scout and former Bristol City assistant manager Tony Collins and distinguished sports writer Len Noad insist that he was in charge of the team as manager when war broke out in 1939, and that he produced much of the talent that formed the nucleus of the side taken over by Matt Busby in 1945.

When I went to see him at home in Torquay Len, now long retired from the hurly-burly of the media, insisted categorically: 'Jimmy Porter was appointed manager of Manchester United in 1938. It's not something I would easily forget because it was my first big scoop for the old *Topical Times*, and we were the only newspaper that knew he had been appointed. The sports pages weren't as important then as they have become, and Manchester United were certainly playing second fiddle to Manchester City at that time, so it wasn't really sensational news at a time when all the publicity belonged to Maine Road.

'But there was no doubt that Jimmy Porter was still manager when war broke out. He had about a year in charge and in that short time proved himself a one-hundred-per-cent football man. I know for sure that he never got the credit in football that he deserved.

'When Scott Duncan left for Ipswich Jimmy took over, and there was no doubt about him being in charge during that year. In fact, I remember when I used to go down to Old Trafford for an interview with him he always used to send Louis Rocca to the kitchens to cook a steak for us both.'

Tony Collins, later to be chief scout at Old Trafford and Elland Road as well as having a successful career in management, backs up Noad's story: 'Jimmy Porter was an amazing man. There was nothing he didn't know about the game, and his contacts were all-embracing. He had a dry sense of humour, and he certainly managed Manchester United before the war, but incredibly you won't find that fact in any record book. I don't understand why it was covered up, and Jimmy never got the credit he deserved, but I do know that the team that Matt Busby took over was Jimmy Porter's team.'

Busby was not much older, at 34, when he took over the reins of the club he was to take to greatness, than Wilf McGuinness when he succeeded Busby in June 1969. Matt had endeared himself to the supporters of none other than Manchester City in the mid-thirties. He first came down to Manchester on 11 February 1928 to sign for City from Scottish junior club Denny Hibernians. As an inside forward he had so little success that he was about to pack his bags when he was asked to play half-back in the 'A' team. His midfield career took off so well that he played 202 League games and two FA Cup finals for City: the 1933 final when Everton beat City 3–0 and the following year when the Blues of Manchester defeated Portsmouth at Wembley 2–1 through two goals by Freddie Tilson.

In the abdication year, 1936, he signed for Liverpool from Manchester City for under £10,000, captaining Scotland during the

Second World War when he served as a sergeant-major instructor. On his demob Manchester United reacted quickly when he made it known that he wanted to settle in Manchester after the war.

Liverpool had tried to tempt him to stay as player-manager; but his destiny lay at Old Trafford, and Jimmy Porter and Louis Rocca had given him a foundation to work on. There was no greater rock for a team to be built on than the formidable Allenby Chilton; while Johnny Carey, a born leader, striker Stan Pearson with his darting runs, the crafty duo of Charlie Mitten and his pal Johnny Morris, and men such as the brilliant Jimmy Delaney and the immaculate Henry Cockburn, a dapper midfield general who one could picture covering the midfield areas with a field marshal's baton under his arm, were all on the club roll call.

Not a bad legacy, and by 1948 Matt had teased and tormented them into shape to such an extent that they trotted out at Wembley and scored a shock 4–2 victory over Stanley Matthews, Stan Mortensen, Harry Johnston and their Blackpool mates in the FA Cup final. It was a victory as important to the career of Matt Busby as was the 1990 Wembley defeat of Crystal Palace that kick-started Alex Ferguson's Old Trafford career. For it was Manchester United's first FA Cup final victory since 1909 and the club's first major trophy since the English championship victory of 1911.

Even then the full realisation of the Busby story could not be guessed at. Sir Matt had started without a ground, Old Trafford having been blitzed in the Second World War so that the peace began with both Manchester City and Manchester United playing at Maine Road.

And as if that was not handicap enough, the Munich disaster of 1958 decimated the Busby Babes who would have changed the face of European football had they been allowed to flower. Real Madrid's proud record of having won the first five European Cup finals, from 1956 to their fantastic 7–3 defeat of Eintracht Frankfurt in Glasgow in 1960, would surely never have withstood Duncan Edwards and his team for five years.

The man who had started his managerial career with an office in a £30 Nissen hut at bombed Old Trafford, saw one dream disintegrate in the horror of Munich, recovered after having the last rites read over him in hospital and, thanks to the football wisdom, loyal support, graft and craft of his dedicated number two Jimmy Murphy at his side, rode the dream again right through to the 1968 European Cup final victory over Benfica at Wembley, when United became the first English team to lift the trophy.

It took 26 years and another fiercely dedicated Scot, the abrasive Alex Ferguson, before United won the English championship again. Sir Alex built a team that would consistently match the greatest in world football. How could you compare the Matt Busby story with the sensational, trophy-winning Alex Ferguson era?

As historians later asked the interminable question – Who was the greatest, Busby or Ferguson? – there were so many imponderables that the answer was as difficult as finding the meaning of life itself.

Bobby Charlton will never forget the excitement of his days at Old Trafford – from his early days with the Busby Babes through to the recovery period from Munich in the sixties, culminating in that glorious 1968 Champions' Cup final run, and then after his own foray in management his continuing association with Manchester United as a director, and an icon of the club and of English football.

There was, perhaps apart from George Best, nobody worshipped the world over in football more than Bobby Charlton. The classic story has been told hundreds of times over. In foreign lands where nobody spoke a word of English, British travellers upon revealing their nationality would find themselves greeted with the words: 'Ah, Bobby Charlton, Manchester United.' It was the passport to friendship for an Englishman anywhere in the world.

Bobby has had a unique viewpoint of Sir Matt Busby and Sir Alex Ferguson as player and club director. And, much as he treasures his memories of a team that brought him worldwide fame, he admits that he has never been as excited and thrilled as with the modern Manchester United under Sir Alex Ferguson.

He told me: 'Alex has fostered the same kind of spirit that fights to the last drop that the '68 team showed in Madrid when coming back from 3–1 down. There's certainly never a worry about players going out on to the field with the wrong attitude. He's proved a great manager, maybe the best ever. He is adventurous, but the top and bottom of it is that he just wants to win, and the philosophy of the determination he transmits to his players off the field is carried over on to the field by his captain Roy Keane.

'If I'm asked which player bears his stamp most I would have to say Keane. He drives and torments his teammates to greater heights on the field, just as Sir Alex drives them forward in preparation.'

The cry after the 1999 Champions' Cup final in Barcelona was 'Lucky United', when in injury time they won a game that Bayern Munich looked to have signed, sealed and delivered. But Sir Bobby continued: 'If you were in the ground as a Manchester United man the '99 European Cup final was phenomenal. We just could not get into their penalty area, and I was thinking, if only we could get up there to disturb their composure, when in the closing minutes Peter Schmeichel started to throw himself forward. It was fantastic because for the first time in the game the Germans panicked. It didn't matter that if Peter had got hold of the ball he'd probably have kicked it over the stand: the point was that he was disturbing them. He simply broke up their defensive patterns, so that suddenly the ball fell to Sheringham and then Solskjaer, and it was over. One of the most coveted trophies in world football had been won again by Manchester United.'

Now, on the morning after the annihilation of Spanish champions Deportivo la Coruña in the 2002 quarter-finals at Old Trafford, Bobby said as we sat high in the deserted stand: 'Although we had lost to Deportivo twice in the earlier stages of the competition I don't think that means it's easier now for the big teams to succeed. While it's hard to compare teams from different eras, and considering the ability of any of the previous Manchester United teams or our 1968 team, I wouldn't suggest that any team of the past was better than what Alex has produced in the last decade.'

In view of Sir Alex's fiery reputation in the dressing room when haranguing his players, I asked how much was there an element of fear in the relationship between the manager and the players, both in the Matt Busby regime and the current Alex Ferguson reign, which to some outsiders seems more like a reign of terror.

Said Manchester United's other knight: 'There has never been any fear in the dressing room in either regime. There was no fear of Matt, even if we almost stood to attention when he spoke. Utter respect is the right description, not fear. It's the same with Alex. But there are no alternatives when Alex gives an order, that's for sure. Very few people leave Old Trafford compared to other clubs, and under Alex they know they'll get a fair crack of the whip despite the big squad system. They all get a chance. He gives you responsibility as a player and if you don't respond then that's it; but you've had a chance. If anybody stops the flow of where we are going then the manager's philosophy now is that the quicker they leave the better.

'Fans have spent since November 1986 saying a mistake has been made by the manager, only to be proved wrong time and again when his methods and his decisions have been seen to be spot on.'

As captain of Manchester United for several years, Bobby Charlton never desired to be anything other than a footballing man, remembered by his pals for his idiosyncrasies and all. Along with Shay Brennan, it was Bobby who palled up with Nobby Stiles to put him at ease after Johnny Giles, his brother-in-law, left for Leeds United. The short-sighted Nobby, whose own hero was 'snake hips' Eddie Colman, was always a favourite with the crowd, and they loved the youngster of whom Jimmy Murphy admitted: 'He doesn't look like a footballer until he starts playing.'

Remembers Nobby: 'The three of us played cribbage a lot on trips, playing for challenges, such as washing each other's socks. I look at him now as a gentleman of football who helped me when I first played for England, was once the best player in the world, and would play until his heart dropped out. He could go either side of you, and used to glide away from people attempting to chop him down. He gave me confidence, telling me not to doubt myself – and, believe it or not, he did a great take-off of Frank Sinatra.

'It was typical of the feeling for him in the game that when he had his name taken in one match, the players of both sides swarmed round the referee demanding to know why he'd been booked. The referee told us it was the only thing he could think of doing to shock both sides into calming down as the match was getting out of hand. Even on probably the only occasion he was booked it was really done as a tribute to him, and his powers of example.

'He would never lose his rag on the pitch, but he could on the golf course sometimes. He can hit every shot in the book but he can't string them together, and it really annoys him. Not that I can talk – he has good cause to know that I can throw a club further than I can hit a ball.

'But he will do anything for you. He's a fantastic ambassador for Manchester United and football, and he just enjoyed playing so much.'

European Footballer of the Year in 1966, Charlton saw during his England career how difficult it was for national team managers to succeed because of the massive expectations. Of course, he saw at first hand the brilliance of Alf Ramsey, the man who finally won the World Cup in 1966, and similarly he has sympathised over the years over the crushing weight of expectations that made it so difficult for successive managers at Old Trafford to give the supporters and the media the lasting success that they craved for.

Either side of the genuinely talented managers who tried, and failed, to bring the Holy Grail of the championship and then the European Cup back to Old Trafford, there was no doubt that Sir Matt and Sir Alex were twin colossi. When they talked about the twin towers of Wembley being pulled down, my instant thought was that they should put fifty-foot-high twin statues of Busby and Ferguson on the entrance to Old Trafford and bring the national stadium north. The Angel of the North would have nothing on the Angels of Old Trafford.

There has certainly been enormous respect for both men throughout the national, European and world game, and Bobby Charlton agrees that although the two icons of Old Trafford, on the face of it, seem totally different personalities there are many similarities; that Sir Matt was as driven and ruthless as Sir Alex.

He said: 'Matt would take longer to make a decision, and then he would have a real purge. He cleared the great '48 team out almost at one go the same year that I came in with such as Wilf McGuinness and Tony Hawksworth.

'But it's true to say that nobody in the game is quicker and more decisive than Alex.'

Like Sir Alex's times, there was no doubt that the Busby era was not all sweetness and light. Stories were rife that Sir Matt could have been more generous in looking after Jimmy Murphy financially, and that he could have rewarded his players better; but Bobby says: 'Matt loved Jimmy Murphy like a brother. He wouldn't stand up if Jimmy wasn't at the side of him, but maybe handling money wasn't Matt's greatest asset. For example, he wanted Mike England from Blackburn Rovers, but pulled out of the deal because of an £8,000 difference in valuation.

'But his personality and his presence were awesome. He was an amazing motivator, while Jimmy did the coaching, especially in the later days. If he had a weakness it was that he didn't keep up with new tactical trends, and as a player it's the manager you look to for guiding the team in new techniques coming into the game.

'When Alex came to the club he had the background of having broken the Rangers–Celtic stranglehold on the Scottish game, and he'd also won the European Cup Winners' Cup in 1983 with Aberdeen against Real Madrid in Gothenburg, and there was no doubt that he was a tracksuit manager. He's a brave decision maker, many times putting his neck on the line, notably when dropping David Beckham for the game at Elland Road when if Leeds had won they would have gone on to take the championship; but Alex once again made the right decision.'

Has he a weakness? 'Yes, he drives too fast,' was the reply.

Who was the greatest Manchester United manager? At the end of this opening chapter the jury is still out.

End of the 'Waistcoat' Managers

Former Liverpool chief executive Peter Robinson always described Bill Shankly as the man who ended the reign of what he called the 'waistcoat' managers, who ruled in a smart suit, with a flower in their buttonhole, and spent more time in their office than in any other part of the football club.

A famous former Portsmouth manager was noted for wearing 'spats', a form of short gaiter covering the ankle and the shoe, and it was true that until the late fifties, and even during the start of the Swinging Sixties, managers generally were desk-bound. Even Bill Ridding, manager of the much-feared Bolton Wanderers side that beat Manchester United in the FA Cup final of 1958, just weeks after the Munich disaster, would have been stepping into unknown territory as a manager if he had donned a tracksuit.

But even earlier, in 1945 to be exact, when Matt Busby reported for his first day as a rookie manager at Old Trafford, he set the style of today, creating a buzz of excitement among his new players as they witnessed a new phenomenon, the boss joining in practice games, showing them by example exactly what he wanted them to do.

Most managers of the time looked throughout the day as though they had just stepped out of Burton's window. Scott Duncan, the longest-serving United manager of the thirties, was certainly a snappy dresser who would never dream of soiling his patent leather shoes or highly polished boots covered by the regulation spats, by going anywhere near the training ground.

But Matt's attitude could be summed up in the footballing mantra that you will hear to this day among managers: 'Managing is a great life, but it's only a poor substitute for playing the game.' He wanted to be involved on the field as long as possible and, along with his faithful second-in-command Jimmy Murphy, he had no intention of throwing away the boots that had done him great service in League and Cup football.

His enthusiasm and attention to detail, as he talked individually to his players, illustrating what he wanted them to do, soon saw them climbing towards glory. But, for three successive years – in fact for four years out of five – United agonisingly had to be content with the runners-up spot in the English championship.

The team was evolving as he transformed the careers of Johnny Aston and Johnny Carey by moving them into defence from midfield and it was the start of greatness for United when, in the 1946–47 season, they were pipped for the title by just one point by Liverpool. Next season it was Arsenal who pushed them into second place. Portsmouth followed, beating them to the championship in 1948–49. And Matt's agonising wait for the title continued when United were again second in 1950–51, this time behind Spurs.

Along the way, there had been the confidence boost of the great 1948 FA Cup final defeat of Blackpool that ended the wilderness years – the last trophy for United being as long ago as the championship win from Villa in the 1910–11 season. The 4–2 Wembley defeat of a superb Blackpool team – Rowley (2), Pearson and Anderson were United's scorers – was described as 'Wembley's finest final', and Matt was supremely confident that he was progressing along the right lines.

That '48 side lined up: Crompton; Carey, Aston; Anderson, Chilton, Cockburn; Delaney, Morris, Rowley, Pearson, Mitten. Only three players had cost the club a transfer fee: Carey had arrived for £250, Jimmy Delaney for £4,000 and Jack Rowley for £3,500. They were all heroes, but spectators who saw him reckon that Delaney was the greatest bargain of all time.

He had left Scotland, where he had been playing international football for a decade, with the experts claiming that he was 'over the hill'. But he was magnificent, perhaps as big an inspiration to that United side as Eric Cantona was to be over forty years later.

Delaney went on to play around 200 first-team games, and teammates in United's forward line, Johnny Morris, Charlie Mitten, Jack Rowley and Stan Pearson, spent the next thirty years reminiscing about him. But then the team was packed with characters and stars. Bolton Wanderers legend Tommy Banks had his own favourite, remembering: 'Stan Pearson was the opponent I admired most.' Only one man, keeper Jack Crompton, was without an international cap. And who could forget Cheeky Charlie Mitten? Nobody loved a bet more than dazzling winger Charlie; when he was manager of Newcastle United he even purchased an extra heat lamp for the medical room so his greyhound could be given regular pre-race treatment.

If Delaney was inspirational, however, there was one phrase that, because of Matt Busby's art as a manager and coach, came to apply to the whole team: Super Reds.

Perhaps nobody was more important than Johnny Carey, whose poise and calm approach epitomised that of his boss, a combination reminiscent – albeit in contrasting style – of another Irish player and Scottish manager some fifty years later, when Sir Alex Ferguson said of his captain Roy Keane: 'He is probably the most influential player we have had at our club ever.'

It was a sign of the esteem that Carey commanded in the game that he was chosen to captain the Rest of Europe against Great Britain at Hampden Park in 1947, and during his career at Old Trafford he filled every position on the field apart from goalkeeper and outside left.

And finally, in the 1951–52 season, came the breakthrough. The League championship trophy was at last on the Old Trafford boardroom table, with Spurs and Arsenal beaten in the scramble for the finishing line by four points. Charlie Mitten had controversially left for Bogotá, so he was not at Old Trafford to enjoy the fruits of a post-war run that (until they came eighth in the 1952–53 season) saw United never out of the top four.

As usual with a Matt Busby team, the title was won in style. At the end of the season a packed Old Trafford saw them destroy their nearest rivals Arsenal 6–1 in a final match that would have seen the title decided on goal average if Arsenal had been able to win. United had led the championship race since going to the top in February and had held on grimly, before slaughtering an Arsenal side with the double in their sights. And in the end the dispirited Londoners lost both League and FA Cup after Newcastle's George Robledo scored the only goal at Wembley.

It was the season that also marked the debut of two of the first 'Babes', the great Roger Byrne, who eventually took over from Carey as skipper, and Jackie Blanchflower. Byrne went on to win twelve England caps in the three short years he had before Munich claimed him, and scored his seventh goal of the season in that final game of the championship year, a game in which Jack Rowley brought his season's total to 27 with a hat-trick.

While 21-year-old Byrne was winning his place in the team that season it marked the end of the ever-reliable Jack Crompton. United's keeper in the 1948 FA Cup final was making way for Reg Allen, although he stayed on as a player until the late 1950s and afterwards joined the coaching staff.

In fact Sir Matt's first championship was achieved on, so to speak, the cusp of two teams, at the time of the transition between his first team from 1945 and the Busby Babes. The old guard who had set Matt Busby on his way were gradually being sifted out, men such as stalwart full-back Johnny Aston, who always enjoyed a laugh when in the sixties it was said that a new system had been invented, employing what were described as overlapping full-backs. Johnny, whose son John was a hero of the 1968 European Cup final at Wembley, his burning speed a vital factor in United's victory, loved to get forward and twenty years before that triumphant Wembley night had scored 30 goals for Manchester United as well as winning 17 caps for England. But he was not lost to Manchester United, and was employed for scouting duties and coaching long after he retired from playing.

The Babes were coming together, accompanied by some shrewd signings, thanks to the tireless journeyings throughout the Football League of Matt and Jimmy Murphy, Joe Armstrong and a band of scouts. So often these days when a player is put under the microscope, you hear analysis of his speed, his bravery, his charisma and his character, all factors in the end product of a good player. But all too rarely is mention made of the basic factor the old-time scouts used to start out from – in other words, can he play football? That was always the starting point for Matt Busby and his band of talent scouts.

Matt used to laugh as he looked back on the time he gave a 'bribe' to an employee of another club, that day at Oakwell when he crossed the palm of a Barnsley employee with silver – or a pound note, to be precise – to save Tommy Taylor being burdened with a £30,000 price tag. Matt wrote out a cheque for £29,999 for the 21-year-old hot shot who had played just 44 games for Second Division Barnsley, and gave the extra pound to the Oakwell tea lady who had kept Matt and Jimmy supplied with tea and biscuits, and her anecdotes of life among the mining villages, while they waited. Around twenty clubs had been tracking the sharp-shooting Yorkshire star, and most of them had made offers. But Tommy had his eyes set on moving to Old Trafford, and Matt admitted: 'It was one of the best signings I ever made.'

He probably remains as the greatest centre-forward ever to turn out for the Reds, a wonderful mixture of Mark Hughes and Ruud van Nistelrooy. And in five short years before Munich claimed him Tommy scored 112 League goals in 166 appearances for Matt Busby's Babes, having joined the club in the same year, 1953, that ground-staff boy Duncan Edwards, at the age of sixteen, was given his first-team debut at Old Trafford. And to add to the feeling that 1953 was a watershed in the life of Old Trafford, Johnny Carey was announcing his retirement after seventeen years' service to Manchester United, having signed in 1936 for £200 from an Irish side, St James's Gate, for the start of a career that saw him voted the Football Writers' Player of the Year in 1949.

Amid all the signings made and players developed there were failures by Matt Busby and his scouting team. Notably there was an attempt to sign a man who still challenges Bert Trautmann and Gordon Banks in goalkeeping's hall of fame, the great Frank Swift, who as a newspaperman was to die in the Munich crash.

Having played with Swifty in Manchester City's 1934 FA Cup final defeat of Portsmouth, and having been a teammate for several years, nobody knew better than Matt of the ability of the keeper with a hand span of fourteen inches, who was already a legend at Maine Road.

Manchester United twice attempted to sign the former Fleetwood keeper who started his career by having to borrow his brother's boots to play in a trial; but City's directors knew that they would be lynched by their fans if they dared to let Big Frank join the 'enemy'. It was reminiscent of a period in Matt's own career; United had tried to sign him from City in the thirties, but had been unable to find the transfer money when they were asked for a fee of £150.

But Manchester United were not short of legends, and First Division championship wins by the blossoming 'Babes' were achieved in both the 1955–56 and 1956–57 seasons. Sweeping, innovative football was being produced, although the players were still not invincible: in the 1957 FA Cup final they were defeated 2–1 by two goals from Aston Villa's Peter McParland, the villain of the match after his reckless charge of keeper Ray Wood ended with the United man needing surgery for a fractured cheekbone.

Ray had played over 450 League and Cup games for United. The incident hastened the end of his career, and saw the blossoming of that of one of Manchester United's bravest keepers, Harry Gregg. The man who survived Munich and went on to be named Goalkeeper of the Tournament in the 1958 World Cup in Sweden, was recognised at the time – just as Peter Schmeichel, another of United's World Cup and European Cup heroes, was later to be recognised – as the world's best.

Poignantly the 1957 FA Cup final losers lined up: Wood; Foulkes, Byrne, Colman, Blanchflower, Edwards, Berry, Whelan, Tommy Taylor, Charlton, Pegg.

Twelve months later Matt Busby had recovered sufficiently from his life-threatening injuries at Munich to hobble into the Bolton Wanderers dressing room at Wembley and congratulate manager Bill Ridding and his team on their 2–0 victory over the remnants of his 'Babes' team who somehow had fought their way to the final, despite heavy hearts, and nightmare memories of the previous three months. In twelve months Manchester United's Wembley final team had changed to this line-up: Gregg; Foulkes, Greaves, Goodwin, Cope, Crowther, Dawson, Ernie Taylor, Charlton, Viollet, Webster. Only Bobby Charlton and Bill Foulkes made it to Wembley again.

One of the newcomers was Ian Greaves, later to become a distinguished manager with Bolton Wanderers, among other clubs. Like a number of players in that final side who had seemed to have no hope of being named for the first team when the club started their FA Cup bid in the third round in January, Ian was thrown into a makeshift side which included Stan Crowther, a stopgap transfer from Villa who was not qualified to play in the final when he signed, but was given special dispensation. Defender Greaves admits: 'I didn't know who was in our dressing room that day. It was all just a blur to me, and I can't remember whether Sir Matt came into the dressing room before the game or not.

'But I can remember Jimmy Murphy, who was in charge of the team, coming round the room, as was his custom, talking individually to every player and reminding them of their priorities in the game.

'We had mourned for our friends and shuddered at the horror of Munich for a long time: now we had to try and get the images out of our brain, and play a game of football at Wembley. We had to get on with life.'

But there was to be no fairytale ending. Two goals from Nat Lofthouse plunged United to their second Wembley defeat in two years.

As I spoke to ex-Bolton defender Tommy Banks before Arsenal's defeat of Chelsea in the 2002 FA Cup final, he remembered Matt Busby limping into the Wanderers dressing room at the end to congratulate Bill Ridding and his team on their victory. He says: 'Matt cost me a glass of champagne because with the glass in my hand I looked towards him as he congratulated us, and as I was thinking what he had gone through in the previous few months, our manager snatched the glass of bubbly out of my hand, saying: "You've been sweating all afternoon. It won't do you any good."'

One of Tommy's teammates that day at Wembley was co-defender Roy Hartle, now still on match-day duties at the Reebok Stadium, hosting the hospitality suites, and also chairman of the Bolton Wanderers Former Players' Association. He vividly remembers Sir Matt coming into the victors' dressing room to praise Bolton for their performance: 'The first thing that came into my consciousness as he stepped through the door was how ill he looked. He was struggling to get round the dressing room and shake the hands of each player, and his spirit and genuineness made me feel so small in my triumph. I still think he must have expended more energy, and more mental and physical strength, in coming to our dressing room than we had all produced throughout that tough ninety minutes. His resolution remains a wonderful memory of my footballing days.'

But even while his doctors were still telling him he must rest and properly regain his strength and that he was still not well enough to work, Matt Busby's shrewd football intellect was working overtime. He had been impressed by Tommy Banks, already an experienced England World Cup international, and had seen him as the man to hold the fort for three years or so while young Tony Dunne matured.

The following week Banks received a letter from Paddy McGrath, a close friend of Matt's, a nightclub owner and an important man in the social life of the city. Matt did not intend that Manchester United should break any rules by approaching Tommy illegally, so McGrath did it for him. Recalled Banks: 'The letter said that Manchester United wanted to sign me and that Matt saw me as the ideal man to take the club through to the time when Dunne was ready, and he asked me to go down to the Cromford Club in Manchester to talk things over.' But Bolton manager Ridding would not let his prize defender move on at the age of 29. In the end United signed Noel Cantwell, who was to become captain of the Republic of Ireland side.

Cantwell played in the 1963 FA Cup final defeat of Leicester City when David Herd (2) and Denis Law were the goalscorers. Nobody had expected it to be so easy. Leicester had Gordon Banks in goal behind a defence with one of the best goals-against records in the First Division, and they had finished eighteen points ahead of United in the League after the Old Trafford men had only just missed being relegated. But United romped to their first trophy since Munich.

And if only they knew it, waiting in the wings was a youngster who, along with Denis Law – who had been dynamic in the defeat of Leicester – Bobby Charlton and a blossoming side of internationals, was to produce a sensational five years leading up to Matt Busby's Holy Grail, the Champions' Cup.

George Best was the name. He was poised to make his first-team debut in September 1963 along with another seventeen-year-old, David Sadler, a one-club man who went on to play over 400 League and Cup games for United.

Before Christmas George was making his international debut for Northern Ireland, and in his first season Best's inspiration was such that United finished in the top two for the first time since 1959, runners-up to Liverpool, and ready to become champions the following year. He had come to England to try his luck as a footballer, and one of the magnets, aside from wanting to play for Manchester United, was wanting to be in the same team as one of his heroes, Denis Law.

Both men were great, world-class footballers at their height, but were otherwise totally dissimilar. Law was a footballer through and through, and nothing would get in the way of his career, while George marked the moment when football became showbiz as well as a sport. You were just as likely to see George's photograph in the papers escorting a film starlet, modelling clothes, being thrown out of a nightclub or posing for a lucrative TV commercial, as playing football for Manchester United. Don't get me wrong, George's overriding passion was his football...but he had lots of other passions as well, and beauties they were too.

And I was reminded of how life and times change, but human beings remain very much the same, when I interviewed Annie Kaye, one of the club landladies. Her house was just round the corner from The Cliff training ground in Salford, United's training headquarters for many years until the vast Carrington complex took shape across the south side of the city. Her words reinforced just how much even the greatest icons have their own heroes. She told me of the day a young lad called David Beckham, fresh from school in London, had knocked on her door, little realising he was to become as famous and adulated as George Best. Joe Brown, then in charge of youth development and scouting, said to her: 'Look after him. We don't want to lose him. He's a great prospect.' Prospect or not, to Annie they were all special, her boys, a long way from home, and in need of home comforts; but she told me: 'You've never seen a youngster so starry-eyed.

'When I showed him his room I told him that for the previous six years it had been Mark Hughes's room. Apparently Mark was his special hero, and when I said who the previous occupant of the room was tears came into his eyes. He looked as though he had been pole-axed, and said that he worshipped Mark. So you know that when he gives his own autograph now to a young fan he knows what is going through their minds, because he's been there.'

Joining up with the ever-growing Manchester United family in the sixties, Annie went on to play an important part in the development of the club under the rule of all the managers at Old Trafford from Sir Matt Busby to Sir Alex Ferguson. And she certainly did not have much time to stand and stare as she boarded homesick young lads who had travelled from all parts of Britain and Ireland to make their name.

Remembering her time as David Beckham's surrogate mum, she said: 'Even then he had a great dress sense, and he arrived on my doorstep with seven suitcases of clothes. What a difference between Mark and David, although they were both wonderful lads.

'Mark would just leave his clothes in a heap on the floor, and if it was up to him they would still stay where they'd dropped from one month to the next. But immediately David arrived he neatly stacked all his clothes in the drawers, tidied his room every day, and there was never an item out of place all the time he lived with me.

'But it wasn't all plain sailing. I remember one of my lads, Deniol Graham, who had only passed his driving test the week before crashing his car.

'He came from Llandulas in Wales, and was used to a very different way of life. I remember he used to leave the back door open, even at night, and I told him that we would find everything in the house gone if he carried on doing that. He said they never closed their back door in Wales, and he was amazed at the security we had to go through even ten or so years ago.

'He was shaking at the thought of having to go into the club and tell the boss that he'd crashed his car. He begged me to go with him to tell Sir Alex. I wouldn't have felt comfortable in going to see any other manager in that way; but he had always told the landladies that he was accessible, and regularly checked with us that everything was OK with his boys. He was marvellous when Deniol fearfully told him what had happened, and I can truthfully say that no manager, not even Sir Matt, ever took so much care with the young players under his control.'

Annie was also quite certain that the success the two Scottish managers achieved was because, despite their fanaticism for Manchester United, they were also very much devoted family men. An important aspect of that success was their ability to mould their teams into a Manchester United family. When the training headquarters were moved from The Cliff to Carrington at the turn of the millennium, and young players needed to be boarded on the other side of the city, the landladies who had served the club for so long were not released before it had been made clear how much their work was valued. Sir Alex and Ken Ramsden took five landladies and their husbands to a special dinner in the Platinum Suite at Old Trafford.

Said Annie: 'One of the most prized possessions of my life is the wristwatch the club gave me, inscribed "Presented by Manchester United to Annie Kaye in appreciation of your service to the club".'

Mrs Kaye saw great similarities between Sir Matt and Sir Alex: both displayed the caring touch that gave the club the vital feeling of being one big happy family. She rated the two knights of football 'the tops', not only as managers, but in the way they treated the little people of the Old Trafford empire.

She told me: 'Ron Atkinson was a personality, but he didn't have any time for ordinary people like landladies, and I don't think he ever spoke to me. Wilf McGuinness was only in charge for a short time, and had plenty on his plate, while Frank O'Farrell was a quiet man, and similarly there was no contact with him. He seemed a bit of a cold fish.'

She recalled that for all his ebullience there was little contact either with Tommy Docherty, while Dave Sexton was similar to O'Farrell, a 'thinker'. But she said that Busby and Ferguson showed that they were determined not to neglect the smallest area of the club. Said Annie: 'I must admit that as far as I was concerned Sir Alex was the best of the lot. One of the first things he did when he arrived at the club was increase the wages of the landladies! Sir Matt was such a nice man too, always had time to have a word with you. But Sir Alex was even more approachable. When they were training at The Cliff he always used to toot his horn and wave when he passed my house. Little things mean a lot.'

No Coaching Certificates, But They Were Fantastic

What a long haul it was: there were plenty of blood, sweat and tears to be shed between the start of the George Best era and the last three years of the Sir Alex Ferguson era that embraced Beckham, Keane, Scholes, Giggs and all the other stars of the nineties and the new century.

The great Denis Law straddled British football as he was voted European Player of the Year in 1964, despite having failed to inspire United to the FA Cup final after three titanic quarter-final battles against Jim Montgomery and Sunderland. Phil Chisnall put them in the lead in the third game for the first time in the Cup extravaganza, with the Law man scoring a hat-trick in the ultimate 5–1 victory. It looked as though the Reds were going to become the first club to win successive FA Cup finals since Newcastle United were successful in 1951 and '52; but West Ham United and Bobby Moore had other ideas, and not only kayoed Matt's team 3–1 but went on to beat proud Preston 3–2 in an electric final.

But what a season was 1964–65. There had been mayhem early in the season when Sporting Lisbon humiliated Manchester United 5–0 in Portugal after Law had claimed another hat-trick in the first-leg 4–1 victory, Busby for once losing his temper in the dressing room after the match. But eventually he was reconciled with his players as they built up a head of steam that ended with the English championship coming back 'home' at the end of the season.

It had been eight long, sometimes painful years since the pre-Munich team had lifted the title for United. Now only Bill Foulkes and Bobby Charlton remained; but they had a team of Manchester United patriots with them, none more so than Nobby Stiles, who once told me that in those days in the sixties every time Manchester United lost the critics would say that it was because they had no method, and victories for such as Liverpool and Leeds United would be because of their superior teamwork and planning. It was a popular cry of the time that Manchester United were not living up to their name because they had no tactical plan to utilise the talents of such as Denis Law, George Best and Bobby Charlton.

Says Nobby, now a popular and successful figure on the after-dinner circuit: 'Looking back to my first European games in the mid-sixties I can recall the thorough preparation. In Europe we generally used one system to contain the opposition in the first twenty minutes or so, and then changed the shape later to be more attack-minded. John Connelly and Best were match-winners for us with this system, and John scored some great goals, especially in the First Division championship season, 1966–67, that earned us our chance to go on in 1968 and win the European Cup.

'No team was better prepared for matches than Manchester United, and we went on to prove it by beating Benfica in 1968 in the Champions' Cup final at Wembley.'

Quite simply, Jimmy Murphy and Matt meticulously built their game plans on adapting to make the most of the team's talents against the strengths and weaknesses of the opposition.

They did not have coaching certificates – and neither did Bill Shankly, the father of Liverpool – but they were fantastic at carrying out the essential requirement of a coach: getting the very best out of the players at their disposal.

After Munich Matt had bought Albert Quixall for a record fee of £45,000 from Sheffield Wednesday, and he'd played his part in the resurgence with an FA Cup winner's medal in 1963; but he had ended his Old Trafford career by the time Matt Busby tasted the fruits of League championship success again in the 1964–65 season, beating Leeds United on goal difference.

Let his own words at the time tell the story: 'Never can I forget that emotional night last April when Manchester United, running neck and neck with Leeds in a grandstand finish, won the Football League championship by overcoming Arsenal. My emotions, I know, were shared by everyone in the thrilled 50,000 crowd at Old Trafford who invaded the pitch, sang and danced and shouted: "We are the champs!"

'What a tremendous occasion it was, and what memories it aroused for everyone – players, fans, and even absent admirers. I was deeply moved by the proud thought that United had become English champions again and were back where they rightfully belong, in the top class of European football. The European Cup has always been our target. My ambition is that Manchester United shall be the first British club to win it.'

The words that the man who fathered United's achievement spoke after that '65 championship win were just as pertinent after Benfica had been beaten three years later. He said: 'Rebuilding the team after Munich was a task that called for great faith and patience. We had lost eight brilliant footballers cut off in their prime, and replacing them was not easy. But slowly Manchester United began the climb back. There was some splendid talent in the Old Trafford nursery. We are now able to field a side of eleven internationals; but with the exception of Alex Stepney and Pat Crerand our boys are mostly home products who have proudly made the grade.'

The fight to get Manchester United back to the top had been no cakewalk for Matt Busby. He had been forced to endure criticism that he was finished, that he could not control indiscipline in his team – Law had a bad record in that respect and Nobby Stiles was constantly in the headlines for his – and for his apparent inability to control the excesses of George Best.

But the answer had been given to his critics. The '68 Champions' Cup win had actually been prefigured two years earlier by an incredible performance in Lisbon where, against a Benfica team who had never previously been beaten at home in Europe, United scored a devastating 5–1 victory in the 1966 European Cup quarter-finals. Best was hailed as world class after opening the scoring in six minutes and notching a second before John Connelly, Pat Crerand and Bobby Charlton completed the rout. And there were two more League championships, culminating in the defeat of Liverpool, Arsenal, Spurs and Chelsea in the race to become the first English club to be crowned European champions.

Meanwhile, it was another Scot, the great Jock Stein, who beat Busby to his ambition, winning the Champions' Cup for Scotland with a magnificent Glasgow Celtic side. The Lions of Lisbon, fielding eleven players all of Glasgow origin, beat Inter Milan, twice winners in the previous three years, 2–1 on a truly wonderful night for football.

Finally, twelve months later at Wembley, it was Manchester United's turn. Yet only weeks before, Matt had given up hopes of finally landing his Holy Grail. Having beaten Real Madrid 1–0 at Old Trafford, United were trailing 3–1 in the semi-final second-leg game in Madrid when he looked at Jimmy Murphy and said: 'We've had it, Jimmy.' But the resignation of an imminent defeat left his face as he stepped into the dressing room at half-time. He reminded his boys, who still seemed stunned from a shattering blitz of three goals in twelve first-half minutes, that they were only 3–2 behind on aggregate, and said: 'Just keep playing football all the time. You are doing great, and we are going to win this match.'

There was nothing negative in his outlook as far as his team were concerned, even though he'd just had the bitter disappointment of seeing Manchester City edge past them to snatch the League championship United had won the previous year.

The response was electric as Real were pushed back in the second half. The resilience of the Old Trafford men was unstoppable: with twenty minutes to go David Sadler pulled back the score to 3–2, and incredibly Bill Foulkes moved upfield on a long, loping run to arrive in the danger area just at the right time to side-foot home George Best's centre. The equaliser took United to Wembley and another confrontation with Benfica, already twice winners and twice beaten finalists in the sixties.

Foulkes, whose 58 appearances in Europe was a record for a United player, and who after his playing career went on to coach in the USA, Norway and Japan, as well as on the United training staff, scored only nine goals in his distinguished eighteen-year career at Old Trafford. Reliving the match some years later, he remembered: 'I was on the halfway line, and something came into my head to go into unexplored territory in their third of the field. No one seemed to want the ball and I thought my run would create some space for

George, who had been double-marked and given rough treatment throughout the game.

'Pat Crerand played it through to George, and by the time he was ready to centre he found I was the only United player in the penalty area, a fact I still find hard to believe. But he pulled a perfect cross to me, and all I had to do was side-foot it into the corner.'

Law was not recovered from injury for the reprise with Benfica at Wembley for the '68 final, while Connelly and Herd had left the first-team scene at Old Trafford; but Best and nineteen-year-old Brian Kidd were the heroes of a great win. There was to be no revenge for the Portuguese stars, just another lockout for the great Eusebio who was so tightly marshalled by Nobby Stiles that he hardly got a touch of the ball. United won in extra time, George Best crowning victory with the second goal, dribbling around the six-yard box as though playing a schoolyard kick-about before planting the ball in the net en route to the 4–1 defeat of Eusebio and his mates.

After the match and the celebration banquet that night my wife and I went with the players and their wives to Danny La Rue's nightclub, where he was introducing a new 'rookie' comedian called Ronnie Corbett. Ronnie was to go on to become one of the greats of British show business for over thirty years. But where were Manchester United going? Who would have guessed that within six years they would be relegated to the Second Division and it would be 31 years before they won the European Champions' Cup again?

Doug Ellis, omnipotent chairman of Aston Villa, was then in the travel business and helping to organise Manchester United's itineraries from his agency in Manchester. Matt had told him after the famous fightback 3–3 draw in Madrid, 'You saved me from freezing to death,' after in bitter conditions he found there was a 'no alcohol' restriction in the stadium. Ellis talked to me about the old times as we sat in his resplendent office at Villa Park: 'Matt asked me to get him some whisky. I went outside the stadium to find a shop, eventually managing to get a bottle of brandy, and risking being nabbed by the stadium police and locked up; and managed to warm him up with surreptitious sips.'

Had somebody 'shopped' Doug Ellis it would have made good headlines for the Spanish media. He was well known in Spain, having been given the Golden Key of Benidorm – the freedom of the city – by Generalissimo Franco for being the first tour operator to start package tours there, an enterprise that heavily boosted the economy of an impoverished area.

The Villa chairman remembered the day when Matt made his first appearance at the ground after Munich. 'He came into the box on crutches, and as the crowd stood to welcome him back there wasn't a dry eye in the stadium. I spontaneously shook his hand as he passed me, and tears were streaming from his eyes.'

In his darkest hour, Matt Busby could hardly have envisaged that Manchester United would become the first English club to win the Champions' Cup. But in June 1968, after that victory and two post-Munich League championships, as well as being championship runners-up on seven other occasions, he was just a year away from retiring for the first time. It had been a long, hard journey from the ruins of the runway at Munich to the glories of Wembley 1968, but there was to be no follow-up. In defence of their European title United fell at the semi-final stage, blocked out 2–1 on aggregate by Milan. Goalkeeper for the Italians was Fabio Cudicini, whose son Carlo was to join Chelsea over thirty years later, ultimately to play in their losing FA Cup final against Arsenal in 2002.

Defeat by the cynical Argentinian side Estudiantes in the World Club Championship, and the disgraceful treatment of Stiles by the referee in South America, did nothing to erode the aura of greatness around Old Trafford, and additional lustre was given through Stiles and Charlton also having been key members of England's 1966 World Cup-winning side. But it was with alarm initially that the news was greeted that the United manager, knighted for his services to football after the European Champions' Cup success, was to resign as manager and move 'upstairs' to the position of general manager.

Sir Matt said in January 1969: 'Manchester United is no longer just a football club. It is an institution, and I feel that the demands are beyond one human being. I have informed the board that I wish to relinquish the position of team manager at the end of the season.'

At the age of 58 he was stepping back; but would still devote his talents to ensuring that Manchester United remained one of soccer's greatest teams. He had put together three outstanding world-class teams, built the worldwide prestige of the club, and made Old Trafford a World Cup ground and one of the most modern and comfortable in Europe. During the 24 years he had been doing the job, he had never failed to accede to any request for his time on behalf of Manchester United, whether it be speaking to the media or the supporters or ceaselessly trying to raise the status of his club.

Once his decision had been digested by the public and the press the optimism was that his move could start an even greater era. But nobody realised what a job it was going to be to replace him, and there was at least one of Sir Matt's old boys who felt strongly that Matt and Manchester United had made one big mistake.

Ian Greaves looks back and says: 'The most ridiculous thing any club can do is keep an old manager on in some other capacity. How can the man who has been in the managerial hot seat possibly resist the temptation to make a comment if he sees something that he thinks is going wrong?

'When Frank O'Farrell was sacked I remember Matt ringing me out of the blue and asking me how I was, commenting that I seemed to be doing well at Huddersfield as manager. We chatted, but I sensed there was another agenda, and that he was weighing me up for the Old Trafford job. I rang Frank O'Farrell and asked if I could have a chat with him. In fact I went down to Torquay and spent three days with Frank, who was very disappointed about what had happened with him at United.

'He told me how difficult it had been working with Matt hovering in the background. I remember him now describing the pinprick, and then another pinprick, and then another... and then the knife. He was very upset at not being given the time he felt he needed to turn Manchester United round. But the lesson served me in good stead, because when I took over from Jimmy Armfield at Burnden Park the board outlined a plan for keeping Jimmy on at the club in some capacity. He is well respected, and rightly so, throughout the game, but I had to dig my toes in against such a move before I accepted the job. I'm glad to say that Jimmy understood my thinking, and that he and I are still good friends.'

Ian Greaves makes it plain that he had nothing but respect and admiration for Sir Matt throughout his own career as a player and manager, and that he felt that the man who had virtually given his life for Manchester United should not have been put in such a situation. He pointed out: 'How could he not care when he thought something was going wrong with the club he built?'

He played for Matt Busby from 1951 to 1959, turning out in 70 first-team games, including the patched-up side that Jimmy Murphy provided for the emotional return to League football in the first game at Old Trafford against Sheffield Wednesday after the trauma of Munich. He admits that he had looked set for a life as a gardener as a teenager, until a scout saw him playing Sunday football, and asked him if he fancied playing for Buxton at Glossop the following Saturday.

He had played only a handful of games for Buxton when he was signed by Manchester United at £5 a week. He soon caught the eye of Matt Busby in a third-team game, after which the boss called him across and told him that he was going to sign him on full professional terms. He was then 21 and remembers: 'Then it was a question of getting to know Matt Busby at a distance, and even the big-name first-teamers seemed to me to be on another planet. Initially only that great little midfielder Henry Cockburn gave me any encouragement as I tried to show that I was as good as the next man as a centre-half; but one particular incident reminds me that not everybody agreed with me. No player had a car in those days, in the fifties, and after training one morning I was waiting at the bus stop, and found myself next to Allenby Chilton, Mark Jones and Ronnie Cope.'

These stars recognised him from the training ground. Chilton, a craggy, aggressive man who played twice for England, and was in United's classic 1948 FA Cup final against Blackpool and Stanley Matthews, said: 'Who are you?' When Greaves replied that he was hoping to make the grade as a centre-half there was little encouragement; Chilton told him without a flicker of a smile: 'You're wasting your time. I'm the number one centre-half and here you have Ronnie and Mark who are the next two in line.' In modern times a young player would probably go for counselling after such a snub from his elders and betters; but this was the tough, competitive climate that the greatest team ever, the Busby Babes, was growing up in.

Admitted Ian: 'As a late starter, and with an earlier ambition to be Percy Thrower, I was 21, having completed my National Service.

'So I was never what you would call a Busby Babe, although I had the honour of playing in the same team as Duncan Edwards, Roger Byrne, Dennis Viollet and the like. But I certainly had a wonderful chance to view at close quarters the man who was to become Sir Matt. And it was an educational series of master classes for my own future career in management.' Looking back on the management style of the man who ran Old Trafford for around a quarter of a century, he said: 'I never heard him raise his voice. He was one of the calmest men I ever knew in football or indeed in life.

'In fact the only man in those days who ever dared talk back to him was our captain, Roger Byrne, on the occasions when we were talking at team meetings on aspects of the game. If he told Matt that he disagreed with any of his ideas we would all flinch as though expecting a bolt of lightning to strike us all down.

'And it should be pointed out that such an attitude, which must seem laughable to today's footballers, was born out of respect and awe rather than fear. For our manager was a benevolent dictator, and he never lost his temper.' But for once young Greaves did question a decision after he'd been dropped following a game against Bolton Wanderers, where he was ultimately to have several happy and successful years as manager. The match was played in thick fog, and Ian had been responsible for United's defeat by putting into his own net in trying to save a goal. But he had played well, and he considered it an injustice that he'd lost his place in the team. So he knocked on Matt's office door. 'Why have I been dropped?' said Ian hesitantly. 'You couldn't even see me because of the fog.'

Replied the manager: 'If you've nothing else to say, son, you can go now.'

You did not need bombarding with a plateful of sandwiches, a hair dryer or a tea cup in those days to be kept in your place. Even if they were not getting into Matt Busby's team, it was obvious that his players thought the world of him. And like all his players who went on to become managers or coaches, the first person they went back to for advice, and help, was their old boss.

Greaves told me: 'I went to see him for a long talk when I got my first job as manager at Huddersfield, and he gave me as much time as I needed. There was a magic about him as a manager and a man, and the magic remained there right until his death.'

When Matt Busby finally relinquished the reins that had welded him to Manchester United for 26 years, and Manchester United to him, the football world queued up to pay tribute. Don Revie, manager of a great Leeds United team that provided tremendous rivalry to the Old Trafford side, said: 'We have tried to model Leeds United on Matt's club. There have been many managers, players and coaches who have turned to him for advice, and he has always readily given it. I went to him myself when I was made manager at Elland Road, and his advice was always sound and constructive.'

Nobby Stiles, one of Old Trafford's greatest sons, said: 'It's going to be very strange for me as I have only ever played for two managers, Sir Matt Busby and Sir Alf Ramsey. I never thought the day would come when he would retire. He's been more like a father to me.' Bobby Charlton added: 'It's a great blow to the players who have been with him all their playing lives. I'm glad to hear we shall not be losing him completely.'

Bill Shankly said emotionally: 'Obviously his record is unequalled. Liverpool, Spurs and Wolves have all enjoyed spells of success for five years or so. United have had it for twenty years and have probably the finest club ground in the country.'

Tributes poured in from anybody who was anybody in world football, but at the end of the press conference back at Old Trafford when Matt Busby made his announcement, he was talking of the reaction of his family, saying: 'Like me they feel a kind of loneliness. In a way it is like the day which comes to every player, the day you realise you cannot play any more. You just have to accept it.'

My Heaven is in Manchester

When he decided in June 1969 to hand over the reins of the club he had made great, Matt Busby had made his decision with a heavy heart. And it was also with a heavy heart that I wrote at the end of his life of the end of a glorious era, the culmination of a quarter-century of crusading years on behalf of Manchester United. It was not just the death of a revered sporting personality; but the passing of an age.

For, great as his sporting achievements were, Matt Busby the man transcended even Matt Busby the sportsman. His inspiration, his unremitting devotion to United was what made Old Trafford the Theatre of Dreams. Through it all, the highs and the devastating lows, he showed humanity and humility, and was always able to talk man to man with supporters around the stadium that was virtually a bomb crater when he took over at the end of the Second World War. He was the father of the modern Manchester United. Matt Busby made the dreams of a legion of supporters throughout the world come true.

Let it not be forgotten, though, that Busby had begun his rise to the pinnacle of English football on the other side of Manchester. When Sir Matt died only Jimmy Heale remained from his Manchester City teammates of the thirties, and he told me: 'He was a quiet man, but always had the air of authority. You rarely heard him swear, and he was a wonderful man to have in your dressing room.'

Matt Busby's playing days were overshadowed by a management career that made him world famous; but he never became a

35

demagogue, and his homespun approach and the fatherly way he looked after his players was as important as his ability as a manager, coach and leader of men.

He made the club an institution by treating everybody, from his greatest players down to the laundry women, like one big happy family. Duncan Edwards, Tommy Taylor, Bobby Charlton, George Best, and such as Johnny Carey, Henry Cockburn and Jimmy Delaney before them, made Manchester United great; but Matt Busby's family spirit made the club legendary.

Harry Gregg, who scrambled from the wreckage of Munich, stood over his boss in Germany when they gave him the last rites, and also saw him at his peak. He said to me at the time of Matt's death: 'I knew Matt Busby in triumph and tragedy, and in adversity, but no matter at what level I have seen him in football or in life, I always saw the same face and the same values. In the ten years in which I played for him I only heard him raise his voice twice.'

Matt's son Sandy lives in the shadow of Manchester Airport, in a beautiful cottage up a country lane close by where his father set out on that fateful journey to Munich in 1958, and like any Manchester United supporter he has been thrilled to see his father's feats replicated in the Alex Ferguson era.

As he told me: 'Twenty-six years takes some beating, but Alex never had the mountains to climb that Matt had. The place was certainly stagnant when Alex arrived, and the youth set-up left something to be desired. He quickly showed himself a strong-willed man, shaking everything up and telling staff that they had better start working or else. But what he had was great backup, with 40,000-plus gates already in place, and honours won in Cup competitions, with exciting European performances, whereas Matt started with the club bang in trouble, and a bombed team and bombed stadium, only to be hit by Munich just when he had got a dream team together.'

In fact Sandy revealed that two years before Munich his father was made an offer to leave the club that most people would have taken, and had he done so the Busby Old Trafford years could have disappeared in never-never land. 'Real Madrid president Bernabeu asked him in 1956 to take over the club, just a matter of months before the start of a run of incredible victories that saw the Spanish maestros win the first five European Cups.

'The Real president had said to Matt, "I will give you a paradise." And Matt replied, "My heaven is in Manchester."'

'Manchester United had been underinsured and were struggling badly for cash after the crash, so Matt asked Real Madrid to play his team in a fundraising game. Bernabeu said, "You have a nerve to ask me after turning me down," and then turned to his secretary and told her to find a date in the club's schedule as soon as possible to go and play Manchester United just for the expenses of the trip.'

There was no doubt that Matt Busby always had the best interests of Manchester United at heart. The wellbeing of the club consumed him – even though, like Alex Ferguson, he couldn't have done the job he did without hurting people, because hard decisions simply have to be made when running a football club.

Billy (Liam) Whelan, the fabulous Irish inside forward who became one of the great heroes of the crowd, once in his early days nervously knocked on the manager's door, asking to be dropped because he was getting regular barracking from the fans.

His request received an angry riposte from Matt, who told him: 'Don't you know I'm the manager of this side? Nobody tells me who to pick for the team. If I select you it's because I think you are doing the job I'm asking you to do. Keep on playing that way, and don't ever come knocking on this door again with such a request.'

The men who belonged to his own generation had now departed from the team, and the boys from the 1957 FA Cup final, when Aston Villa triumphed after Peter McParland had knocked out keeper Ray Wood, had grown up with Matt as the boss.

Sandy carried on his story: 'There was of course Besty to come, and how Matt loved him for his football skills and his natural ability; but the little Irish imp was the first of his kind. There had never been a personality let loose in football like George, quite simply because the 1960s was a new era and new times. The Swinging Sixties were hard to understand for people who had been involved in the carnage of the Second World War. So, while it's an understandable parallel to draw, it's not realistic to ask if Alex Ferguson would have made a better fist of handling George Best.

And after all, Matt got more great football out of George than anybody ever got out of Paul Gascoigne, who surfaced at a time when the free-spirited, high-living footballer was no phenomenon.

'But he was frustrated at seeing George Best ending up so badly physically after being one of the greatest players in the history of world football. It distressed him, and United could have lost him completely at the beginning but for Matt acting like a father to everybody on the staff.

'Watching some youngsters training at the club one Sunday he noticed fifteen-year-old Best, and when two weeks later he was down again at the Sunday training session he noticed George was missing. "Where's the little fellow?" he said. Apparently he'd gone home. Matt immediately rang his parents, who told him that George had returned feeling homesick. Matt told them that when he wanted to come back everything would be put in place, and he would be looked after, and he kept in close touch until George did return.

'He showed he cared, and his approach was similar to the way Alex kept in contact with Ruud van Nistelrooy when his injury breakdown made it look as though it might end his career before he had even signed for United.

'It was a cruel fate that made George an alcoholic, because plenty of people drink as much but aren't alcoholics and it doesn't hurt them.

'But George was a gem as a person, and would do anything for Matt, the club or the supporters. I remember once Matt found it hard to get one of his players willing to referee a preparatory schools game in South Manchester; but George volunteered immediately he heard of the problem, and then stayed on after the match for another ninety minutes signing autographs at the head of a queue that went twice around the school grounds.'

Said Sandy: 'Matt was a man who had overcome great problems and achieved the greatest success in his professional life. He would have been able to cope with modern-day millionaire players and the problems of the present era. One of the main problems is that some who are now on more per week than the sixties players used to earn in a year, just don't seem to care about giving their all. He would have dealt with them.

'But he would have had no grumbles about seeing that a player got a millionaire's wages if he deserved it. He always said that if a stage artist could get £2,000 for a show, and a footballer only a maximum £20 for ninety minutes' play and a week's training, there was something wrong. He was pleased when the wage structure was changed.'

He added: 'Matt's great strengths were his knowledge, dignity, and the respect he created. He was a great man for treating all kinds of people the same; but he wouldn't stand fools gladly, pauper or prince.'

Just as Alex Ferguson could not make his son Darren a star player, Matt could not make Sandy a star. He admits: 'I certainly wanted to be a player, but he wouldn't let me sign for Manchester United because he insisted that I complete a four-year engineering apprenticeship, during which time I played as an amateur for Oldham Athletic. Manager George Hardwick offered me pro forms when I was seventeen only for Dad to advise me not to sign. Then I played for Lancashire Under-18s against Yorkshire at Maine Road and Blackburn Rovers showed interest and signed me on my twenty-first birthday. But being the son of a legend is a bit of a burden; although I did make some kind of mark at Ewood Park, unfortunately it was on Denis Wilshaw of Wolves.

'Dave Whelan, who's now the multi-millionaire owner of JJB Sports, remembers playing in the same reserve team as me against Wolves when the boss had told me to look after Wilshaw. He'd also told the more experienced Whelan to look after me looking after Wilshaw, and see I didn't get into any trouble. I did what I thought the boss wanted me to do and kicked lumps out of Denis, leaving Dave Whelan to come up to me after the match and say that the boss should have told him that I could look after myself. That was a real tribute from Dave because he certainly was a tough guy. But to succeed I needed more than a tough approach. My biggest problem was that I lacked a yard of pace.

'Matt certainly never put any pressure on me over my football, and I couldn't have wished for a better father. He loved to talk about the family, Manchester United and golf. He was also fortunate he married a great woman. She bossed the house, and Dad bossed the job, and made a great family of Manchester United Football Club. He only smacked me once, and that was for throwing potatoes at our garage; but he was great if you were worried about something, and would talk through things with me, and I could see afterwards that he would be just as caring if any of his players had problems.

'One of his other great strengths was his rapport with the press. The trust and respect was mutual, and clearly that aspect of the game isn't the same nowadays.'

Fiercely loyal to the memory of his great father, Sandy indignantly denies stories that Matt Busby interfered in the management of the playing side of the club after he retired. And I can back Sandy up in that. Certainly, while I was down at The Cliff training ground every midweek day during the seventies and eighties I never once saw Sir Matt Busby there.

He told me: 'True supporters and those close to the club know that it wasn't so. If one of the past managers said that he did interfere I would take action. The accusation was never made in the press until he died. I know Frank O'Farrell bought all his own players and was given a free hand by the board.'

Said Sandy: 'If in that 26-year period [1967–93] there had been one League title win there would have been no talk of Matt interfering, but the rumour kept surfacing, and I feel it was used as an excuse for failure by some of the managers. Of course he was a hard act to follow, but I know there was nothing he wanted more than that the managers who followed him be successful. There was no question of him being the man who wouldn't let go. He told them all: "You are the manager. All I will say is that you're welcome to knock on my door any time you want to."

'Alex certainly respected him, and would always poke his head round his office door and say, "Hey, auld yin...you OK?" And when Alex was down in the dumps in the early days of his career with the back pages of the newspapers full of hate against him, Dad would tell him: "The solution's easy. Don't read the back pages. It isn't worth getting yourself upset about. You have more important things to do than read newspapers."

'But it needed a supreme effort for Matt to keep going after Munich. It was probably the ambition to bring the European Cup to

Old Trafford as a memorial to his boys lost at Munich that kept him going and was always in front of him.

'It was his innate physical strength and strength of character that I'm sure kept him alive during those uncertain days after the crash, and that no doubt came from his early days playing village football in Scotland. In those days the religious divisions meant that if things got tough you had to put your clothes where you could see them during the match so you could get them and run if things got ugly.

'He could certainly handle himself, and that early hard upbringing enabled him to come back after Munich determined to do what he knew was his destiny.

'And when he retired he knew that he'd done his part. He'd seen his Babes team as the one capable of stopping Real Madrid, then the greatest club in the world. I vividly remember when we were talking with Bob Paisley about Madrid's European successes, the Liverpool boss scoffed, and said: "Five successive Cups! The Babes would have won everything for a decade."

'It's also fair to point out that there was never in my mind any truth in the popular theory that he wasn't sufficiently ruthless to replace his 1968 team quickly enough or that it was a factor in the club not going on to further glory for twenty-six years. There was still ample gas in the tank, and Matt never looked back with regrets about his decisions on that score. Tony Dunne, Shay Brennan, Pat Crerand, Bobby Charlton, Dave Sadler, Nobby Stiles and Brian Kidd were all internationals at the time, and still in their national teams.'

Protective and proud of his father's reputation, Sandy cannot help showing his anger at some questions: 'It was utter bullshit to suggest that Matt wasn't ruthless in breaking up the '68 team, and pass this off as the reason for the long run of failure.'

Sandy remembers his father as Scottish national team manager as well as Manchester United boss before Munich, picking Denis Law to play against Northern Ireland at Hampden Park. Denis was given his instructions 'to look after Danny Blanchflower'. At the end Danny Boy limped off the field black and blue; seventeen-year-old Denis had kicked him all over the park. So successfully had young Denis followed instructions that even Matt was embarrassed at the torment the great Blanchflower had been subjected to.

But Sandy reckons that his father never had more tactical torment himself than when he was trying to come up with the right name as his successor at Old Trafford. He said: 'He had sleepless nights thinking who should take over, successively recommending Wilf, Frank O'Farrell and Tommy Docherty. The crowd loved Tommy, and after some of the players didn't get on with him when at first he tried playing defensive football, he signed Steve Coppell, Gordon Hill, Stuart Pearson, Lou Macari, Stewart Houston and Jim Holton when they dropped into the Second Division, and then went from strength to strength.'

Immersed as he was in football, however, Matt had other interests, and Sandy fondly remembers his love of the old variety music halls, especially when his grandad took him to the Glasgow Empire, said to be the graveyard of stars.

One of the greatest comedians of the time was on the bill that day, but suddenly his fans had turned against him because he had been quoted in the newspapers saying that the miners should not have come out in a national strike. Up in the balcony they whistled and jeered, but Grandfather Busby stood on his seat, rattled his walking stick and shouted to the audience: 'This is one of the all-time greats. You aren't fit to lace his boots!' Such family stories stuck in Matt's mind.

And he also used to love to get up at parties and sing. Said Sandy: 'He intended entitling his life story "My Way", and was a tremendous fan of Frank Sinatra, but his party piece was Satchmo's song: "What a Wonderful World". He always felt that way about life, and his philosophy in football and in life was to be honest and true to himself.

'His seven grandchildren were his delight, and he obtained great joy from many things; but he was a serious man. He had tremendous compassion and humanity, and would love it when ex-players, especially lads who hadn't made it to the top, came back to see him. I remember when Frank Haydock brought his family round to see the club, and when Matt saw him he made a real fuss of him, took him in the office for a cup of tea, yarned over old times. He was clearly made up when they came back to the club.

'In the FA Cup semi-final at Hillsborough, a match played on a bog, we lost 3–1 to West Ham United, and we all met as miserable as sin in the Cromford Club in Manchester after the match. But as we walked in somebody said Nobby Lawton was in the club. Now Nobby had played for Preston North End that day in the other semi-final and had won through to Wembley. Matt choked back his own disappointment, sought out Nobby, and there was genuine pleasure in his face as he congratulated his former player, who told him: "I wish it was United we were playing in the final."

'He was very sentimental, but there was one thing he would not forgive and that was not giving one hundred per cent for Manchester United.'

The Sir Matt Busby Fact File

1909:   26 May, born in Bellshill, Lanarkshire.

1928:   Joins Manchester City from Denny Hibs FC.

1933:   FA Cup final loser's medal with Manchester City.

1934:   FA Cup final winner's medal with Manchester City.
Scottish debut v Wales.

1936:   Transferred to Liverpool.

1939–45: Army service with Physical Training Corps.

1945:   16 October, appointed manager of Manchester United.

1948:   United win FA Cup.

1952:   United win English League championship.

1956:   United win League championship.

1957:   United retain League championship and reach European Cup semi-finals, runners-up in FA Cup.

1958:   6 February, Munich air crash. Eight players killed, Sir Matt seriously injured.
United FA Cup runners-up, European Cup semi-finalists.
CBE in Honours list.

1963:   United win FA Cup.

1965:   United win League championship.

1966:   United reach European Cup semi-finals.

1967:   United win League championship.

1968:   United become first English team to win the European Champions' Cup.
Knighted in Honours list.

1971:   Became Manchester United director.

1980:   Became Manchester United president.

1994:   20 January, died in his sleep.

Everything is Beautiful
Until It Isn't

Wilf McGuinness was in the hot seat at Old Trafford from June 1969 to December 1970, and although he came to the job inexperienced in management, he was certainly experienced at the age of 31 in the ways of Manchester United.

He spent the first season as coach, Matt Busby telling him: 'You will probably be appointed team manager next year.' But his spell in sole control lasted just eight months, and at the time perhaps people both in and out of the club did not recognise how distinguished was his record, despite being invalided out of the game early in his playing career. With his happy-go-lucky nature, however, he was no mystery to the public and his teammates, and he never let a superstar aura develop about himself.

But judge for yourself by skimming through that record career how far along the road he was to becoming a superstar. Wilf McGuinness was captain of England Schools at the age of fourteen, and went on to play for England Youth, England Under-21s and Under-23s before gaining two full England caps for his country in 1959. One of the Busby Babes, he played for the pre-Munich team, making his first-team debut for Manchester United at the age of seventeen against Wolves, and earned a full England cap before Bobby Charlton or Eddie Colman. After breaking a leg in 1959 at the age of 22 he never recovered full match fitness, but he was soon drafted into the England setup and became the first manager of the England Youth team, then assistant to Bill Nicholson with the Under-23s after being on the England training staff under Alf Ramsey for the 1966 World Cup.

Wilf's own international debut had been against Northern Ireland alongside new teammates such as Billy Wright, Johnny Haynes, Tom Finney, Ron Clayton and Bolton's hard-tackling Tommy Banks. He had played for England at every level, something only a very select band of players have achieved in a century of football. Now who was that man who questioned Wilf's superstar aura!

He was asked to take over from Matt Busby, a man who was acknowledged to be an impossible act to follow. Wilf's failure during his short period at the helm, and a measure of the level of expectation laid upon him, was that he only took United to three Cup semi-finals, which comprised seven semi-final games. He did not manage just that extra stride that would have given him a longer breathing space to carry through his agenda.

He first took his team into semi-final action in December 1969 against Manchester City in the League Cup, losing 2–1 at Maine Road and drawing at Old Trafford, leaving City to go on and beat West Bromwich Albion 2–1 in the 1970 final. Then against Leeds United in the FA Cup semi-final it was goalless at Hillsborough, goalless at Villa Park, before Billy Bremner scored the 1–0 winner in a tense second replay at Burnden Park.

Came the 1970–71 League Cup when Aston Villa were the Reds' semi-final opponents. The two-legged clash should have seen Villa stage the initial game, but it was the time of the power strike, and because United had their own generator it was decided that the first leg should be staged at Old Trafford. With United's advantage of playing away second lost, Villa were left to win the second game on their own ground after a draw at Old Trafford.

Seven semi-final games in just over twelve months, and not a sausage to show for it!

Grouse shooting traditionally begins on the Glorious 12th of August. But directors of major football clubs seem to train both barrels of their shotguns on their managers at Christmas, the time of goodwill to all men – except football managers. And sure enough, after a Boxing Day 4–4 draw against Derby, who were to go on and win the First Division by one point from Leeds United and Liverpool, Wilf was relieved of his duties on 28 December 1970 after a long talk with Matt Busby.

Wilf was far from the first man to find that a three-year contract was not worth the paper it was written on; but it felt like the end of the world to him.

Let the man himself take up the story: 'I thought the contract would give me time to do a good job. But at Manchester United you live in a fairytale world. Everything is beautiful until it isn't. Matt tried as hard as he could to let me down gently, but it was a terrible shock to me. We had a two-hour meeting, and I tried to cast my mind back, reminding Matt of our talks when I took over from him. I remember as vividly now as the day it happened when I said to him, "I thought we were going to go through it together."

'But the decision had been made. The plan would have been right in terms of continuity, but I'd needed more maturity and experience. I'd left Bobby Charlton and Denis Law out against Everton in my first year, and it had upset people. Perhaps I should have adopted a more gradual approach. On the other hand, if I'd had the experience to force my opinions on the board more I might have had my own way with signing players. But it was so different economically than it is now, and then we didn't have the money to compete with everybody. Even so, the fact was that the only player we signed during my term of office was central defender Ian Ure. I had wanted to sign Colin Todd from Sunderland. He was the name I put to Matt, only to be told that he was too expensive. It made me wonder whether it was a case of the club not having the money or not having the will to sign the players I wanted to take us forward.

'Sir Matt was general manager, and let me make it clear he didn't interfere, but just did what any general manager would do. It was never a question of him not wanting to let go, and with my lack of experience I needed his wisdom behind me. But it was clear to me that the team needed freshening up, and as well as Colin Todd I told the board I wanted to sign Mick Mills, with whom I had had experience during my time as England Under-23s coach, and Malcolm McDonald of Luton Town.

'I'd seen Malcolm play at Mansfield while Matt and Jimmy Murphy watched from the crowd, and I was very impressed with his play, thinking what a wonderfully direct player he was. I told Matt he was the man I wanted, and strongly recommended that we sign him. Luton manager Harry Haslam said we could have an option on him, along with Liverpool, but said they wouldn't let him go until the end of the season. Which only underlined the uncertainty of football, because Newcastle United signed him well before the end of the season.

'Another signing to fall flat was Ron Davies, who always did well against us. I had to look back and feel that had I been given the go-ahead to sign those players the continuity of the team would have been kept going, with the quality we required, because undeniably some of the established players had reached the veteran stage. I also felt that these players would have helped George Best feel more settled, and he wouldn't have to be relied on too much to pull the fat out of the fire time and again for us with his great virtuoso skills. He had to carry the team on occasions and too much was asked of him.'

It was tough for Wilf. Despite his sunny exterior, and although he stayed on as reserve team manager for a while until he found another job, the inner turmoil produced by the termination of his contract from his beloved United showed when, in his first overseas job in Greece, he woke up one morning to find that he had lost all his hair overnight. He certainly had a good head of hair two years earlier when his delight was so transparent at the press conference announcing his appointment as United's heir-apparent manager.

Perhaps his agony was compounded by the thought, when he looked back, that if there had been no Munich disaster, and he had not sustained his leg injury, he would have been part of a United super team that would have gone on to win the Champions' Cup three or four times, and at least have shared the honours of the first decade of European competition with Real Madrid, Benfica and the Milan clubs. As well, most likely, as being in England's 1966 World Cup-winning team.

But he might also have remembered that he would have been on the plane to Munich, having played against Borussia Dortmund earlier in the competition. In fact he was booked on the flight, but had torn a cartilage in a reserve game the week before the ill-fated trip to Germany.

Recalled Wilf: 'I was at Old Trafford having treatment when they brought the bodies back from Munich, and Gordon Clayton, our reserve keeper, and myself represented the dressing room at the funerals.

'It was a time when we were all walking about in a daze, and felt as though we were treading water, expecting we would wake up from a nightmare any minute. I also knew that but for being injured I would have been on the trip.'

But life had to go on after Munich, and so it did for Wilf after hearing he was no longer in charge of the team in December 1970. Could he have approached the job differently? Should he have adopted a more measured approach? His answer: 'It was a combination of factors, and maybe I should have discussed things more with Matt; but to be fair to myself I've never been one to think I was right all the time.'

Whatever else, his affection for Matt Busby never faded: 'Matt was our leader and our father. And when the team won the Champions' Cup at Wembley against Benfica they were all as one: the win was for Matt and for the boys who had died at Munich. It was all so emotional. There was a feeling that we had scaled every height there was to conquer, and that perhaps some of us felt there was nothing else to achieve. There was no doubt that if the Busby Babes team hadn't been destroyed they would have been the greatest ever Manchester United team, right up to the present day. Looking back you would have to have any of those players, along with Law and Best.'

But, at the end of 1972, Wilf McGuinness, with a young family, had to look forward, and he was helped by his own optimistic nature and good humour. He worked in the Greek League with Aris of Salonika and Panahiaki of Patras for three years.

It was a period which, he says, 'provided me with some of my most successful management times, probably because they couldn't understand what I was saying! The three years were very enjoyable, and enabled me to get my confidence back. But with the children growing up the time was ripe for returning to England, so I worked for Billy Bingham at Everton to give me time to look around for a management job, eventually succeeding Tom Johnston with Second Division York City. Tom had taken a job at Fourth Division Huddersfield Town, and it seemed strange to me that he should move down two divisions. But I soon found out that his strategy was good when after battling to keep York in the Second Division the first season we eventually fell to the Third and then the Fourth Division.'

Out of work again, Wilf was offered a short-term contract managing the Jordan national team for an international tournament – a trip which proved highly successful – before returning as coach under Ken Houghton at Hull City. Following two years on Humberside he started an eleven-year love affair at Gigg Lane with Bury, a club that had beaten Southampton 4–0 in the 1900 FA Cup final and Derby County 6–0 in the 1903 final, both at the Crystal Palace, and in later years produced a stream of stars headed by Colin Bell and Terry McDermott.

Said Wilf: 'I joined Bury in 1980 as assistant manager to Jim Iley, then went on to do just about every job at the club: manager, first-team coach under Martin Dobson, trainer, physiotherapist, during which time I fed the office cat on Sundays because I was at the club treating players injured from Saturday's game.

'I was also caretaker manager, and acted as secretary for a month, making up wages etc., when the regular secretary was ill. I had a great time at Bury, and the club will always be close to my heart.'

Talk about 'Always look on the bright side of life'. The ditty could have been written for Wilf. He certainly would never be described as one of the game's moaners.

Eventually Wilf joined the after-dinner circuit, and later became host at corporate hospitality events thanks to the prompting of Danny McGregor at Old Trafford. He says: 'I've always enjoyed life, but I've never had so much fun as I have going around the country with stars such as John Conteh, and many big names from other sports, making people laugh.'

He certainly had a richly varied career to look back on to make up the scripts for his shows, and there is no doubt that in recalling his management career at Old Trafford he could console himself with the thought that more experienced men than he struggled to follow the Busby legend. He told me: 'It was hard to envisage in those days what the club was to become. It seemed in the sixties that we would always be behind clubs like Real Madrid, who had the best team in the world with a combination of home-grown players and the pick of the foreign stars. By government decree we weren't allowed to sign foreign players, and it's so great, despite the pride we have in our home-grown players, to have seen world-class stars such as Schmeichel, Cantona, van Nistelrooy and others brought into the United family.

'I think I could even have afforded Colin Todd if the same setup had been in operation when I was in charge of the team. But the last ten years have been so exciting, and the icing on the cake that we're waiting for now is for the European Cup to be a regular visitor to our trophy room. If any British club can do it in the next decade Manchester United can.'

It is easy to say that the managers who succeeded Busby were not helped by the fact that Best, still in most supporters' minds the greatest ever Red, became such a loose cannon. Seemingly it was an aspect of the malaise caused by the club's failure to capitalise on the advantage of winning the Champions' Cup. It appeared to some observers that rather than strengthen from strength the club was content to rest on its laurels, waiting, before strengthening from weakness. It was a fair question to ask which came first: George Best's increasing wantonness or United's apparent agenda that everything possible now had been achieved? Surely the time to strive for heights hitherto never touched in British football was *after* winning the European trophy in 1968 at Wembley.

Looking at the issue of Best, Wilf McGuinness said: 'I was lucky to some extent with George because he had some great moments in my time. Remember that great day at Northampton when he scored six. He hit some wonderful goals in his day, and it was a tragedy that Northern Ireland didn't reach the finals of the World Cup and European championship while he was at his peak, so that he could really show on the world stage that he was the greatest.

'But perhaps the club could have motivated him more. He was certainly disappointed that we hadn't signed new quality players to strengthen the team when we needed them; but there were some great times in the sixties as Matt and Jimmy Murphy built the team. It's easy to forget that we had three European Players of the Year in Charlton, Law and Best. It was such a privilege to be associated with them.'

The oft-repeated question seemed appropriate. Would Alex Ferguson have dealt any better with Best than Matt Busby?

He said: 'If Alex had been doing the job in the sixties I don't think he would have handled George any better. At the time George was a one-off, a new development in the game, and through his antics managers of all clubs developed a different outlook in handling players in future.

'We've had two great, world-class managers at Manchester United and both were father figures, worshipped by their players. While on trophies alone you can make an argument for Alex being number one I am sure in the recent era Matt would have won as many trophies. I think it's also important not to forget that the managers between these two all had something to offer. A lot of the success in football, and sport generally, can come down to being in the right place at the right time.'

Running his rule over the men who followed him at Old Trafford, Wilf said: 'Tommy Docherty was a bit of a rascal, but I liked him, and he was a good manager. He had great self-belief, was very knowledgeable, and had a wonderful sense of humour. I sometimes think people don't realise how much he says outrageous things to wind people up, to get a reaction, when he doesn't really believe himself what he is saying. He might have had more clubs than any other top manager in the game, but he's given something special to every club he's been with. The team was progressing to greatness. He was developing a good squad that could have provided our first English title since 1967 if he had stayed on at Old Trafford.

'In fact it should have been done before Alex Ferguson arrived. Big Ron was a great personality and he had that fantastic start, but after winning the first ten games it must have felt like finishing third in a two-horse race. Ron had the opportunity; he produced an exciting team that won Cup finals and he brought more European football to the club than any other manager in between Busby and Ferguson; but he couldn't travel that extra mile. It's easy also to forget that Frank O'Farrell was top in December during his time at the club, and the team was going like a train in his first season.

'In fact you couldn't argue about the quality of the managers before Ferguson came on the scene, because Dave Sexton also had enormous respect in the game; it's a tribute to his stamina and his ability to put over his coaching points that he's still coaching at international level in his seventies. It probably didn't help him that he was a Southerner coaching a Northern club and, while he had a lot of supporters in the club, things just didn't spark for him. Dave and Frank were good pros, and right in the top rank in the game. Their contributions probably made it that little bit easier for Tommy and Ron, who in turn took us another step forward in quality and purpose towards the Ferguson era.'

Wilf would not argue with the theory that Matt Busby let things slide after 1968, and that the production line faltered. For a few years, the quality of players being brought into the club was undeniably not what it had been. After all, he had only been allowed to sign one player, and although Wilf gave youngsters a chance, the club could not be expected continually to be unearthing players of the calibre of Duncan Edwards, Bobby Charlton, George Best and Nobby Stiles.

Said Wilf: 'Until Dave Sexton came we hadn't once finished in the top two in the First Division after the Busby years, and the first eighteen months of the Doc's reign were a nightmare until his groundwork started to produce results. But the club must have felt they couldn't keep changing managers, and he was able to enjoy some success for his hard work. In any case, what better example could there be of giving a manager plenty of time than Alex Ferguson.

'Certainly whoever follows Alex when he decides to retire, United are better placed to achieve continuity than they were in the seventies and eighties. The club is financially so strong, and has such a good power base on the field, that it's hard to see it regressing, although you never know in football.'

Let us leave the last word on Wilf McGuinness to Ian Donald, former chairman of Aberdeen and now the club's vice-chairman, and a man closely associated with Alex Ferguson. He was a player at Old Trafford during Wilf's time in charge, and says: 'Wilf had always been my pal, and for a man who was a former player and had moved up from being a coach, to step into Matt Busby's shoes was practically impossible.'

The Wilf McGuinness Fact File

1937:   25 October, born in Collyhurst, Manchester.

1952:   Selected for England Schoolboys' team and went on to captain England, Lancashire and Manchester Schools.

1953:   Signed on schoolboy forms for Manchester United on the same day as Bobby Charlton.

1955:   Made first League appearance for Manchester United, a 4–3 win against Wolves, and went on to play for England Youth, Under-21s and Under-23s before gaining full England cap.

1958:   Missed being on Munich disaster plane because of a knee injury.

1958:   Made his England debut against Northern Ireland, and Mexico.

1959:   Broke a leg in reserve match against Stoke City.

1961:   The leg break ultimately forced him to give up playing and he became assistant trainer of Manchester United for eight years, although remained registered as a player until 1966–67 season.

1963:   First appearance as part of England training set up, and became national youth team coach.

1966:   Part of Sir Alf Ramsey's coaching team for England's triumphant World Cup winning team.

1968:   Coach to England Under-23s team under manager Bill Nicholson.

1969:   June, appointed chief coach to Manchester United.

1970:   Appointed team manager at Old Trafford in July, but not given time to develop his policies, and was relieved of his duties on 28 December; but carried on coaching the young players at the club until Feburary 1971 while he decided his future.

1971–72: Managed Aris of Salonika for two years in Greek League.

1973–74: Managed Panahaiki in Greek League.

1975:   Appointed manager of York City in the Second Division, but left Bootham Crescent in November 1977 with the club in the Fourth Division.

1978:   In charge of Jordan national team, preparing them for Middle East tournaments. Worked on the coaching staff of Hull City under manager Ken Houghton.

1980–81: Appointed assistant manager to Jim Iley at Bury.

1981–92: Continued in a number of coaching and administrative jobs at Gigg Lane before retiring for knee and hip operations, and then started his career in corporate entertainment and after-dinner speaking.

Not Accepted by the Senior Players

There was no longer any doubt that the good times at Old Trafford were going to be hard to recapture, but nobody envisaged just how hard. Wilf McGuinness had failed to re-create the thrills and glory years of the Busby times at the drop of a hat, and Matt spent another six months in the hot seat, from December 1970 to June 1971, after the man he had chosen as his successor was relieved of his duties. Now, experienced and tactically sound as Frank O'Farrell was, he found that the jury were sent out before he'd had sufficient time to present his case, and the verdict was 'guilty of not producing a miracle in eighteen months'.

According to Ian Donald: 'After Wilf we had Frank O'Farrell, who brought a great reputation with him from Leicester City; but Frank and his assistant Malcolm Musgrove just didn't seem to have the spark that was needed.'

Bobby Charlton was captain at the time and admits: 'The players couldn't appreciate Frank and Malcolm Musgrove. Frank spent a lot of time in his office, and we wanted him at the training ground. There was no doubt he knew the game, but in the end the club weren't prepared to give him time. The problems with George Best eventually caused him worries too. But I certainly wouldn't blame Frank O'Farrell for problems on the field. We simply didn't play well enough for him.'

Frank O'Farrell will not go down in the Old Trafford hall of fame as one of the club's more successful managers, that's for sure. His reign, lasting from June 1971 to December 1972, was surrounded by controversy; but only now has he commented on the stories that have abounded for thirty years about interference with his management.

O'Farrell, the stylish Cork-born former international, a great midfielder in his own right, was head-hunted by United from Leicester City where he was being lauded as one of the brightest young managerial prospects in the game. But it all went wrong when he took over from Wilf McGuinness, and he quickly found that he had no real chance of doing the job that he was hired for.

Even now, however, he does not look back in anger or bitterness. Happily living in Torquay now in his retirement, he admits: 'I was hurt and puzzled at what happened. My brief when I signed for United was to change the team round, and while I knew it was a difficult job to indicate in subtle ways that the best days of some great players was behind them, and rebuild the team, the job was one I relished from the outset. Bill Shankly had done it successfully at Anfield. He'd grasped the nettle and produced an even greater team, after building one great team, by making changes when they were needed. But Matt Busby had proved that after building three great teams he couldn't do it again.'

It was said that Busby interfered, that O'Farrell's job was made almost impossible because there was always an outlet for complaints. World-renowned players, it was claimed, who had to be dropped as they were coming to the end of their great careers, took their grouses down the corridor to United's legendary former manager. And who could blame Sir Matt for listening? After all, these were the boys he had brought through all manner of handicaps to the greatest trophy in European football.

Said Frank: 'He'd gone through so much with his boys, some of whom had survived the horrors of Munich with him, and it was understandable. He should have given me a chance by stepping right back, but he didn't. He was still at the club every day, and still somebody for the players to go to behind my back. I was brought in to make changes, to look for a new dawn for Manchester United, and the established players knew that I was brought in to get rid of them sooner or later: so if a higher authority was there they'd go to him. And naturally Matt was that higher authority, and Bobby Charlton was a case in point.'

O'Farrell had arrived at Old Trafford full of hope, excited at the thought of being able to fashion the future of the first English club ever to win the European Champions' Cup. But he claims that he quickly found that the presence of the man who for thirty years was Mr Manchester United was a hurdle difficult to negotiate. As Ian Greaves points out elsewhere, when such a situation arises it is the fault of those who have made the decision to keep the ex-manager in-house.

Frank told me as we chatted on Torquay seafront: 'It became apparent that there was no way that I was going to have a long-term chance unless I got good results and nothing but. The difficulty is that in situations like this, when major surgery is needed, it's often a case of getting worse before you get better.' But there was to be no bedding-in period, no allowance for new ways and new directions to start taking effect.

It is tempting to compare O'Farrell's situation with that of Alex Ferguson, whose first two years produced great hostility from the fans. Campaign after campaign was mounted to get him out, but Ferguson survived because he had the support of a chairman with strength and vision. Had Martin Edwards learned of the need to give firm backing to a manager with the right ideas when he was a young board member, watching the assassination of O'Farrell while his father Louis was chairman?

Frank explained: 'I quickly realised I was up against it when I found Matt Busby out on two matters that I can only say showed a streak of vindictiveness.' And he warned: 'What happened once could happen again, and this is why I would look with great reservations at any decision for Sir Alex Ferguson to remain part of the club when he finally retires. It's hard for anybody to let go of a situation that they have created, such as the wonderful way Sir Matt built up the club after the Second World War. If you had written the story in 1945 people would say it was too wild a dream even for fiction.

'Similarly, Sir Alex, with his record number of trophies in the nineties, will find it almost impossible to remain a part of the club and resist still being a counsellor and a guru to his old players.'

Frank O'Farrell, however, found early on in negotiations for the job of manager at Old Trafford that Sir Matt was not on his side. He remembers: 'The first news of their interest came from Matt Gillies, who told me that Matt Busby wanted to speak to me. I talked to my chairman Len Shipman, and eventually I arranged to see Matt at my home in Loughborough Road, Leicester, meeting him just off the M1 so he could follow me to my house. It was cloak-and-dagger stuff. We didn't even walk to my house together in case we were seen.' In fact the meeting was so secretive that Frank walked into the house first and then after an interval Matt walked in through another door.

The arrival of the doyen of Manchester United brought an instant reaction from Frank's young daughter Catherine, who told her father excitedly: 'That's Matt Busby. I know because I've seen him on television. Oh Daddy! Are you going to sign George Best?'

Meanwhile Busby was starting the talking: 'We'd like to sign you, Frank. It will take at least three years to turn things round. We can offer you £12,000 a year and a five-year contract.'

After a long meeting, O'Farrell asked for time to think things over and talk with his own chairman; but within days the deal was done, although not before he found out for the first time that Matt Busby was not a man he could trust.

He said: 'On Monday Len Shipman told me that Manchester United had posted their bid for me to become the new manager at Old Trafford, and arrangements were again hush-hush; there was going to be a meeting on the road between Manchester and Derby.

'The meeting took place with Louis Edwards's Rolls-Royce leading the way to a lay-by, and I climbed into the car to talk to Matt and his chairman. We started when I asked them to repeat the terms. Matt immediately said that the terms would be as he said, namely £12,000 a year salary and a five-year contract, but chairman Edwards looked surprised, and said, obviously instinctively, to Matt that he'd got it wrong, the board had agreed the figure would be £15,000.

'Right at the start I'd found that Matt Busby couldn't be trusted, and I was in a dilemma: could I trust him to be telling the whole truth about the fact that I would be totally in control? At the time, I took the chairman's interjection as being due to a misunderstanding with Matt Busby, but later Jimmy Murphy, Matt's faithful assistant, showed that Matt had tried to slice £3,000 off the top of my salary.

'Murphy said that he knew the story was true when I told him because he told me how Matt had said to him that he could have got me for £12,000 "until that stupid bugger" said that it was £15,000 they were offering.'

He found out all too soon that the incident should have been a warning signal: 'Then came the second warning as he told me that he would need a little office at the ground. When I started the job I found that he was still occupying the manager's office, and a much smaller one down the corridor would be mine.

'It was the second contretemps before I'd had time to find my table, never mind put my feet under it, and I knew I had to make a stand.' There was no row, no bust-up. Frank O'Farrell has never been a tub-thumper, and he said quite calmly: 'Matt, that's not going to look right for you or me. The press have already been speculating that it would be difficult for a new manager with you still at the club. It will be seen as significant symbolism if you stay in the room that has been the manager's office.' After thinking for a while he said that he understood, and would move his stuff out.

'When he heard of it Jimmy Murphy couldn't believe what had happened, and it was only when he told me that it had always been the manager's office that I realised the magnitude of what I'd done. Yet it seemed the only thing I could do if I was going to be in charge of the footballing side of the club.

'But it set the tempo of my career at Old Trafford. It was going to be hard enough battling to put the club back on its feet; I didn't need another battle with the former manager. At least I knew now that we both knew the score between us. He must have realised that I had no intention of being his poodle. I'd seen behind his image a bit. He'd tried to cheat me out of £3,000 a year, and now I'd had to fight to get the manager's office from him. He said that he was going to be a junior director; but had he been truthful in his presentation of the job I was taking? I began to realise that he wouldn't be satisfied with being a junior director.

'In fact it became clear that if he had thought the Manchester United team I had inherited was going to win more trophies he wouldn't have resigned.'

Despite his forebodings about the spectre of the man who had carried the club on his shoulders for so long, O'Farrell had stepped into the job feeling he was the man the Old Trafford club needed, and that he would be a worthy successor to Sir Matt. Soon after his midsummer appointment he was into pre-season training, getting to know the players, and starting the season so well that by October Matt Busby, the man who had signed Denis Law, George Best, Bobby Charlton and so many great stars, was quoted as saying: 'Frank O'Farrell is the best signing I've ever made.'

Indeed, by Christmas, six months into his management of an ageing team that was eventually, under Tommy Docherty, to face relegation, O'Farrell's United were five points clear at the top of the First Division. Perhaps there was success ahead after all the early misgivings.

It had been a hard road to the top. His distinguished playing career with West Ham United, Preston North End and the Republic of Ireland continued in non-league football where for a spell he was player-manager of Weymouth. He went on to manage Torquay United, where his success as one of the bright young managers in the game – a product of the West Ham school of soccer thinkers – led to offers to manage Bolton Wanderers, Carlisle United and Ipswich Town before he finally took the plunge to step up and join Leicester.

In his first season he took the Midlands side to the FA Cup final. Neil Young's goal gave Manchester City a 1–0 victory at Wembley, and it was altogether a sweet and sour season for Leicester because they were relegated. But Frank soon had them top of the Second Division in 1971, and they returned to the First Division as champions along with Sheffield United, taking the place of the relegated Lancashire clubs, Blackpool and Burnley. In that summer came reward for his cultured management style and his success in remodelling the Leicester team, as the interest of Manchester United grew.

His first signing for United was Martin Buchan, a cultured central defender from Aberdeen, who added quality and solidity to a creaking defence, while flying winger Ian Storey-Moore, craggy Welsh striker Wyn Davies and Ted MacDougall from lower-division Bournemouth were other signings. Frank gave 'last of the Busby Babes' Sammy McIlroy his first-team debut, and brought Arthur

Albiston into the side. And by Christmas of his first season at Old Trafford the future seemed rosy indeed. The Reds were top of the English League and seemingly back on song. In fact the eminent Frank Butler, writing in the *News of the World Football Guide*, had previewed that season with an erudite, studied article about the end of the Busby era and the possibilities of the future. He wrote:

> Sir Matt Busby is no longer 'The Boss' at Old Trafford. The greatest manager of the post-war era, and perhaps of all time, will sit back and relax this season more than he has done for a quarter of a century as a director of his beloved United.
>
> Only one man, Frank O'Farrell, seems young enough, and of the right breed, to take on the toughest assignment of all time – to be as successful, or even nearly as successful, as Matt had been over two decades.

Butler's article was headlined 'Farewell to a Genius'. But Frank O'Farrell had another headline for the man whose shoes he tried to fill: 'The genius who would not let go'.

It was a wonderful start for the new boss, but it could not last. The old guard were still in residence. George Best began to lose concentration, causing problems off the pitch by disappearing when O'Farrell thought that he was getting the best out of the Irish star.

Said O'Farrell: 'George had carried the club for several years, and told me that he went missing because he was worried about the safety of his parents during the troubles in Northern Ireland. So I checked with the club what we were prepared to do for his family, and then went over to Ireland to speak to his parents. I put a proposal to them, offering to settle them in Manchester with a house, and asked them to think about the proposition. I came back to Manchester, but there was no sign of George at training, and no word until late on Friday when I had a call asking what time George needed to meet the following day for the match at Molineux against Wolves.

'I knew he hadn't been in Belfast because I had just come back from there, and when it was no-show Best for two days at training I had already decided that I just had to drop him for the match. It was a tough decision to make; but if we were to go forward, make the club all we wanted it to be, such decisions had to be made. The long term was what we were talking about: after all, Matt Busby himself had told me it would take three years to turn the side round, and he had given me a five-year contract. In any case, contract or no contract, if I was to be true to myself, and the club, I had to make what I considered the right decisions. In terms of the Best situation somebody had to say "stop" over something that was rapidly getting out of hand.

'I told the players what I'd decided, and urged them to go out and win without George Best. There was no happy ending: we lost 3–0. Even so, what I did was morally right, although it was clear I was in a no-win situation.

'The decision had to be made, and having made my point he went back into the side next week at Southampton where we drew 0–0 in a cup tie. Then, in the replay, George produced two bits of his special magic, and we won through to the next round.'

Unfortunately George Best had gone beyond the control of a mere manager. If anybody could have controlled him it was Matt Busby, the man who had him from a boy, but the whole tenor of the Swinging Sixties was against even a giant such as Matt. Society had been transformed. Discipline was out, sex, booze and pop music were the gods, and a handsome fellow such as George Best, who was as big as the greatest of the pop idols, was prepared to live the *dolce vita* to the limit. Despite his almost limitless talents as a footballer, the end of his top-level career at the age of 26 showed that even his great ability could not be used to full effect when his fitness was ebbing away ten years too soon.

Admitted O'Farrell: 'It was so sad. He had a moral obligation to use his talents to the full, but the culture of the time lured him away. Even though in most people's minds he was Britain's greatest ever footballer, he could have been so much greater.'

But the wonderful, sad, fantastic, tragic Best was not the biggest of O'Farrell's worries: 'After a match when we lost 3–0 at home to Spurs in October 1972 we had a party for the groundstaff boys, and afterwards my wife Ann told me that Matt Busby had taken her on one side, and told her: "Your husband is an independent sod. Why don't you tell him to come and talk to me?" What was behind that I do not know, because whenever he came past my office I always asked him in, offered him a cup of coffee, and we had a chat before he went on to his own office. So next time he passed I made the usual offer, and then told him that Ann had spoken about his conversation with her.

'Then he blurted out that he didn't think I should have dropped Bobby Charlton, and said that Martin Buchan wasn't playing well, and that he was responsible for the goal against United last Saturday. I was staggered. But I gave him my reasons for dropping Bobby, and then pointed out that Martin had been marking Martin Chivers and had jumped with him, while the man David Sadler should have been marking had lost him and scored the goal. Quite simply Matt just wasn't making valid points. Even if it had been his position to come carrying tales from his old players, he wasn't making sense, and to be quite frank I was pissed off.'

Two months later, on 19 December 1972, Frank O'Farrell was just plain off, and his great adventure, the thought of which had thrilled him so much, was over. At the end of his one full season United had finished eighth, with champions Arsenal, Leeds United, Tottenham Hotspur, Wolverhampton Wanderers, Liverpool, Chelsea and Southampton in front of them, after having a clear lead at Christmas. Halfway through the 1972–73 campaign O'Farrell was given his cards when third from the bottom of the First Division, after a 5–1 defeat at Crystal Palace and eighteen months into his five-year contract.

He recalled: 'I had plenty of people commiserating with me. A friend of Matt Busby's asked me out to dinner at the Midland Hotel, and told me that I'd had a raw deal. A director told me that Matt had been sitting on his backside for the last three or four years, letting the team run itself, and added that he brought in other people to do the hard things that had been neglected, and then didn't support them when they tried to do the job.

'It was Matt who said, when we were top of the League, that I was the best signing he'd ever made; but he left Louis Edwards to tell me they were terminating my contract. I'd been called into a board meeting. I asked for the reason for the decision to end my contract, and the chairman replied: "No reason." So I said that if they thought I was fool enough to go out of the room without being told why, then they were wrong. Eventually I was told by the chairman that it was because we were near the bottom of the League, and I insisted that secretary Les Olive put it in the minutes.

'When I left they were arguing over a pension for Jimmy Murphy, one of the most loyal servants they ever had. This was a man who had given his life to Manchester United and Matt Busby. And for a time I had to sign on the dole in Salford because it was ten months before Manchester United paid me up.

'The whole sorry affair was, I felt, more damaging to Manchester United's reputation than mine; but I was determined never to make myself vulnerable to that kind of situation again.

'For I had a fruitful time left in football, and a good period as national team manager of Iran, with the remit to prepare them for the Olympic Games and the 1978 World Cup in Argentina as well as the Asian Games, after which I enjoyed a return to Torquay United as general manager.'

He was also offered the managerial post at Newcastle United in 1976, but after considering at length he turned it down, resolving: 'I'm never going to put myself in the position I was in at Old Trafford where I couldn't trust people.

'It was an injustice to the people who came after Matt Busby that while deservedly taking all the plaudits for the wonderful things he achieved for Manchester United, doing something I am sure nobody else before or after him could ever have done, he was never held accountable for the decline of the club that he let go so badly after winning the Champions' Cup of 1968.'

Frank summed up his feelings concisely: 'One period of disappointment in a wonderful lifetime of being involved in the greatest game isn't bad; but I learned the best lesson of my career: that there is more to life than Manchester United.'

Perhaps nobody could be more sympathetic to Frank O'Farrell's unhappy term at Old Trafford, a job that he accepted with such relish and high hopes, than his first signing, Martin Buchan, who now works for the Professional Footballers' Management Group. For if

Frank's Manchester odyssey proved to be a rocky ride, his protégé looks back with even more regrets at his own brief period as manager of Burnley.

And Martin's prophecies were also not something you'd want to have a bet on. He remembers that when going for his first job, learning the managerial ropes at Turf Moor, he was tipped to go back to his old club Aberdeen to take over when Alex Ferguson took over the national team job with Scotland. At the time Martin said: 'Alex is too young to want to manage a national team, *and he certainly wouldn't relish moving south across the border.*'

Martin had a call from Alex on his first day as boss at Turf Moor, wishing him good luck and telling him: 'Always make yourself available to the press, and never engineer a confrontation because confrontations will arise in the course of the job.' Ruefully Buchan related to me: 'I had to tell Alex his advice was too late. I'd already punched one of our players in pre-season training to show who was boss. I couldn't believe myself what I'd done. In thirteen years as a pro I'd only had four yellow cards and never been sent off, but in 1986 I'd clouted one of my own players within weeks of starting as manager. How it never got into the papers I don't know. Alex was probably surprised to hear what I was telling him because when he'd played for Rangers against me at Aberdeen I got nothing from him but bruises, but he finished on the losing side despite scoring their two goals.

'But it was great to be signed by Frank O'Farrell from Aberdeen because I'd had such a wonderful grounding at Pittodrie under Eddie Turnbull, who was their manager between 1964 and 1971. If I was disappointed in anything in my football career it was that I failed to carry on my managerial ambitions, because no man could have had a better grounding than working with Eddie Turnbull.

'I felt I'd let him down by not putting myself in a position to pass on all the knowledge he instilled in me. When I left Aberdeen I could have played in any defensive formation in the world, Italian, Spanish, German, you name it. He made Aberdeen a force in Scottish football rather than the rest home it was for old pros from southern Scotland when he arrived. He was a wonderful manager and coach, and you can always assess a man by what he tells his team at half-time. You don't have long to change things, but he didn't need a video replay: it was all in his head, instant recall, every second of the game up there in his head. He was brilliant.

'And finally, when United came for me, I was certainly ready. United needed a replacement for David Sadler who had a knee problem. Leeds and Liverpool were also after me; but Frank O'Farrell came up with Les Olive and Johnny Aston to sign me on 29 February 1972. And by Christmas Frank was out of a job after a big defeat by Crystal Palace and Tommy Docherty was appointed.'

Had Frank O'Farrell been overwhelmed by the United job? Had he not been given enough time? Was he not extrovert enough, under the shadow of Matt Busby? Buchan's answer pierced straight to the heart of the matter, underlining that O'Farrell was let down by players who did not want to realise that times had changed and natural ability alone was no longer enough for success.

He said: 'The simple fact was that Frank wasn't accepted by the senior players. Football had changed from 1966 when England won the World Cup with Alf Ramsey's 4-3-3 formation, and more than just natural ability was needed at the top.

'Alf had found a system to suit his players. Too many clubs tried a formation that didn't suit their players, and that caused problems. But more organisation was shown to be needed, especially at Old Trafford, and the players couldn't accept it. They said that Matt Busby had told them just to go out and enjoy themselves on the field.

'They couldn't accept the new needs of the game. Other teams proved to be better prepared, even if they didn't have such good players. But in trying to change to better habits Frank O'Farrell got no support at all from the senior pros. Maybe some of them had been allowed to stay on too long. They should have been eased out. How did I rate Frank? I never got a chance to find out. He wasn't there long enough. He was an honest man, but not a hands-on tracksuit manager like Eddie Turnbull. Frank's number two Malcolm Musgrove was a man I got on well with, and maybe if he'd had more authority things would have worked out. But I was a wide-eyed 23-year-old busy settling in Manchester, and probably at the time just didn't see the big picture unfolding in front of me.'

Added Buchan: 'There was no doubt that our manager had done well at Leicester City, and one of the main reasons that he got the job was that his television interviews showed him to be an honest straightforward man who came over well, and had the track record with results to show for it. I have to give him credit for being a decent man, and he looked after me when he signed me, giving me good advice about getting a pension, from which I'm reaping the benefit to this day. But the bottom line was that he didn't have the confidence of the senior players. There was clearly a faction there working against him.

'And, of course, the cry was that Matt Busby wouldn't have done it this way or that way. I don't recall personally thinking there was anything wrong with Frank's tactics, rather I remember questioning the ability of some of my teammates, who in my opinion wouldn't have got a game in Aberdeen reserves. I was amazed. We had ageing players there plus young players who just were not Manchester United quality. I often wondered how Eddie Turnbull would have fared if he had been given the job. I'm sure he wouldn't have stood any nonsense, and would have handled the job as he saw it. He would have been first class.'

The Frank O'Farrell Fact File

1927:   9 October, born in Cork. Started career as a player with Cork United in the League of Ireland.

1948:   Signed for West Ham United.

1952:   Made international debut for Republic of Ireland against Austria.

1956:   Signed for Preston North End and scored in first game against Manchester City; finished third in First Division.

1957–58: Second in First Division.

1959:   Last international appearance for Ireland against Czechoslovakia, scoring two goals in nine games.

1961:   Moved from Preston to Weymouth as player-manager for four years.

1965:   Appointed manager of Fourth Division Torquay United.

1968:   Appointed manager of struggling Leicester, and experienced the agony and ecstasy of football, being relegated and reaching the FA Cup final in the same season, before losing at Wembley 1–0 to Manchester City.

1969–70: Finished third in first season in the Second Division.

1970–71: Won Second Division and promoted.

1971:   June, appointed manager of Manchester United.

1972:   Went into the New Year top of the First Division, but finished the season eighth. Made his first and most successful signing this year in Martin Buchan, who cost £135,000 from Aberdeen.
Told by chairman Louis Edwards at Christmas he was being sacked for being near the bottom of the Division.

1973:   Managed Cardiff City for a short while to gain breathing space to map out his future.

1974–76: Appointed Manager of Iran national team, preparing them for the Asian Games and the Olympic Games in Montreal.

1976:   Became general manager of Torquay United and remained at Plainmoor for six years, during which time he turned down major football jobs including management of Newcastle United.

1982:   Retired from football, and did some property developing before retiring completely on a golf handicap of 21. Still lives in Torquay.

Always So Upbeat

Eddie Turnbull may not have become manager of Manchester United, but Martin Buchan was still to find that his next boss was a fellow Scot. The Tommy Docherty era saw a massive clear-out, while important players in Old Trafford history such as Lou Macari, Stuart Pearson and Steve Coppell – a great player who could easily have later become manager of the club himself – were signed as the new broom swept clean.

Tommy became United's manager in December 1972, head-hunted from his position as national team manager of Scotland, and in his first season he saved United from relegation. It was only a stay of execution, however – they went down to the Second Division in his second season. But he went on not only to produce once more the kind of entertaining football that Manchester United had always been renowned for, but to take the club both to their biggest Wembley shock and one of their greatest domestic Cup final victories.

As Buchan recalls: 'Tommy certainly rejuvenated the club, although it took a relegation season for the breakthrough to start. Enjoyable as periods were under him, I was under no illusions about my status: I know I was never a favourite of the Doc, and perhaps the fact that the press portrayed me as a loner – an easy tag – helped, because I preferred reading a book to playing cards, and I didn't gamble. So I wasn't in any of the easily identifiable groups. What I was proud of was that after playing thirteen games up to the end of my first season, I only missed one game in four 42-match League seasons. Not many players can say that nowadays, in the era of squad rotation. The rotation system wouldn't have suited my tastes. One of my theories is to always play your best team.'

Manchester United were relegated in the 1973–74 season alongside Southampton and Norwich City, just six years after being crowned champions of Europe; but they bounced back in one season, winning the Second Division championship with Aston Villa in second place and Norwich third, while Chelsea, Luton Town and Carlisle United were relegated from the top flight to take their place. It was the prelude to some heady entertainment for the United faithful. According to Martin Buchan: 'Our new manager certainly wasn't short on charisma, and he could have won the championship the season after we won promotion from the Second Division.'

There were undoubtedly signs of the old sparkle returning. The new United were confident enough on their return to finish third in the First Division with 56 points – behind Liverpool (60) and QPR (59) – although there was a shattering drop back to reality in May 1976 when Bobby Stokes scored the winning goal for Second Division Southampton in the FA Cup final as what looked like a foregone conclusion for Manchester United turned into one of the biggest post-war FA Cup shocks to that date.

United were odds-on favourites in the 1976 final against Saints, who had reached the final via two replays before beating Crystal Palace 2–0 in a Stamford Bridge semi-final. The Southampton fans had experienced a roller-coaster ride to Wembley, their team beating Villa at the second attempt in the third round and then Blackpool before needing a fifth-round replay to overcome West Bromwich Albion, the prelude to a sixth-round 1–0 cliffhanger against Bradford to reach the last four. Not that it had been easy for United either; they had defeated Oxford United, Peterborough United and Leicester City, but had nearly fallen when drawing 1–1 at Old Trafford against Wolves before winning a sixth-round replay en route to a comfortable semi-final win over Derby County at Hillsborough.

Approaching his fourth full season, Tommy Docherty had welded together a team that looked capable of beating anybody, but now, eight years after their historic Champions' Cup victory, it turned out they could not beat a nobody. It seemed that the team from The Dell were just going to Wembley to make up the numbers, but then all hell was let loose as one of the FA Cup's greatest upsets unfolded. Confirmation that names and reputations mean nothing in the Cup. But it was Liverpool's turn to find out that old truism twelve months later, after beating Moenchengladbach to win back-to-back European Cups (with a follow-up victory against Bruges in 1978), a feat Manchester United have so far been unable to duplicate. The Doc's team grabbed a wonderful 2–1 win in the 1977 Wembley final, ending the Merseysiders' treble hopes through goals from Stuart Pearson and Jimmy Greenhoff, with Jimmy Case replying for the Anfielders.

Two months after that great triumph, and with signs that there were more trophies to come from his young team, Tommy Docherty was on his way out of Old Trafford after falling in love with Mary Brown, the wife of the club physiotherapist.

Buchan continued: 'I'll go to my grave thinking we should have won the title. We were distracted by the FA Cup, and underestimated Southampton. We went to pieces from winning the early rounds after twice being behind against Wolves.

'We were certainly good enough to win the League. We had a good mix of youth and experience, and had the Doc stayed after winning the Cup when we returned to Wembley the following year, I think we would have gone on to win the championship. But you never know: it's all about opinions, and perhaps we'd had our chance.

'Although the fans loved him for the excitement he had brought back to football at Old Trafford, there were players who didn't get on with Tommy Docherty; but I must admit that at the end of the day the two happiest years of my life, and the most entertaining, were those first two seasons back in the First Division under Tommy.

'I always wonder if we could have kept that momentum, and gone on to level up some of the glory years that Liverpool enjoyed in the seventies and eighties. They were more pragmatic than we were, and could grind out 1–0 wins, whereas we were more cavalier, and never learned to close teams down. But the Doc produced a great family spirit right through the club. Everybody was a part of it, and Tommy Cavanagh played a big part alongside him. My select team from that era would, I think, have matched any United team in history.'

Buchan had a point. Docherty's United were certainly not without star names. Every member of the Doc's side was an international, apart from the best United player never to win a cap, electric-heeled Jimmy Greenhoff. Against Southampton the Wembley line-up had read: Stepney; Forsyth, Houston, Buchan, Brian Greenhoff; Coppell, Daly, McIlroy, Hill; Pearson, Jimmy Greenhoff.

'If the Doc had stayed, would we have won the League? I discussed it with Johnny Giles, and he didn't feel we had enough mature players to do it, whereas Leeds and Liverpool were always so tight and hard to beat. But our boss was always so upbeat. He preferred to let the opposition worry about us, although still to be aware of major threats. Some managers frighten their own team to death with dossiers on the opposition.

'And yet Tommy's ways could be just as effective. At one team talk before an important match against Sunderland he insisted on calling their defender Dick Malone, who was a noted hard man, "Dorothy Malone" – which not only lightened the atmosphere but made sure that we approached a ninety-minute battle with the fiery Malone with a smile rather than a whimper.

'He also encouraged people like Eric Morecambe and Freddie Starr into the dressing room before a match, even though Eric followed Luton Town and Freddie was an Everton supporter. There was never a dull moment.

'What a difference we had in managers in terms of personality. For instance, when there was a press conference at The Cliff the media boys left the Doc wondering what to leave out. With Dave Sexton they left wondering how on earth they could make his words sound interesting and newsworthy.'

Around Old Trafford there was no better informed person outside the inner circle of the board and management than the late Jim Barker, restaurant manager and catering manager at the club from 1975, when he was appointed to oversee the building of the new restaurant complex. He ran the restaurant and catering of the club until retiring in 1991. And some of his best stories concern the Doc.

It is worth digressing briefly to tell Jim Barker's own story. His connection with the club went far beyond his period of employment at Old Trafford, for the Grand Hotel in Manchester city centre, and the Brook House Hotel in Fallowfield where he worked before that, were both haunts for Manchester's footballing fraternity.

The Grand was a famous watering hole where managers would meet for a Saturday evening drink after their respective matches, while visiting teams also often stayed overnight in preparation for games. It was there that he first came into contact with Matt Busby and his assistant Jimmy Murphy, and where he developed close connections with many famous footballing names, notably the great Liverpool boss Bill Shankly. Remembering those times, he related to me a particular example of the respect and awe in which Busby and Shankly were held, especially by their players – an awe that is no longer evident nowadays, in an age of multi-millionaire players.

'When Shankly came into the dining room the talking stopped. You could hear a pin drop as his players, internationals and young hopefuls alike, and even the directors, would fall silent. Not even the toughest of them dared to incur a withering glance, or a sharp Scottish reprimand from his lips. In fact they dared not even select their own meal for the night before a match, or their lunchtime snack!'

Explained Jim: 'A typical example of the way Bill held his players on a tight rein was that while they were sick to death of the same pre-match meal wherever they played, not one of these world-class stars had the nerve to complain. He would not bend, always telling me he wanted the same meal: soup, fillet steak, fruit salad and ice cream.

'But one weekend the lads must have felt extra brave because they delegated Tommy Smith to buttonhole me. Tommy said he knew I was Bill's pal, and that I could get round him. They knew he would agree if I, from the lofty heights of my culinary expertise, suggested a change of menu.

'Foolishly I agreed to help the lads. When Bill told me that he wanted the same old meal I asked him if he didn't think it would be a good idea to have something different, and suggested various alternatives.'

Bill Shankly's reply was delivered without a change of pace or a twitch of the facial muscles. 'That's a good idea, Jim. I tell you what, we'll have soup, fillet steak, fruit salad and effing ice cream. I think they'd like that.'

Added Jim: 'He didn't miss a trick, and nothing threw him out of his stride. He knew what his boys were thinking before their little grey cells started to work. They could never beat him to the punch. And his fellow Scot Matt Busby was equally on top of every twist and turn, every nuance of the squad of players he ran with such precision.'

Jim looked at the fashion in modern times of having a two-man management team. Such arrangements were ostensibly popularised by the Brian Clough and Peter Taylor combination at Nottingham Forest and Derby County, but in truth Matt Busby and Jimmy Murphy set the style, and as with Matt's youth policy, football generally only caught up decades later. Jim also pointed out that the team behind the team included the chairman as well as the manager, but added: 'Louis Edwards, the chairman at Old Trafford, always did as Matt told him. Matt was capable of running anything and everything. He was a born leader. And as a businessman, the chairman knew that Matt would make the right decisions about every aspect of the club, and that he was an ambassador supreme for the club.

'He had that knack of making the club one happy family because he treated everybody the same, high and low. He always had time to have a word with people. In all the time I was at Old Trafford I never saw or heard a row among the staff. Everybody respected everybody else. It wasn't like that with every manager.'

He continued: 'What a contrast we found when Ron Atkinson took over from Dave Sexton. There was no resemblance to Matt Busby's style of management. Tommy Docherty certainly had his own way, Dave Sexton and Frank O'Farrell were quiet men; but Ron Atkinson, quite simply, despite his happy-go-lucky press image, was an arrogant man. He was a successful manager in many ways, did well in Cup competitions, and undoubtedly produced one of the most entertaining teams of all time at Old Trafford, but he had no respect for the little people at the club. I had a good staff in the restaurant, but I would always have them coming to me and complaining about Ron upsetting the waitresses with his complaints and rudeness to them. He was never liked by the backroom staff at the club. A typical incident occurred after a Cup final win when we were at our London hotel.

'The chairman told me to close the bar at nine o'clock to ensure everybody was in the dining room by then. Big Ron had Malcolm Allison as his guest in the bar. When the time came I told the bartender to put the shutters up, but Ron called the waiter over and insisted loudly that he be served with another round of drinks. I quietly told him that I'd been asked to close the bar and pointed out that he could order his drinks with his meal when he moved to the dining room. But he became most offensive towards me, to the embarrassment of everybody in the room, cursing and really making a spectacle of himself. It wasn't the behaviour expected of a manager of Manchester United. I'm sure his players at Old Trafford were always very much on his side, but he was never really liked through the rest of the club.'

Jim Barker told me that he always got on well with Alex Ferguson, a man generally thought to be much more abrasive than Big Ron, whom I have always found approachable, caring and good company. But he said: 'Sir Alex was easy to get on with, and although they were very different people on the surface there were many similarities between Sir Matt and Sir Alex. Mind you, I retired early in Sir Alex's career, and the pressure hadn't got to him in his first two difficult years as much as it seems to have after seven Premiership titles and a Champions' League final win.'

Despite those similarities, however, Matt was a different kettle of fish to Sir Alex. Jim Barker told me: 'Although he never let pressure get to him, Matt certainly had an iron fist in the velvet glove when it came to winning matches for his beloved Manchester United. I'm sure that the old man wouldn't have made the same mistake that his successor made of spending £49 million at the start of what was originally going to be his last season.

'And I also think he would have realised what Sir Alex didn't realise, that a wake lasting a full season would be something that neither the players nor the manager could stand the strain of. When

the time comes Alex Ferguson will, I'm sure, end his long reign as
the boss of Old Trafford just like Matt, with people saying that he is
an impossible act to follow.'

What will be needed to provide continuity and take Manchester
United to further success?

'It seems more than likely that Sir Alex's successor will be the fall
guy just as Wilf McGuinness was, making it that little bit easier for
the next manager but one to get the club back on the trophy trail and
save the club from the fate of again being relegated only six seasons
after being crowned European champions at Wembley. Sounds an
outrageous possibility, doesn't it? But there's no place like a football
club for illustrating the old saying that what goes round comes round.'

Many Scotsmen seem to be better educated than their English
counterparts. Even Fergie's notoriously abrasive manner belies the
fact that he is well read, and capable of speaking with authority on
many subjects other than football and horse racing. Said Jim:
'Busby was a very clever man, a lot cleverer than people gave him
credit for. It was a near impossible act to follow, and it was tragic
that a good guy like Wilf McGuinness should have the heartbreak he
suffered in following him. When the time comes, the man who
follows Sir Alex after such a fantastic run will need very special
qualities to keep the club going forward. He'll need the composite
talents of Matt, Alex, Brian Clough, Bill Shankly, Bob Paisley,
Arsène Wenger and Joe Harvey.

'I never saw a player step out of line with Matt. Shankly, too,
moulded an extraordinary discipline into his team, and always had
an answer to every move the opposition made. And Paisley was
exactly the right man to follow him – he was a rigorously solid
football man. Joe Harvey at Newcastle in the late fifties and sixties
wouldn't stand the slightest messing about, and ruled his team with
a rod of iron. Clough just had such an extraordinary personality yet
a wonderful tactical sense, while Wenger has impressed me with his
own personal control and the calmness that seems to permeate his
team, just as Sven-Goran Eriksson's calm personality gives new
strength and purpose to England.

'Perhaps after Sir Alex there might also be the need for a lighter
touch, the type of touch that Tommy Docherty gave to the team before

his private life destroyed his chance of becoming the first manager since Busby to win the League title for United. He was a good manager, knew the business inside out, and there was no doubt the supporters loved him; they were chanting his name long after he left.

'It might be the wrong vibes that some of us inside the club received, but there was a feeling that Matt was the man responsible for Tommy Doc being swept out of the club because of his affair with Lawrie Brown's wife. Sir Matt was never a big pal of Tommy's. Perhaps he resented the fact that he was so friendly with Matt's own big buddy, chairman Louis Edwards.'

But it seemed that the Doc was born for fun and controversy. Concluded Jim Barker, who, sadly, after a long illness died between my interview and publication: 'I'd only been at the club five weeks when Tommy arrived. Immediately he was a person anybody could talk to, a personality big enough for Manchester United. But he loved his double whiskies, and I remember one particularly tough time when I had to sober him up.

'He was due to speak at a dinner arranged at the club by director Denzil Haroun, who asked me where he was when time was getting late and there was no sign of Tom. I went to Tommy's office, and found him in a bad way. I had to give him gallons of black coffee, but he still argued that he couldn't possibly speak. I went to tell Mr Haroun that his prize speaker was under the weather. I was told in no uncertain terms that that was nothing to the weather he'd be under if he wasn't ready to speak in ten minutes.

'After an uncertain start Tommy came up trumps as usual. It was probably one of the best speeches he ever made, and the following morning he didn't even remember he'd made a speech.'

The Last to Know

Physiotherapist Lawrie Brown was a constant presence in the Manchester United dressing room for twelve years. He was there during the latter period of Sir Matt Busby's reign, the brief period when Wilf McGuinness was in charge, and then through the regimes of Frank O'Farrell, Tommy Docherty and Dave Sexton. Only when Ron Atkinson instituted a purge and brought in his own men did Lawrie's tenure end.

For a physiotherapist Lawrie, whose first match with Manchester United was the semi-final of the European Cup United were defending in 1969, has been in the middle of some turbulent times. But he has come out of it well with some tremendous sporting memories, and a reputation for being able to keep a secret.

But one secret he was not privy to for a long time at Old Trafford was that Tommy Docherty, the manager, and a man he thought was a firm friend, was having an affair with his wife. And eventually, when the affair came to the attention of the board of directors and chairman Louis Edwards, and was subsequently made public, it became a cause célèbre, leading ultimately to Docherty's sacking. Lawrie bit the bullet and stayed at the club for another four years, giving sterling service and becoming recognised as one of the top remedial physiotherapists in the game.

Lawrie had been working in the practice of Ted Dalton, another long-serving Old Trafford physio, when he came to Matt Busby's attention. At Ted's retirement, Lawrie Mawson had filled his shoes briefly. Brown took over when Mawson in turn retired, and soon found it was a job he relished. As we talked in the lounge of his house, around a long goal kick from the Stalybridge Celtic ground in Greater Manchester, he remembered: 'I'd done some work previously with Ronnie Allen at Wolves. I wasn't used to football at the Manchester United level, but I soon found my feet, marvelling at how the top players like Nobby Stiles and Pat Crerand motivated themselves, and how superstars like Bobby Charlton, Denis Law and George Best didn't need anybody to talk tactics to them. They knew the game inside out.'

So much of it was common sense, backing up Matt Busby's and Bill Shankly's frequent claims that 'Football is a simple game, made difficult by the coaches.' The coaches, they used to say, would take an hour on the blackboard, spend an age talking about it, and two days a week shadow play to try and prove that football was a mystery.

Said Lawrie: 'Denis Law, however, took just a few minutes to work out how to beat teams trying to man-mark him out of a game by going and standing with another defender, taking his marker with him, instantly leaving the opposition a man short, leaving his teammates to utilise the extra room. He reckoned it didn't need a rocket scientist to work that one out.'

Having joined the staff on the cusp of Matt's brief handover to Wilf McGuinness, the new physio was able in the heartbreaking eighteen months that Wilf was in charge to see just how tough a job it was following in the footsteps of a legend. He reflected that it will be no easier for the successor to Sir Alex Ferguson.

According to Lawrie: 'Wilf had a tremendous enthusiasm for the job, and he tried desperately hard. Being new to the job myself, and perhaps a little naïve, I didn't know anything about there being somebody in the background pulling the strings. Of course stories surfaced afterwards – and they were repeated during Frank O'Farrell's time at the club – that there was interference against their attempts to run the team their way. But it was news to me.

'I worked from The Cliff training ground where the players did all their training, and after Matt Busby retired as manager I never once saw him there, whereas some newspapers talked as though he was there every day of the week, interfering in tactics and training. They seemed unfair comments to me.

'But I could see how upset Wilf was when things didn't work out for him. Although he stayed on briefly to take charge of the second team after he lost his first-team job, he obviously felt uncomfortable. Perhaps he was too enthusiastic.

'The case of Nobby Stiles and John Connaughton when they were in St Joseph's hospital for cartilage operations, was perhaps an example. While they were still in hospital under the charge of the consultant, Wilf went down to see them and give them fitness tests. When the consultant found his two charges running high temperatures he wasn't pleased. Wilf's overenthusiasm created more than a few waves on that occasion.

'But in my view Wilf showed that he had everything needed to make a good manager if he had been allowed time to build up more experience. There was no doubt that he wasn't helped by the more experienced players not taking kindly to the harder training routines that he introduced. But you only develop a complete man-management style by gaining experience. That was all that was lacking, and Wilf wasn't given time to learn the ropes.'

So Frank O'Farrell took over. He didn't wear his heart on his sleeve as Wilf did, and he always seemed composed, but he also had a rough ride.

'There was no doubt,' said Lawrie, 'that Frank O'Farrell believed in being well organised. Of all the managers I worked under he was the only one to ask me if I was a qualified physiotherapist. He also tried to look after his staff. Previously I'd been at the ground seven days a week, but he told me he wanted me to get some rest, and that he didn't want me there every day of the week just for the sake of it.

'Under the new manager, George Best, who had begun to be a bit erratic in his time-keeping, was in fantastic form and completely reliable. The manager must have wondered what all the fuss was about when people said that George was difficult to handle. He did all he could to make sure George was handled right to get the best out of him, and was amazed when the wayward element in Best's lifestyle began to resurface. He was shocked and distressed when George went missing again from training, but that wasn't the main reason for his downfall.

'Quite simply players were brought into the club who weren't of the right calibre, and weren't as good as the men they were replacing. But it was a difficult period, and for all the thousands of people who knew, or thought they knew, what the problem was, it was a period when nobody else came up with any better answers over who should replace Law, Best, Charlton, Crerand and Stiles. For my money Frank O'Farrell was a decent man, and I felt sorry for him, because he didn't get the support he deserved. It was hurtful to find that when he arranged a farewell dinner for his coaching and backroom staff, few of them bothered to turn up.

'But the new manager, Tommy Docherty, was much more streetwise, and quickly seemed to know everything that was going on at the club. He collared me within a week, saying he knew I was a Frank O'Farrell man because I'd gone along to his farewell dinner.'

Docherty quickly became a favourite with the supporters. But, as Martin Buchan hinted, they were not the only ones to show favouritism. Shortly after the Doc arrived he surprisingly made Scottish international Willie Morgan captain. Says Lawrie Brown: 'When Docherty started he would often be out lunching with Willie Morgan while the rest of the team were training under Tommy Cavanagh, and it appeared that the manager and his captain had become bosom pals. But it became apparent that this was the Doc's weakness – he would play favourites with certain players, thus creating cliques in the side, and it would all end in tears because when the manager fell out with anybody he fell out big time. When Willie left the club he described his former friend and manager as the worst boss in the world.

'The end had come when Steve Coppell was signed from Tranmere Rovers and Willie was relegated to the subs' bench. Steve was brought on for his first game, and we scored immediately from his inswinging corner. It was impossible to get Steve out of the team after his performance, and what a good pro he turned out to be.

'He was one of the earliest players to voluntarily stay in the afternoon and put in extra training by himself. In fact, before him Alan Gowling was the only other player who did this. Perhaps the fact that they both went to university before becoming pro footballers had something to do with their dedication.' Steve was such a success, going on to win 42 full England caps, that Willie Morgan was never missed.

Within twelve months United were back at Wembley. Coppell and company had a chance not only to make up for that shock defeat by Southampton, but to beat League champions Liverpool, who had also overcome Borussia Moenchengladbach in the European Champions' Cup final in Rome.

It was almost the same United team that had been humbled by Lawrie McMenemy's men, but there were new full-backs in Arthur Albiston and Jimmy Nicholl, who had replaced Stewart Houston and Alex Forsyth, and Dave McCreery came on as sub for Gordon Hill as he had done the previous year. And it was a fantastic performance by United, Stuart Pearson and Jimmy Greenhoff scoring against the lone reply of Jimmy Case. Beating Liverpool at Wembley gave the Doc's boys unparalleled pleasure, for it denied the Merseysiders a treble.

Lawrie Brown continued the story: 'Players seem to come in clumps at Old Trafford. The club had a great build-up of star quality players leading to 1968 after the sad loss of all those great players at Munich, and now there was another talented group coming together with such as Albiston, the Greenhoffs, Coppell, Pearson and Macari.

'Little did we know that my private life was heading for disaster. I suppose it's not uncommon in these circumstances, but I was the last to know what was going on between the manager and my wife. It all came out in the open, however, after the Cup final. Initially it looked as though Docherty had survived when Louis Edwards said that it wasn't a football matter. But apparently other directors didn't agree with the chairman.

'Perhaps it was no surprise to the Doc that he had to go, because looking back later that summer I recalled that he'd often talked about when he would leave the club, and Derby County, where he eventually ended up, often figured in his talk of the future. What was a surprise to me, though, was that no mention was made that I should leave as well.

'Obviously I was the innocent party in all of this; but it would have been easy for the directors to feel that I would find it difficult to stay under the circumstances. But nothing was said to me, and as I was determined to stay if I could, it was a pleasant surprise that I didn't have to fight to keep my job.'

Added Lawrie: 'What wasn't said was that Tommy was living on the edge, and that there were other problems that were never revealed. I heard it said that the "Sacked for Love" scenario was a nice excuse to solve an escalating problem. There was certainly a lot going on behind the scenes, but then when has there not been a lot going on behind the scenes at Old Trafford?'

One man who could back up that view was John 'Scoop' Maddock, former Northern sports editor of the *People* newspaper. He was an eighteen-year-old cub reporter in 1961 on the *Daily Express* when he had his first connection with Matt Busby, although he admitted to me that it was not until he made contact with Tommy Docherty that he made full acquaintance with the most bizarre aspects of football.

But there were plenty of eye-openers even at the start of his career in newspapers. His first experience of Matt Busby was an immediate illustration of the power of the man who ruled Old Trafford. He recalled picking the phone up to hear Matt's voice on the phone, asking: 'Is Bill Fryer in the office?' Bill was a distinguished sports writer, and like all sports writers, distinguished or not, Bill was usually to be found in the pub round the corner from the office.

'Matt told me to get him out of the pub quickly. When I got the message through to Bill he came back like a shot, telling me abruptly that if ever I got another message from Matt I should get it to him more quickly. He knew if Mr Busby, as he was then, said it was urgent it could only mean one thing, he had some transfer news for him. That was the first time I realised how people jumped if Matt said jump, and the more I became involved with the players the more I understood what a grasp and command he had over them.

'Make no mistake, whatever the players say, they literally lived in fear of him, and the respect for him was total. A typical example was when one of them gave me an exclusive story the season after the 1968 European Champions' Cup success. They weren't doing well the following season, and Matt had given them a strong lecture at a team meeting, telling them they were relaxing, resting on their laurels, and he wasn't standing for it. He also added at the end of the talk that if anybody told the press about what he'd said to them then he would fine every one of his players.

'When the story came out he went crazy, and he didn't let the players off the hook for a long time; but in the end he relented on the fine when the form improved, probably because of the fear he'd put into them over the leak from my mole in the camp.'

Added Scoop Maddock: 'When he retired the first time, I ran a story that Brian Kidd, nineteen years old at the time, and one of the heroes of the defeat of Benfica, had asked for a transfer.

'Wilf McGuinness, then in charge of the team as coach and manager-in-waiting, cornered me in the VIP lounge at the club, and before a crowd of people he shouted angrily across to me: "Your story is a load of bollocks! Matt knows nothing about it, and he's been to see Brian Kidd."'

Replied Maddock: 'That must be the first time that the Mountain has gone to Mahomet.' And at that he rested his case.

But within days Wilf approached the *People* man in the same room and apologised, saying that Matt had after all known about Kidd's transfer request. 'The incident certainly showed who was in charge.'

An example of the skill with which Matt used the media was shown when Wrexham came to Old Trafford for a Cup tie as potential giant-killers. Maddock takes up the story: 'Before the match Matt asked me to point out the Wrexham press men, and told me to inform them all to come into the lounge after the match and, win or lose, he would give them an exclusive interview. He was there as promised after the game and asked them their names, shook their hands, and then said he would give them ten minutes and to fire away their questions. He gave them some great copy. I was puzzled, and later I asked him why he had put himself at their disposal, when it was unlikely he would ever see them again.

'He told me that he knew none of those people, and he didn't know if they knew him, but they would do now, and then he added that you never knew how far people were going to go in life.

'Nobody knew how to work a room better than Matt. He was always asking who a certain person was if he hadn't come across them before, and he would ask the name of the man's wife if she was with him, and then walk up to them, addressing the wife by her Christian name, and she'd think what a wonderful man he was. He'd made another conquest, and the husband would be delighted at being recognised.

'He was a very purposeful man. He rarely went to the Football Writers' annual dinner in London; but he went one year, taking two directors with him, and he came back with the name of a new manager, Frank O'Farrell. Unfortunately that signing wasn't a success. Judging by the comments of the players Frank should have been a priest rather than a football manager. Both he and his assistant Malcolm Musgrove were reclusive figures at the club. Hard as they tried it wasn't made for them. I don't think either of them realised what an institution Manchester United was, and they certainly never built up any kind of rapport with the fans.'

Maddock's own big falling out with Busby came when he played politics with United, revealing in his own column in the *People* that although Busby was officially 'upstairs' now, he was still a big influence in the club, and that he called the shots.

Maddock told me: 'Matt's friends outside the club advised me not to print the story. One of my most respected colleagues, Tom Holley, got me on one side and said, "I wouldn't do it, lad"; but I printed, and it caused a massive rift with Matt.

'Shortly after, at a dinner, he came into the room alongside Manchester City chairman Peter Swales, who tried to intervene and smooth things over, but Matt said the equivalent of "Get lost". But within six months the United supremo was giving me four FA Cup final tickets as well as regaling me with whisky.'

On another occasion Maddock had got hold of a story of a rift between chairman Louis Edwards and Matt Busby over a previous agreement between the two men that their sons would join the club board together. Martin Edwards and Sandy Busby were due to become directors at the same time, and chairman Edwards had made a firm promise to this effect.

When Matt Busby heard that Maddock was going to print the story, he greeted him like a long-lost friend and asked to read the

article. The story was first class, he said, having perused it; but told
Maddock to rub out the bit that stated he would resign over the
issue, adding: 'I will never resign!' Maddock is sure to this day that
he will never meet a man again who is as calm, as capable at playing
politics or as ruthless as Matt Busby.

But he will always remember too that, even in the often eccentric
world of football, Tommy Docherty was a very special case. He
said: 'I first met Tom when he signed to write for the *People*, and
we travelled down on the train to London with Matt who was going
to an FA meeting. After we'd signed the contracts Tommy took the
party from the *People* to a favourite Greek restaurant that he used to
frequent in his Chelsea days.

'We went in for dinner at about eight o'clock, and at one a.m. he
started throwing plates over his shoulder – apparently a Greek
custom – and continued nonstop until one-thirty. Where all the
plates were coming from I don't know to this day, but Tommy kept
picking them up from the table, whirling away as though he was an
Olympic discus thrower. Bizarre! It certainly wasn't the normal
introduction the press got to a new Manchester United manager.'

Tommy Docherty by now had his feet firmly under the table at
Old Trafford. *Joie de vivre* was returning on the terraces, in the
dressing room and the boardroom, and it became a regular Friday
habit for John Maddock to write the Doc's weekly article.
Accompanied by Tommy Cavanagh, Gordon Clayton and Lawrie
Brown, they would meet regularly in a local restaurant, where
Tommy would read his weekly column and talk about the following
day's match. It must be added that before Maddock selected the
venue for their Friday luncheon he warned the proprietor to lock up
all the spare plates!

Perhaps it was lack of target practice with the plates that led to the
Doc generally rounding off lunch with vast amounts of red wine and
several gin and tonics. Maddock told me: 'One Friday he decided to
drive home, and we did all we could to stop him, wrestled with him
to get his keys, argued with him, but he got the better of us, and
drove off down Stretford Road on his way home. Sure enough he
was stopped by the police, and breathalysed with about two bottles
of red inside him plus a good few glasses of gin. When the constable

An historic photograph – one of the last of the team before the Munich crash – that even half a century later brings a lump to the throat and a tear to the eye. It shows Sir Matt Busby briefing the team in a Belgrade Hotel in 1958 before they played what was to be their last game. Shortly after leaving Belgrade they lay in the wreckage of their home-bound plane in Munich. We will never forget them.

Wembley, 1968: Sir Matt, realising a life's ambition, holds the European Cup after Manchester United had beaten Benfica in an extra-time final. Triumphant, but still remembering the events of just a decade ago, Sir Bobby Charlton and the team had but one thought: 'We did it for Matt and the boys who didn't survive Munich.'

Opposite page
Top: Flanked by Jimmy Murphy (left) and Jack Crompton, Sir Bobby Charlton – a World Cup winner two years before – embraces 'the boss' after collecting his 1968 European Cup medal.

Bottom: Manager Sir Alex Ferguson, president Sir Matt Busby and chairman Martin Edwards, 1993. As he receives yet another accolade, Sir Matt, aged 84, still has the broadest smile.

SIR MATT BUSBY WAY
FORMERLY WARWICK ROAD NORTH

Ain't life grand? Sir Matt always enjoyed a cigarette, especially when he was talking about football and his beloved Manchester United…

… But the man who first introduced youth policies to professional football with his Busby Babes enjoyed even more seeing young players grow. Here in his kingdom he stands with Jason Lydiate and Ryan Giggs after presenting their 1989 Manchester United awards as Young Player of the Year and Reserve Team Player of the Year.

Wilf McGuinness: Hair today…

…and gone tomorrow.

Above: At a Testimonial match in the 1970s, with Ian Rush (left) and Sir Bobby Charlton. (Was Sir Bob hiding something under that hat?)

Right: After losing his job at Old Trafford in 1970.

Above: A proud moment –
Frank O'Farrell *(left)*, who was
soon to become Manchester
United manager, leads out
Leicester City in the 1969 FA
Cup final at Wembley against
Joe Mercer's Manchester City
(Manchester City won 1–0,
scored by Neil Young).

Right: O'Farrell in 1971 with
Malcolm Musgrove, the coach
he took to Old Trafford as his
right-hand man.

told him the tube showed negative Tommy blurted out: "You must be joking." He must have felt affronted; but the police had the last laugh because they booked him for driving at 70 m.p.h. in a 30 limit.

'It was so irresponsible, although it wasn't seen as such a crime as it was twenty years later. And it must be added that those Friday meetings were a real education about the serious side of football, because he knew everything that was going on in the game, and nobody could get the better of him in his knowledge of the game...after all, his education had started when he played alongside Bill Shankly at Preston, and what could be a better start?

'But the Doc stories go on for ever. There's one about a visit to the Malta branch of the Manchester United Supporters Club. I used to look after the outside activities of some of the players, and I took three of them on a goodwill trip to the George Cross island. I asked Tommy if he wanted to come but he'd planned a tour with the team. The day before we were due to leave we got a call from Tommy in Bermuda, saying that they'd still got two matches to play, but sandwiches were £3 a time, and it was very boring there. He'd decided to come with us to Malta.'

He continued: 'The first thing Tommy did when reaching Newcastle Airport, where we were flying from, was to ask a stewardess how many bottles of champagne were on the plane. The answer was six, and he told her that wouldn't be enough, and to stock up again. When we were airborne with a plane full of Geordies, he ordered champers for everybody, over a hundred holidaymakers. Most of them probably hated Manchester United when they got on the plane, but they arrived at their destination as another ambassadorial triumph for our manager.

'I told him to cool the drinking as we had a raft of TV and radio interviews lined up for him immediately we landed; but he breezed through it all when we arrived, couldn't do enough for the media, and charmed everybody.'

If John Maddock thought things were going smoothly he might have changed his mind when he was given a double room with Tommy, and found at first hand just how much energy the man had. Apparently the man is the world's best catnapper. He could go full throttle for 24 hours at whatever task he'd set himself – lecturing, interviews, the lot – and a two-hour nap would have him up at full revs again.

Maddock was shattered and went straight to sleep, but at two-hour intervals he found the Doc screaming in his ear, 'Bugger Derby!'

Lawrie Brown's revelations to me later indicated that Derby County had perhaps been asking Docherty to take over as manager at the Baseball Ground, but John Maddock never found out the reason for his behaviour. He quickly found another room, only to endure another two nights of Tommy standing outside his door shouting: 'Maddock, you're a coward!' He was obviously looking for a partner for a drinking spree.

Let the scribe himself end the story: 'He was outrageous, but the Maltese supporters loved him because he just could not do enough for them. They couldn't tire him out with their requests. Say what you like about his lifestyle, he was the perfect ambassador for the club. But I eventually found that he did sometimes become depressed, despite seeming such a likeable rascal; when United were relegated in his second season after he'd saved them from relegation as successor to Frank O'Farrell, he was absolutely at his lowest ebb. He told me that he would give £25,000 of his own money to get the team back in the top flight. But he soon cheered up; you couldn't get him downhearted for long. He said: "What am I talking about? We'll be back in one season in any case." And of course they were.

'He was a terrific motivator, and knew what was happening to the players, on and off the field, before they knew themselves. But there were always intrigues around Tommy. On Bobby Charlton's last trip as a player – to Verona – I sat next to the captain, George Graham, and told him to watch his back, informing him that he wouldn't be captain next season. The Doc was getting too close to Willie Morgan, I said, and I was right. Willie did take over the captain's armband.

'But their friendship ended with a nasty court case. Tommy sued Willie, unwisely in the view of my colleague Norman Wynne and myself – we told him that he might as well go up Blackpool Tower and throw £30,000 to the winds. [Morgan had said, 'They'll be dancing in the streets of Manchester when Docherty is fired.']

'He went ahead anyway, and then as a follow-up to the case he landed himself in trouble again when he was up before a judge at the

Old Bailey on a count of perjury. The judge was clearly not charmed by the Doc. But Tommy was luckily cleared of the charge through a brilliant barrister.

'Tommy broke down in court at the end. When he recovered, and we were on our way home in a taxi fully expecting the usual outrageous celebrations to start, we found him just filled with total relief, realising what a close shave he'd had. All he wanted was a cup of tea. He'd been through the mangle, and it had been all his own fault. It seemed a sobering experience for him, and believe me it took something extraordinary to dampen his spirits.

'But there will never be another Tommy Docherty, and the good far outweighed the bad side of him.'

I can certainly say amen to those sentiments. Once I was talking in a group of eminently sedate high-ranking officials in the Old Trafford VIP suite when I almost broke the world high-jump record. The Doc had crept up behind me and ferociously 'goosed' me. You never knew what might happen with the man, but one thing you could be certain of: he loved to embarrass his friends.

The Best Signing of My Life

Either side of Thomas Henderson Docherty's controversial, but largely highly successful time at Old Trafford were two introvert managers. Frank O'Farrell and Dave Sexton were both genuine, sincere men who did their best in difficult circumstances, but neither was able to provide the personality and charisma essential in managing such a big club as United, with its larger than life personalities as players.

In the old days many retired footballers used to make a living by running a pub. But now they either go into the media as pundits or join the after-dinner speaking circuit, having a laugh about football and often shattering a few illusions for the punters with tales about other footballing names. Famous for his one-liners and sense of humour both as a player and a manager, it was an easy transition for the Doc to the media and the speaking circuit after he rounded off his management and coaching career at Preston, Wolves and South Melbourne, Australia before warming down by helping out non-league Altrincham. Nevertheless, in an era when image is everything, Tommy will probably look back and think he could have done with a spin doctor.

Now, decades after the United board decided Tommy had to go, he is still together with Mary. They live in Compstall, a happily married couple, and the Doc says: 'She was the best signing of my life.'

As we talked at his hillside home, looking back on his career at Old Trafford, he told me: 'It was a pity that it all ended just as we were getting the team together that the fans wanted and the club needed; but I got the best of the deal, even though it was disappointing to be pushed out. It came so soon after beating the best team in Europe, and the defeat of Liverpool in what wasn't a classic final was certainly tremendous consolation for the defeat at Wembley the previous year. We really thought we were going to beat Southampton, couldn't see them overcoming us, and perhaps we were too confident. But I believe in that feeling of "if your name is on the Cup", because I had that feeling against Liverpool even though I couldn't really see how we had a chance against them.'

Recalling his arrival at Old Trafford from the Scotland team manager's job, he said: 'It was ironic that the Wednesday before the match against Crystal Palace Matt Busby spoke to me and indicated that something was wrong at Old Trafford. I was able to see what was happening to United that week because I had told Palace that I would be at Selhurst Park on the Saturday for the match with Manchester United to run the rule over the form of a couple of Scottish players.

'Even more ironic in view of what was to happen later was that inside the ground before the match I was talking to Frank O'Farrell. We were friends and former teammates at Preston, and my seat was way back in the stand; but Frank told me to sit with him in the directors' box as he had a spare ticket. The match was a nightmare for United as Don Rogers ran amok and Palace won 5–1, putting Frank's team down among the relegation-threatened teams. At the end of the game Basil Graham came up to me, and said that Matt and Louis, the chairman, wanted to see me in the boardroom.'

Matt came straight to the point: 'There's a lot of trouble in the camp, and it looks as though it's going to come to the boil on Wednesday. Would you be interested in the job?'

Tommy grimaced as he looked back, and then said to me: 'This is the dirty side of football; but it happens throughout the game. Frank was a friend of mine, but if I didn't take the job somebody else would. I told them that they would have to speak to Willie Allen, the secretary of the Scottish FA, if they did decide they wanted to make me an offer. So it was no surprise on the following Thursday in the office when Willie told me that Louis Edwards had asked if Manchester United could approach me to offer the job.

'I left with Willie telling me that I had done a fantastic job for Scotland, and wishing me luck.'

He soon settled in at the club, knowing that he had a tough job. Looking through the record books at the men who have followed Busby, he says: 'It was difficult for Wilf McGuinness, who had played at Old Trafford all his life. I know just the almost impossible situation he must have gone into because I had a similar situation when I took over at Chelsea at the start of my management career. I moved from coach to manager, and the transition was so difficult. And for Wilf it must have been so much harder. He was undermined by the older players, and never had a chance from the start.

'And the trouble when Frank arrived was that the barrack-room lawyers were still in the dressing room, laying down the law. He did a good job to an extent, but he didn't clear out the older players immediately, when he had the chance, and it rebounded on him.'

In fact the Doc learned from what he had seen happen before him. One of his first tasks when taking over was to clear out the old brigade, although conversely he also brought back one of the oldest of the old brigade into his team. It was not, however, the team on the pitch, but the team off the pitch that Jimmy Murphy was brought back to help. Jimmy, Sir Matt Busby's right-hand man, the man who stood at the bridge to keep the Good Ship Manchester United on a straight course while Matt was fighting for his life after the Munich disaster.

'He was to be a vital part of my scouting team, despite being at the veteran stage, and I just couldn't speak too highly of him,' said Tommy. 'There were people at the club who weren't happy that I had brought Jimmy back; but the chairman told me the decision was up to me, and but for JM I don't think I would have made one of my best signings, Steve Coppell.'

He went on: 'Jimmy was a fantastic judge of a player; he always made a decision about a player by watching him at an away game. Coppell was a rare occasion when I bought a player I'd never seen play, and I did it because I trusted Jimmy's judgement absolutely.'

In fact, despite the millions that Tommy Docherty paid for players during his career, he reckons that four players whom he signed for under £100,000 were among his top buys in a long management career: 'Coppell was virtually unknown when I signed him from Tranmere Rovers for £27,000. He was a manager's dream. He was always a credit to the game in an era when a lot of outsiders get an unfortunate impression that footballers are all just money-grabbers. He would astonish the critics. I remember offering him a rise; he answered that he still had some of his contract to complete, and he didn't think he was worth a rise until he'd completed his contract satisfactorily. He always reckoned it was his job to go out and do the playing to justify his money. Would the public believe it today if you told them a player had said that he hadn't proved he was worth a rise?'

So that puts Coppell top of Docherty's hit parade, closely followed on the list by Dave Watson, Gordon Hill and Gerry Daly.

Continued the Doc: 'I bought Dave from Notts County reserves when I was at Rotherham, and he cost me £1,000. That kind of deal, again for a man who went on to play for England, really gives you a kick. And what wonderful buys Daly and Hill were. I got hold of Gordon Hill at Old Trafford for £70,000 and with his skill and ability to excite crowds he proved a tremendous investment. Then Daly, whom I first bought for £12,000, was one of the great midfield players of the time. You could build a team around a player like that.'

The signing of players like Lou Macari, Stuart Pearson, Jimmy Greenhoff and others, albeit for bigger sums, left no doubt about Tommy's ability in the transfer market, but in terms of value for money there was never a deal like Steve Coppell. And yet there were so many big clubs watching him that he could have easily been lost. Cash-strapped Tranmere were struggling for money, but initially they were asking the going rate of £100,000 for Steve, and the board said it was too much for United to pay for a lower-division player. Yet Jimmy Murphy told Tommy: 'Pay it now. Matt gives that much in a year to head waiters!'

He remembers: 'On Jimmy's word I drove straight over to Prenton Park on the Monday morning and signed him, but bearing in mind the views of my board on the fee, and how desperate Rovers were for money, I managed to beat Dave Russell down to under £30,000.'

Coppell played in the FA Cup finals against both Southampton and Liverpool as well as the 1979 final under Dave Sexton, and then as manager led Crystal Palace to the 1990 Wembley final against his old club, only losing 1–0 in the replay as United scraped through.

Surprisingly the Doc did not rate his Cup final win over Liverpool as the highlight of his five years at Old Trafford: 'The best bit for me was coming straight back up from the Second Division with a young side. There was a terrific spirit, we had a side built for the future, and could perhaps have gone straight on and won the championship if the board hadn't been so stringent in the transfer market.

'Alex Stepney was the last of the European Champions' side. He was never a minute's trouble, and he was a fine keeper, but he was past his best. I knew if I signed Peter Shilton from Stoke City I just about had the final piece of the jigsaw in place. Alex could certainly have gone on playing until the age of forty, but not to the exceptional standards of his peak years. It was an exceptional man I wanted in goal to help us win trophies every year, and I could have had Shilton for £250,000 and Alex in part exchange.

'But the deal failed on the wage issue. Our top whack was £300 a week, and the United board dug their heels in and wouldn't pay the £400 a week that Shilton wanted, so we lost one of the world's great goalkeepers. Instead Brian Clough signed him for Nottingham Forest and went on to win the League championship and two Champions' Cup finals with him.'

There was no doubt that, despite his flaws, many of the Doc's qualities were just what United needed so badly. It looked as though he was going to stay at Old Trafford until the day he retired. He admitted: 'I just loved managing Manchester United, and the feeling with the supporters was brilliant, and not surprisingly because really I was just one of them. After all, they paid my wages and the players' wages, so it was no imposition to go around to Supporters Club meetings and talk to the fans.

'But in the end I got sacked for falling in love when there were people at the club in high places who'd been in more beds than Percy Thrower.'

People at the club had tremendously enjoyed working for Tommy, and the team spirit was great – even in spite of the unnecessary problems that he made for himself by openly favouring certain players. But his first-team backroom staff of Tommy Cavanagh and Frank Blunstone – Pat Crerand's replacement, given a chance after a word from Matt Busby – were loyal lieutenants to him.

He reckons that the best team from his years at Old Trafford was: Alex Stepney (whom, incidentally, he had sold to United when he was at Chelsea); Jimmy Nicholl, Brian Greenhoff, Martin Buchan, Stewart Houston; Steve Coppell, Sammy McIlroy, Lou Macari, Gordon Hill; Stuart Pearson and Jimmy Greenhoff.

He said: 'I chased Jimmy Greenhoff for ten years. He was probably the best uncapped striker England ever had the chance to honour. It was ridiculous that he never played for his country when you see some of the people who get capped now. He screened the ball like nobody else could, he scored great goals, was lightning quick and had such a great touch.

'But I had given up hope of signing him when Tony Waddington [manager of Stoke City] told me that he'd got a player for me. Was I interested in Jimmy Greenhoff for £100,000? Was I interested? Did I want to win the pools?'

Never slow to celebrate an event with a drink or three, Tommy had plenty of events to celebrate during his time at Old Trafford, and he admits that when he joined the club Matt Busby told him: 'Watch your company. The drinking culture in Manchester is lethal.' But Tommy admits he wondered if it was possible that Matt didn't want him to become too friendly with chairman Louis Edwards. Busby and Edwards had been very close for many years as chairman and manager, and, said Docherty, Sir Matt had told him once already that it wouldn't be wise to get too close to Mr Edwards: 'When I was invited to a party at the chairman's house Matt quizzed me about the invitation, and suggested that I shouldn't accept. But when I spoke to Louis he told me that Matt had had his day. He said to me: "You and I run the club now."

'But I would never fall out with Matt. He'd been my team manager when I played for Scotland in the fifties, and if you thought Harold Wilson was a clever politician then you should have seen Matt in action. He would have been a great prime minister.'

Answering Jim Barker's story elsewhere in this book about a drunken escapade at an Old Trafford dinner when he was scheduled as the guest speaker, Tommy told me: 'I'd been ill with tonsillitis, and had some champagne in my office along with Tommy Cavanagh, and this allied with the antibiotics I was taking probably affected me.'

Which, to the cynical, might make Tommy Docherty as good a politician as Harold Wilson and Matt Busby!

He does, however, admit to one or two other escapades. 'I remember we played Coventry City at Old Trafford one Saturday, and at night went to dinner with Martin Edwards and a party of Polish people who had with them Jacek Gmoch, their national team manager.

'They had been watching our training routines at The Cliff during the week. We drank some glasses of champagne, and then sat down to a meal where vodka and caviare featured strongly. I didn't really enjoy the caviare, and the combination made me ill for three days. I've never been so poorly. I thought I was dying.'

After his playing days he had spent seven years as coach and then manager at Chelsea under one of football's legendary chairmen, Joe Mears. Tommy said succinctly of Mears: 'He just let me manage, which sounds simple; but chairmen who were football people used to let you do it, unlike some present-day inexperienced chairmen who come into the game knowing nothing about football, and want to tell you how to run a football team and which players to pick. You would get a straight answer from Joe Mears. He always told me that I made the football decisions, and that was what he paid me for.'

As has often been said, the Doc had more clubs than Jack Nicklaus. After Chelsea the list includes Rotherham United, QPR (twice), Aston Villa, Oporto of Portugal, Scotland, Manchester United, Derby County, Sydney Olympic of Australia, Preston North End (after Nobby Stiles), South Melbourne (Australia), Wolves and Altrincham, as well as a spell as assistant manager at Hull City.

His after-dinner speeches find most of the chairmen of the above clubs getting a mention, famously Jim Gregory, under whom he worked at QPR.

When chairman Gregory finally decided it was time for QPR and Docherty to come to the parting of the ways, he asked the Doc to come into his office, telling him: 'I'm afraid we have to call it a day, Tommy.'

To which the Doc memorably replied: 'Oh, I'm sorry to hear that you are leaving, Mr Chairman.'

Any Manchester United supporter who has not heard that story before should please send me a £5 note in a small brown envelope.

Few people have had greater experience of the great personalities of the game – chairmen, players, managers, coaches – than Tommy Docherty, so it is natural to ask him the perennial question: Who was the greatest, Sir Matt or Sir Alex?

He answered: 'Matt Busby was a great manager without a doubt. He had little money to build his teams, but with the help of Jimmy Murphy he worked miracles, and his players were patriotically attached to Manchester United.

'On the other hand, Alex has won more trophies than Matt and had a fantastic record after the early, difficult years, although it was much easier for him to attract players to Manchester United from all over the world. And he used the Busby formula of creating a production line of talent. The youth policy has paid off so well in blending overseas talent with home-grown stars. He's been lucky in his worst habit of wanting to fix things when they don't need fixing. Some bizarre decisions – to drop certain players, for example – have bounced in his favour.

'Even so, it's a hard one to call, especially when Matt lost a team at Munich that could have gone on to monopolise honours in England and European football for a decade.'

The Doc's punchline, however, comes on the blind side: 'Both were absolutely world-class managers, but in my opinion the greatest British manager of all time was Liverpool's Bob Paisley.'

Statistics do give credence to the Doc's point. United will have to win the Champions' League three more times before they catch up with the Anfield club. He says: 'But you can't compare Busby and Ferguson until Alex has ended his reign at the club, and his desire to control everything is so great that he could still be in place at Old Trafford in 2010 as well as being chairman of the Jockey Club, and doing Sepp Blatter's job in his spare time with FIFA.'

The Doc was never short of a comment on any given situation. Here are a few:

On Alex Ferguson, March 1993: 'He's to blame for losing the championship. He threw it away last year. There is no doubt about that. He chopped and changed a good, successful, attractive, winning team. And he blamed the pitch. He never once said, "Am I not to blame?" somewhere along the line.' Six weeks later Ferguson won the Premiership to end 26 years of failure for the club.

August 1969, after Bob Stokoe burst into the Carlisle United boardroom saying: 'If any team I'm in charge of play like Aston Villa today I'll pack in management and get a job sweeping the streets.' Docherty's reply: 'All this made me think he's a bad loser, and I don't think he'd make a good street sweeper either.'

On Oscar Arce, a ball-juggling Argentinian signed by Villa on a record £70 a week contract, August 1969: 'He may not have been much of a footballer, but he was a great negotiator.'

On Manchester United's £28 million Argentine signing Juan Sebastian Veron, May 2002: 'Making a mistake is easy, admitting it is hard. But I think Sir Alex Ferguson should hold up his hands and admit to two blunders – buying Veron and messing around with his line-up on Tuesday night. Both have cost United any chance of success this season.'

The Doc on Docherty after admitting in court that he 'told a pack of lies under oath': 'How can you believe a word I say?'

On coaches: 'Football is about common sense, not about coaching and blackboard football. I've known players to make the names of coaches, but never coaches to make the names of footballers.'

And at the start of his managerial career with Chelsea: 'My weakness is having too much to say.'

The Tommy Docherty Fact File

1928:   24 April, born in Gorbals, Glasgow.

1948:   Finished National Service and signed for Glasgow Celtic; had three first-team games for Celtic before signing for Preston North End in 1949.

1951:   First of 25 international caps for Scotland, against Wales, and promotion from Second Divison to First Division with Preston in same year.

1954:   Beaten 3–2 by West Bromwich Albion in FA Cup final, and in the same year played in the World Cup for Scotland against Austria and Uruguay.

1958:   Played in World Cup in Sweden for Scotland against Yugoslavia and France, and in August signed for Arsenal.

1959:   Last international for Scotland at Wembley against England.

1962–67: Manager of Chelsea, relegated in first season.

1965:   Chelsea win League Cup.

1967–68: Manager of Rotherham, relegated to Third Division.

1968:   Manager of Queen's Park Rangers for 28 days.

1968–70: Manager of Aston Villa, sacked.

1970–71: Manager of Portuguese club Oporto.

1971:   Assistant manager for a few weeks to Terry Neill at Hull City.

1971–72: Manager of Scotland.

1972–77: Manager of Manchester United, relegated to Second Division but promoted as champions within twelve months.

1976:   United are FA Cup runners-up, third in First Division.

1977:   United win FA Cup, beating Liverpool.
           June, sacked for affair with Mary Brown.

1977–79: Manager of Derby County.

1979–80: Manager of Queen's Park Rangers, sacked and then reinstated before being sacked again.

1980–81: Manager of Australian club Sydney Olympic.

1981:   Manager of Preston North End for five and a half months, sacked.
           Manager of South Melbourne, Wolves, Altrincham.

1983:   Became a media broadcaster and columnist.

Never a Dull Moment

The mood at Old Trafford changed in July 1977 with the arrival of Dave Sexton, a former colleague of the Doc's at Stamford Bridge. The two were as different as chalk and cheese.

For the second time in his career Sexton was taking over from Tommy Docherty. Having begun his coaching career at Chelsea when the Doc was manager of the London club, he had picked up the reins when Docherty departed Stamford Bridge in 1967. Now, after a successful management career including seven great years at the Bridge, followed by a spell leading Queen's Park Rangers to the most successful era in their history, he was replacing his disgraced former boss once again.

Unlike the flamboyant, wise-cracking Docherty, Dave was a deep-thinking soccer coach to his fingertips. Nevertheless, there was a certain Manchester United pedigree about him: he was no stranger to youth policies, having given Alan Hudson his first-team debut at the age of seventeen and put Ray Wilkins in the first team when only sixteen during their Stamford Bridge days.

When chairman Louis Edwards introduced manager Sexton at the press conference held to announce his appointment, he made it clear that he was relieved he had got a man who would make no waves in the social life of Manchester.

Sexton soon outlined his philosophy: 'My idea is that the best way to run a team is to make your own players. There's no doubt that you get a better spirit that way, although sometimes it is

100

necessary to go into the transfer market to fill a specific need. With a big club it's the blend that counts.'

He had demonstrated that he had a shrewd eye when it came to paying out to strengthen a side. At Chelsea he had been blessed with an abundance of creative players, but had needed a bustler up front to put pressure on defences, so he had brought in Ian Hutchinson, Chris Garland and Alan Birchenall; whereas at Queen's Park Rangers, in need of midfielders, he had signed Scottish international Don Masson from Notts County.

He did not have an international cap, but had a good playing background and sporting genes; his father was Archie Sexton, a top-flight middleweight professional boxer who hailed from Bethnal Green. Archie was a legitimate contender for the world championship, long before the present-day proliferation of world titles for which just about anyone can box who knows how to lace a pair of gloves. Dave has always retained an interest in pro boxing and remains proud of the memory of his dad's career, which showed a record of seventeen wins, ten of them knockouts, six losses and two draws in 25 contests. He twice won the British middleweight championship, his first national title victory being appropriately at the King's Hall, Belle Vue, Manchester where he outpointed Jack Casey in 1914.

And despite his quiet style and detached image, beneath the surface Dave Sexton was always a chip off the old block, as Lou Macari, who played under him as well as Tommy Docherty and Ron Atkinson, recalls.

Taking time to talk to me as he hoisted Huddersfield Town into the play-off zone of the Second Division in 2002, Macari admitted: 'On the face of it nobody would rate Dave Sexton as the life and soul of the party, and yet he was good company. And nobody fancied crossing him. When you got to know him it would come as no surprise that his father was a professional boxer. There was no doubt he could handle himself.'

Macari had signed professional forms for Glasgow Celtic in 1966, gaining two SFA Cup winner's medals before joining Tommy Docherty's United side in 1973 in a £200,000 deal. He went on to score 78 goals in 329 appearances for the Reds. He also played 24 times for Scotland, his international career ending after the ill-fated 1978 World Cup in Argentina when he publicly criticised Scottish FA arrangements for the event.

His managerial career started at Swindon Town as player-boss, steering the club from the Fourth to the Second Division in five years, and it seemed he was booked for top management when he moved on to take over West Ham United from John Lyall in 1989. But he resigned from Upton Park, even though the board asked him to stay on, after he was fined £1,000 for breaching rules regarding betting on matches while at Swindon. He returned to management in 1991 with Birmingham City, going on to win them the Leyland-DAF trophy at Wembley and following up with a return trip, taking the Autoglass Trophy with Stoke City.

In 1993 he was appointed manager of Glasgow Celtic, but was there for only eleven months before returning to Stoke after board reorganisations at Celtic Park. Subsequently he took over Huddersfield Town in the 2000–01 season from another recent Old Trafford hero, Steve Bruce, but their failure to escape from the Second Division saw him depart at the end of the following campaign. He has a lifetime of experience in the game and has been in enough hot water to open his own health spa; among ex-Old Trafford stars only George Graham is better placed to talk about the highs and lows of the managerial business.

Virtually a one-off in football circles as a teetotaller and non-smoker, he joined United from a Celtic team managed by the great Jock Stein, and immediately had a massive culture shock.

He reminisced: 'Jock ruled absolutely. He had a tight, close control of every player, and he was determined that I was going to Liverpool. I hadn't a clue that United were interested, and it was only by sheer chance that I didn't sign for Bill Shankly.'

Revealing a soccer secret that has been kept for the best part of thirty years, he told me: 'Jock and Bill Shankly were big pals, and I was sent to Anfield to sign for them. But they made one mistake. They sent me down on match day, and I was given a seat in the directors' box to watch the match. Unfortunately for Liverpool Pat Crerand was sitting two seats away from me, and he told me that Manchester United were interested in me, and were prepared to sign me.'

Despite the fact that Liverpoool were pre-eminent, were winning the championship and set to win the FA Cup the following season, and embark on a fantastic fifteen-year sequence of success in England and Europe, Lou had always been a Manchester United supporter: 'Later I went in for an interview with Mr Shankly, listened to all he had to tell me, and said I would talk it over with my family before making a decision. But once I had heard that United were interested there was no decision to make as far as I was concerned, and even the prospect of an £8,000 signing-on fee made no impact.

'I went back to Glasgow, Pat Crerand and the Doc met me in a hotel there, and we quickly clinched the move – which was a surprise for Jock Stein – and on the same terms that Liverpool had offered. I was in a different world immediately. Jock's management was hands-on. He masterminded everything at the club, probably pretty much the same style as Sir Alex eventually adopted at Old Trafford; but right at the other end of the spectrum from Tommy Docherty.'

Said Lou: 'Jock Stein was cool, calculating and clinical, stood no nonsense, and was a total dictator who dominated the Scottish football scene. Whereas the Doc, despite being a total football man and knowing everything about what was going on in the game, was certainly not what you would call predictable.

'He blew hot and cold, would fall out with people and as quickly fall in with them again. He gave people involved with him a roller-coaster ride, while Jock insisted that match preparation should be rigid and correct. So when I signed for United on a Thursday in Glasgow my urgent thoughts were of getting down to Manchester as quickly as possible so I could get a good night's sleep and a training session with my new teammates on Friday before playing against Bobby Moore and West Ham United on the Saturday.

'But that wasn't the Doc's style. He had no intention of rushing back to Manchester. He wanted to sit down, have a big meal and plenty of drinks to celebrate signing me before he left for England. I had to down eight or nine cokes while the party went on, and got into bed at a hotel in Manchester after midnight. In all the seven years I'd been at Celtic I don't think I'd ever even sat down in Jock Stein's presence, never mind had dinner and drinks with him.

'But despite all that, the week ended well when I slipped past Bobby Moore to get the equalising goal in a 2–2 draw. I'd been welcomed to the world of Tommy Docherty.

'It was Tommy's first season, he'd taken over a relegation-threatened side, and I was his first signing. We survived that season, but the team still needed more players to go on to better things, and it was a big help, ironically, in the formation of a really top-class team that we were relegated the following season.

'The drop down gave us breathing space. There were some excellent signings, we got together as a young team, and despite players coming in right, left and centre we steamrollered through the promotion season back to the top flight. I don't think any of us had ever before enjoyed ourselves so much. The Doc was such a great motivator. He was a funny man, a tremendous wit, but what a football man he was. His great strength was the team spirit he produced. He really geed up his players, and there was never a dull moment in the dressing room.

'His weakness lay in the cliques that grew up in the team, particularly through the way he favoured Willie Morgan, and even went off for lunch with him, leaving the rest of the team training. This business of playing favourites was bound to let him down in the end. You must treat everybody the same in a club, and inevitably it rebounded on him.' But Lou admitted: 'It was a total shock to me when news of Tommy's affair came out and he was sacked. I didn't have a clue what was going on, and it amazed me. But there's always something happening at Manchester United: never a dull moment, and especially so with Tommy Docherty.'

Lou was long past the time when he believed the Bill Shankly maxim: 'Football isn't a matter of life and death. It's far more important than that.' He has had to endure probably the worst tragedy a parent can go through. For he lost his youngest son Jonathan who, after being released at the age of nineteen by Nottingham Forest, was found hanged near the family home in the Potteries. Said Lou: 'If you thought it was a nightmare that your striker had missed a match-winning goal, you soon realise there are *real* nightmares in life. In the all-consuming world of football we sometimes forget that there are people who go through life with bigger problems than winning a football match.'

He'd been coach at Huddersfield's McAlpine Stadium under Steve Bruce before stepping up to manager. It was a long way down the road from his first job. At Swindon he once motivated his players by telling reporters that he would pick the team only after smelling their breath. That was the season they won the Fourth Division with a record 102 points.

He learned plenty of motivational tricks from the Doc, Dave Sexton and Ron Atkinson: 'No one can ever say what might have been nor can they logically compare players from different eras. But it is possible that if the three managers I played for at Old Trafford had been given the time that Sir Alex was given, any of them might have been the first to win the championship since 1967. Although Ron's Champagne Charlie image and wisecracking was close to that of Tommy Docherty, in the case of Ron the image was wrong. He used the charisma angle for PR purposes, and in fact he was more at home with a cup of tea and a sandwich than with champagne and caviare.

'What Ron loved most was the game of football. I never saw a man relish so much coming into the big time as he did when he arrived at Old Trafford. It wasn't a big-time Charlie attitude, he was just happy to be in the kind of environment he'd worked so hard for from the time he was an ordinary Second and Third Division player. My career ended early in Ron's reign, but that was always on the cards. I'd had a good run at that level, and I finished at Old Trafford in 1984 to join Swindon as player-manager. There were no hard feelings when Ron gave me the elbow. My time was due, and it had been a wonderful time.

'Summing up Ron, I'd say he was a combination of the Doc and Dave Sexton. He did well in the transfer market, and United owed him a debt, particularly for signing Bryan Robson and Arnold Muhren. He certainly got everybody ready and psyched up for the game ahead. Sexton was a brilliant coach, superb in the details of the game, and he could hugely entertain the lads with his tales about football, but he hated the administrative side of the game. He couldn't stand the thought of press conferences, or being involved in desk work.

'He just loved to be out on the park, coaching his team, and watching matches. But there was no way he could be absolutely hands-on, and unlike Sir Alex and Sir Matt he didn't want to control every aspect of the club.'

He added: 'Sir Alex's career has certainly been incredible. To keep things rolling season after season has been his greatest achievement, much greater than being the first United manager to win the English title in twenty-six years. To keep all those players disciplined and contented has been a miracle. He never hangs about: if he thinks a player is a problem he clears him out immediately.

'For instance, as soon as I read what Jaap Stam had written in his book I said, "End of story for Jaap". People say the breaking point was secrets he told about the manager, but he had had a go at one of his teammates, and I think that would be the factor that Sir Alex would think unforgivable.'

Was Sir Alex lucky to survive those first difficult two or three years?

'He was lucky to have a strong chairman in Martin Edwards, who could see what other people and 99 per cent of the fans couldn't see, that Alex was putting everything into place from the bottom upwards, and the club reaped the benefit from the chairman's leadership.

'Even from a distance it's clear that Sir Alex Ferguson isn't a man to cross, and it may surprise people to find that probably the other manager you could say that most certainly about would be Dave Sexton.

'Nobody would call Dave an extrovert, and I never saw him lose his temper or raise his fists to anybody. He kept himself to himself, and was a gentleman. But although he never did, you could imagine Dave cutting loose and doing a lot of damage to any of our teammates if they did something that really riled him. In fact he could leave his mark without being aggressive.

'A look was enough, and his eyes could go ice cold.'

Should Have Been England Manager

Most people's choice as elder statesman of English football would almost certainly be Bobby Robson, a man held in the highest affection throughout the game as Britain's most enduring and successful club manager over three decades. Nevertheless, when England went to Asia for the 2002 World Cup with their travelling caravan of families, gurus and various baggage there was still no doubt that Dave Sexton was the leading light in the Dad's Army of football coaching.

In his 72nd year Sexton was still doing his bit for England, heading Sven-Goran Eriksson's backup team of scouts. Nearly all his team had a bus pass in their wallet next to their scout's card; but age did not matter beside the immeasurable experience of men such as Noel Cantwell, John Sillett, Ken Brown and Ted Buxton. Former Brighton boss and Sheffield Wednesday chief scout Bobby Smith was the only member of his team not of pensionable age.

Says Sexton: 'I was a coach at Fulham when Bobby Robson joined the club. He's just a youngster.' But he added: 'What he's doing at Newcastle proves that football management is not just a young man's game.' Reporting to Eriksson or his veteran assistant Tord Grip, Dave's team of golden oldies keep tabs on the fifty or so players who are of international or near international standard, while always on the lookout for rising stars, and do thorough checks on the teams England will meet on the international stage. Eriksson has enormous respect for the former Manchester United boss, saying: 'It is such a pleasure to be with him, talking about football, because he just oozes the game.

'I was very happy to find him working with England when I took over, but I wanted to use his knowledge differently and gave him a free hand to form a scouting team, and he made some excellent choices.'

No man in British football is held in greater respect for his coaching ability and tactical sense than Dave Sexton, and no man stands up more for England – and has done for over thirty years – than Dave.

When still manager of Manchester United he told me, during one of the periodic sessions of breast-beating about English failure on the international stage or in international club competitions: 'It's part of the recession in which even ICI have to cut their coat according to their cloth, just as the corner shop has to. We know it will mean we must limit the number of youngsters coming into the club; that we must be selective, especially if we have a professional staff of forty.

'But it would be silly for people to read into all this something that isn't there. This is all part of the ebb and flow of running the intricate financial empire that a major football club is these days. Anybody who listens to the prophets of gloom about the state of the game in this country could not be more misguided.

'I will say quite firmly we're a lot healthier than most countries in world football. People may talk about Dutch football being something to set up as an example, but in their League programme they only have two worthwhile gates each weekend. They envy us our support, and their supporters envy the excitement our games provide.' Words that could apply just as aptly in 2002 as in 1980.

And he added a comment that could just as easily apply to the exciting ending to the 2002 Premiership season which sent Manchester United's title monopoly crashing before the World Cup with the title success of Arsenal: 'Perhaps the beauty of our game is that even United with their massive gates have no divine right to success. All the big teams have got to keep working and planning to maintain their high positions and this is why the fascination of the game in this country will never really be lost.'

But Dave is not a man to talk about himself, and admits: 'I don't have a huge ego. I just like working in football.'

Despite their different characters, Dave has one thing in common with Sir Alex Ferguson: he would sooner go for a long country walk with a stone in his shoe than endure the inquisition of a press conference.

Friday press conferences before the weekend's big matches have for many years been the norm at major clubs, and while we never had the open warfare that Sir Alex has given us over the years, it was always clear that if he could, Dave would metaphorically keep his foot in the door of the press room so he could make as early an escape as possible. While it is the press who suffer with Sir Alex, it was Dave Sexton who sweated, wriggled and shuffled in discomfort when faced with a group of newspapermen.

It just was not his scene, and we could respect that. He tried to do his best, and was always courteous and pleasant despite the suffering in his eyes. So it was nice to have a chat with him about football, rather than football politics, many years after he left Old Trafford when I bumped into him in the VIP room at Belle Vue, the home of Doncaster Rovers.

But I couldn't help a mischievous joke at Dave's expense, and indulged in some mild mickey-taking by saying to him: 'I bet you miss the old days at Old Trafford when you used to enjoy the press conferences so much. You always used to look forward to our Friday meetings.' Without a twitch, or a change of expression, Dave replied: 'Yes, they were the good old days, weren't they?' I think Dave ended by taking the mickey out of me.

He certainly had his high spots as a manager at Chelsea. Probably there was nothing greater than the 1971 Cup Winners' Cup final defeat of Real Madrid in Athens after a 1–1 draw and a replay, and there was more big-match replay glory in the 1970 FA Cup final victory over Leeds United at Old Trafford.

Yet neither of these ranks as his most satisfying match. He once told me: 'You don't always derive the greatest pleasure from the big games. I can remember at Chelsea losing the first three games of the season when I'd had a row with Peter Osgood and put him on the transfer list. We had a lot of injuries and Ossie played centre-forward practically by himself in the fourth game and we won 2–1 at Huddersfield. That game is one I always look back on when I talk about games that have really thrilled me.'

Dave started his own managerial career when he went from Chelsea to become manager of Leyton Orient, and successfully rescued them from their relegation fight after being second bottom in the old Second Division when he took over. Never one to blow his own trumpet, Dave pointed out that it was his players who were the heroes. With such as Bobby Robson, Johnny Haynes, Scottish international Graham Leggatt, George Cohen and ex-Manchester United star Mark Pearson he certainly had talent to work with, but the debonair Vic Buckingham was quick to point out: 'It was Dave who got the best out of them.'

Dave's increasing reputation as a coach with special qualities was being noticed. He moved from Orient to Fulham but spent only a few months there before Bertie Mee, later to become a double hero for Arsenal, offered him the job as coach at Highbury. Said Dave: 'It was a big step up for me. Anybody would have jumped at the job of coaching Arsenal, and although I was sorry to leave Fulham, I had a fruitful eighteen months before Tommy Docherty left Chelsea in 1967 and I was offered the job.'

That was a period when clubs did not have the same hire 'em and fire 'em attitude that was to become such a feature of life when the Premiership came into being, and Dave was manager at the Bridge for seven years.

It was a mark of his prestige in the game that two weeks after leaving Stamford Bridge he was snapped up by Queen's Park Rangers as their new manager, and he still stands in the records as one of the club's most successful managers. He masterminded Rangers to second place in the League championship in his second year at the club, finishing just one point behind champions Liverpool in the 1975–76 season, and three points ahead of third-placed Manchester United.

It was a fantastic feat by a club regarded as the poor relation of the big metropolitan clubs, and Dave kept the pressure on the elite Arsenal–Chelsea–Spurs axis by taking little QPR to the semi-finals of the FA Cup and the quarter-finals of the UEFA Cup the following season. After three years at Loftus Road he decided to move on and was considering an offer from Terry Neill for a return to Arsenal when Manchester United approached him for the second time, having first tried to bring him north following the departure of Wilf McGuinness.

It was a period when his coaching ability, his results and the way he seemed to be one of the first in the British game to notice new ideas, were being recognised all over Europe. While managing QPR he had already turned down a chance to manage Ajax of Holland. He said: 'The offer from Old Trafford came up just at the right time, and to be managing Manchester United was an exciting prospect.'

Despite Tommy Docherty's disappointment at losing the job when he had won the FA Cup and felt the next sustainable target was the League, he spoke warmly of his former coach at Chelsea: 'I rate Dave Sexton as the best coach in the country. He would make an excellent coach for the England team.'

It was a view that everybody in football seemed to recognise apart from the International Committee of the Football Association, and it is a view I certainly endorsed. I firmly believe that it was a disgrace that Sexton was never offered the job of England team manager. His ability to organise and prepare a team, without the burden of all the extra administrative duties that a club manager has in football, equipped him perfectly to be an outstanding national team manager. In fact he was an English Sven-Goran Eriksson well ahead of his time. Alf Ramsey once said that Martin Peters was ten years ahead of his time; in an international context Dave Sexton could be said to have been twenty years before his time.

I remember him saying: 'The kind of approach that advocates flowing football and an urgency to entertain your club's supporters is great for the game. A manager has to serve three masters in his job. He has to keep the crowd happy, the directors satisfied, and his players content. And that isn't the easiest combination of jobs in the world.'

Aged 47 when he took over at Old Trafford, he soon knew that that was exactly the combination of jobs he had taken on, and that nowhere in football were expectations higher. And until Sir Alex came on the scene Dave Sexton was the only Manchester United manager since Sir Matt Busby to finish in the top two placings in the English League, United being runners-up in a desperately close finish with champions Liverpool in the 1979–80 season. Sexton's team were also runners-up to Arsenal in the 1979 FA Cup final when the Gunners won a thrilling game 3–2, snatching the trophy from under United's noses through Alan Sunderland's late winner. But would second place be enough to satisfy Manchester United?

Despite his quiet manner, his discomfort at having to be involved in press conferences or admin work, Sexton has always been respected as a world-class coach. Even before the era of Eriksson he was involved with various England team regimes and, although he would wince at the description, he has been something of a godfather to a coterie of highly committed football professors in English football such as Bobby Robson, Don Howe and Malcolm Allison.

Howe, himself a highly successful coach throughout Europe and revered for his first-team coaching at Arsenal in the seventies, told me: 'Dave has always been a great man to work with, and despite his sober exterior people who get to really know him find he has a great sense of humour. He is recognised as a terrific coach, perhaps the best, and what a thinker he is on the game. He thinks deeply not only on football but life itself, and is a great talker on England trips, soon getting a crowd round him when he gets into his swing. It's always been a great pleasure to be with him.'

Added Howe, who now works at Highbury in the Arsenal Academy, bringing on the stars of the future for Arsène Wenger: 'Throughout Dave's career, whenever somebody somewhere in the world was doing something innovative Dave would be on to it and he would be the first person we discussed it with.

'Bobby Robson used him tirelessly as an analyst and a match report man, and his coaching was a key factor for England in World Cup 90 in Italy when we reached the semi-final and were unlucky not to progress further. You won't go to any club where he coached without finding enormous respect for him. He was always the leader in spotting what different countries were doing; for example, he was the man who picked out earliest the system of pressing other teams that produced such great success for Hungary in the late fifties and sixties, long before Holland took notice and brought it effectively into their game plan under Rinus Michels.'

I suggested that Sexton should have used his talents coaching top teams in Europe, where a coach/boss setup is in place rather than a manager/boss structure, and that there he would have been able to concentrate fully on working on the field with his players and not had to use up his time in office work. Should Dave Sexton have taken a big club job on the Continent? Don Howe reacted like lightning: 'Without a doubt. Bobby Robson told him he should have coached abroad years ago. He could have had the pick of the jobs, and Bob said he would have a different class of life because they love their coaching and studying the game in depth on the Continent. Dave was the continental-style team coach rather than the English-style team manager.

'He would have been left to concentrate on the coaching and running of the team, while all the extra activities such as organising the club and holding press conferences would have been taken care of by other people. He would have been in his element. In a general sense in the game in England he was probably much misunderstood by the public at large, who didn't see his real character because he was so wrapped up in the intricacies and the depth of the game.

'He was so close to becoming the first since Busby to win the championship for United, losing by just two points to a fantastic Liverpool team, but my feeling is that if you are at Manchester United you've got to win trophies, and when we beat them at Wembley in that 1979 FA Cup final, I remember my first thought was, "We won't have done Dave any good." But he knew you have to understand that when you walk into a job at Old Trafford you have to provide success more than anywhere else in football.

'But I would stake everything I've got that had he stayed longer he would not only have won the championship for Old Trafford but would have taken them to regular success in Europe.

'He was a totally straight man, and there was no messing about with him. He had high standards about the way he should behave, and had a tremendous outlook on life. If somebody said something that he didn't like he would say nothing, and would never criticise anybody in public.

'There are big differences between him and Sir Alex, but they have similarities in that they both have a demanding nature, and would never have a problem or be stressed by the fact that the job demands all your time. Alex certainly has a good eye for players, and his driving force is that he knows he has to keep on winning.'

And top managers are under no illusions about the game they are in. Confidence and positive thinking is the field marshal's baton in their knapsack. Even Sir Alex Ferguson had black moments – on one notable occasion early in his career at Old Trafford he feared the worst after a defeat by Leeds United – but there were no hysterics from Dave Sexton when the end came for him in April 1981, just when he might have thought a run of seven successive wins had given him an end-of-season lifeline.

On his arrival in the summer of '77 he had promised he would quit if he did not win a trophy in three years. He said then: 'I set myself standards and if I don't reach them I will leave. United have given me three years to do the job, and it's long enough to win something. Managers are fighting for their lives all the time, and it's the same with players. If a goalscorer doesn't score, a schemer creates nothing, a defender doesn't defend or a goalkeeper lets in goals then we get someone else.

'It's the same principle for a manager. If he doesn't win something the club must get someone else, and I accept the situation. I only left Queen's Park Rangers because I had been there three years, and though we had gone close to winning a couple of things we didn't have a trophy to show. But if you win something you buy yourself time.'

So it was probably no surprise that when he had been three years and three months in the job, with some outstanding performances but no trophies, he was shown the door. And when he was told by a board meeting that his time was up he reacted with the same equanimity that Antarctic hero Captain Oates did when walking out of his tent to certain death in the snow. The ultimate professional, there were no recriminations, just a brief, 'So that's that then,' before nodding to the directors, leaving the room and driving home without even enquiring about the terms of his dismissal.

But he departed with honour, and lasting respect from the players he left behind.

The Dave Sexton Fact File

1930: Born in London, son of the British middleweight championship contender Archie Sexton.

1948: Started at Newmarket Town and continued via Chelmsford City, Luton Town, West Ham United, Leyton Orient and Brighton to Crystal Palace, where knee injury ended his playing career. His only honour as a player was winning a Third Division championship medal with Brighton in 1958.

1963: Took his coaching exams and joined Chelsea's coaching staff under manager Tommy Docherty.

1965: Appointed manager of Leyton Orient, and went on to have coaching stints at Fulham and Arsenal before returning to Stamford Bridge.

1967: Appointed manager of Chelsea in succession to Tommy Docherty.

1970: Won FA Cup by beating Leeds United 2–1 in replay at Old Trafford after a 2–2 draw at Wembley.

1971: Won European Cup Winners' Cup final replay 2–1 against Real Madrid after a 1–1 draw.

1972: Beaten 2–1 by Stoke City in League Cup final.

1974: Sacked by Chelsea, and within days appointed manager of QPR.

1976: Beaten by one point by Liverpool for Football League championship, and reached quarter-finals of the UEFA Cup.

1977: Resigned from QPR and was negotiating to join Arsenal as coach when Manchester United offered him job as manager.

1979: Runners-up to Arsenal in FA Cup.

1980: Runners-up in League championship.

1981: April, sacked by Manchester United.
Summer, replaced Gordon Milne as manager of Coventry City, beating Manchester United in his first game in charge at Highfield Road.

1983: Dismissed as manager and replaced with Bobby Gould. He had won nothing with Coventry, but during this time was allowed to also manage the England Under-21s, with whom he won the European championship.

1984: Relinquished Under-21s position to become assistant manager to England boss Bobby Robson, and had a variety of roles in Robson's regime, including England B manager and some Under-21s duties.

1990: Retired from coaching duties at national level to concentrate on scouting duties when Graham Taylor took over as England manager.

2000: Given more responsibility when Sven-Goran Eriksson became England manager, and has headed Sven's team of scouts to help prepare for international matches and the 2002 World Cup and 2004 European Nations championship.

115

Never Fully Appreciated

His public persona was to many that of a Flash Harry character, who had a sun bed in his office, would motivate his players by jangling his jewellery, bathed in champagne, dressed in slick suits, and drove top-of-the-range cars. But Ron Atkinson had one of the most decorous exit lines in the long history of dismissal days in British football – a never-ending torrent of days that have seen insults traded in many a club boardroom between sacked managers and directors.

Like Dave Sexton, who simply said, 'That's that then,' to his executioners and walked off with never a backward glance, Ron Atkinson didn't need to apologise or rant and rave. He knew he had given Manchester United five of their most exciting years and some of the classiest football since the days of Sir Matt Busby. He had put together a world-class midfield unit, bringing Bryan Robson and Remi Moses from his old club West Bromwich Albion and adding Gordon Strachan and, from Holland via Bobby Robson's Ipswich Town, the cultured Arnold Muhren. Under his management United had taken several steps forward, especially in terms of competing in Europe.

Sacked after a 4–1 League Cup defeat by Southampton in 1986, he simply said to chairman Martin Edwards: 'Thanks for giving me the chance.'

Like some of the most successful managers in the game, Atkinson had not been his new club's first choice. United had tried desperately hard to sign Lawrie McMenemy, the man who engineered the most humiliating Cup final defeat in their history back in 1976, but he had turned the job down.

That was where sports writer John Maddock came in again, asking Edwards if he would be interested in Ron taking the job.

Maddock told me: 'It was arranged that the chairman would meet Ron at my house, and I picked him up at Manchester Airport, the pair of them discussing the job at a three-hour interview. It was obvious they had come to an agreement, but I knew Ron would have trouble getting his release from the Hawthorns, so I didn't use the story in the *People*.

'The following week United haggled with the West Bromwich Albion board over compensation, and finally the job was done. Ron repaid me for keeping the news quiet by giving me an exclusive that his first signing would be Bryan Robson. What a great way to start his career. Although Bryan wasn't on the international stage at the time, Ron assured the sceptics that Robbo was going to be a great, great player, and history confirms that he was right – he was one of the club's greatest ever signings.

'Along with my *People* colleague Norman Wynne, who was working in Cambridge when Ron was starting his career there, I was very close to Ron in media terms during his time at the club. In my mind he'd got it right with the team, and was on his way to lasting success.

'A manager who'd played for Oxford and Cambridge couldn't have found it easy at the start being surrounded by superstars. That's a good CV for an academic career, but not exactly high flying for a footballer. Some players felt he was too flash and that his knowledge was too shallow; but in the end it was generally accepted that he was very knowledgeable about the game, and that he'd played up to the Champagne Charlie tag to get noticed. He didn't drink a lot, but he would always be keen to fill up other people's glasses.

'His big fault, perhaps, was that he neglected the youth policy, and that became the plank on which Alex Ferguson's success was built.'

That is a popular theory about Ron Atkinson, and yet Sir Alex has always been generous in praising the work Eric Harrison has done in developing the youngsters who have been such a vital part of his Premiership success stories since the nineties. In a press release for the launch of Eric's autobiography, *The View from the Dugout*, Ferguson wrote: 'Eric was a tremendous servant to Manchester United, and he played an enormous part in the club's revival during the 1990s. In fact, I would go so far as to say that it is almost impossible to measure his contribution.' However, he has never acknowledged the debt the club owes to Ron Atkinson for bringing Harrison to the club in the first place.

You only have to read a list of Manchester United and England soccer stars who admit they owe an enormous debt to Eric Harrison to be aware of the role he has played in the club's success. He guided United's youngsters in 1992 to the club's first FA Youth Cup final triumph since George Best's teenage years in 1964, and such as Ryan Giggs, Gary Neville, Paul Scholes, Nicky Butt, David Beckham, Wes Brown and a number of others now with first-team experience bear testimony to his great influence. And it was none other than Ron Atkinson who brought former Halifax Town, Hartlepool, Barrow and Southport wing-half Harrison to the United coaching staff in 1981.

Atkinson and Harrison had done their National Service together between 1959 and 1961. Both had played in the RAF soccer team and they had later been on opposing sides when Hartlepool played Oxford United in a League match that Big Ron will never let Eric forget.

As we sat in Eric's office overlooking The Cliff training ground, still a Mecca for youngsters even in the early days of the new Carrington Training Centre, he recalled: 'We were having a bad time, and Ron was winding me up all the match. Even though it was my pal who was having a go at me, I was really infuriated and ended up trying to kick everything that moved, especially Ron, and I finished the match so bad-tempered that I sulkily refused to have a drink with him after the match.'

But they were soon pals again, and continued to be so, keeping in touch throughout their careers until Eric's appointment at Old Trafford, where he continued his gold-card coaching career during the glorious nineties. Although he officially retired from a full-time commitment towards the end of the century, he carried on as coaching co-ordinator for the United Academy, also becoming assistant manager to one of his protégés, Mark Hughes, with the Welsh national team.

As Eric remembered: 'When I arrived at Old Trafford as youth team manager we had seventeen-year-old Mark Hughes and sixteen-year-old Norman Whiteside up front, with players such as Graeme Hogg, Clayton Blackmore, Billy Garton and Mark Dempsey also in the squad. There was never any doubt that Hughes and Whiteside were going to be big, big stars. They had such terrific determination to succeed, and were technically so good. Both men had outstanding technique, but that was no use without desire, and they had that in abundance.

'I was thrilled that Ron had offered me the job, and it was great to work with a manager who possessed so much personality. But because he was such an extrovert nobody ever gave him full credit for his status as a great football man, full of knowledge, and a man who would talk the game all day. He prepared his teams well and had them playing the Manchester United way. He produced a tremendously entertaining and successful side, and it was unfair that he was pigeon-holed as being flash. His ability as a manager and a coach was never fully appreciated by the world at large.'

Revealing a stoical side to Ron, he said: 'He was always philosophical about it, saying that there was nothing could be done, that it was just a fact of life he had to live with, and that he wouldn't allow it to ruin his life.

'He was absolutely number one as a motivator, always bright and breezy, even if he'd got problems, and if I'd been playing under him I know that I would never detect any nervousness on his part or any feeling that he feared the opposition. He oozed confidence, and it allowed his players to express themselves to the limit. Never would he allow pressure to get to his players. If there were problems flying around he never took it out on his staff, even if things were going pear-shaped.'

Analysing his old boss, Eric told me: 'Sitting at my desk in the coaches' room, preparing my day's training, I would always hear him coming up the stairs singing. The only time I saw him down-hearted was when he was sacked. He was absolutely devastated, no matter how much he tried not to show it. He'd sensed things were going wrong after a bad result against Coventry City, and I'd never seen him so quiet after a match. I think he felt that the end was near for him. It was a great pity because despite his playboy image he was a dedicated professional, didn't cut any corners, and was well respected by his players. He always got a kick out of playing in five-a-side games. And he bounced back quickly after his sacking by arranging a party for his players, and was just himself again, making sure everybody enjoyed themselves that night.

'He'd been so close to ending the championship famine, and enjoyed good runs in Europe. But he didn't show he was in mourning after leaving the club. And he's never been a jealous man. He would have wished Alex the best, and was delighted to see United achieve success.

'The club certainly owed him a debt for bringing some great midfielders together. He formed a good managerial team with his assistant Mick Brown, who was a whole-hearted football man like Ron. And both of them could have a go in the dressing-room – they could take turns at blistering the paint on the dressing-room walls. But Mick, close as they were, was certainly no yes-man to Ron.'

Sir Alex and Ron were both lucky to have such a good youth coach working for them in an important and often unheralded job; but Eric turns it round and says he was lucky to work for two such top-quality managers. 'Alex was a fantastic manager from my point of view. We never fell out, and although Ron had different ways they both had the same philosophy: they employed me to do the job, so they just wanted me to get on with it. Alex was more hands-on, but both were a terrific help to me, in different ways, with my career. Alex certainly made it clear that he felt the way forward was through a good youth policy, and from the start he made it imperative throughout the club that everybody should roll their sleeves up to try and find the best young talent.'

Gary Neville paid handsome tribute some time ago to Eric when he admitted: 'When I first came to United I was a player who maybe hung back a bit. I could have been more confident. I saw lads who had come from the FA National School for Excellence, lads who had played for England Schoolboys, and I probably lacked the belief that I had what was needed to make it as a player with Manchester United.'

But, he revealed, 'Eric Harrison changed my attitude. He used to get the young players in his office individually. In the first couple of months he told me that if I listened to him and did what he said, giving everything I'd got, then I had a chance of playing for Manchester United's first team.

'From then on I believed in him and myself. I believed everything he said and I did everything he told me to do, and that's got me to where I am now.'

But England star Gary knows that his encouraging attitude did not mean there was any softly, softly approach in the way he moulded his young prospects: 'Even now, if there's anything in my game Eric sees he'll come up to me and talk about it. He was the kind of person who, if he had a go at you, could make you feel about an inch tall. You wanted to dig yourself a hole in the ground. But his praise made you feel as tall as the Old Trafford floodlights.'

Ron Atkinson believes strongly that there is no substitute for experience – after all, one of his best friends is management veteran Jim Smith – and he was certainly getting experience on Christmas Eve 1981 when, over a cup of tea at The Cliff, he asked Tony Collins to join him as chief scout. Collins was still there when Ron left Old Trafford and had a year under Sir Alex.

One of the most respected figures on the scouting beat in British football, Collins had earlier in his career been chief scout at Leeds United under Don Revie. Earlier still he had achieved one of the biggest giant-killing runs in England when taking Cinderella club Rochdale to the final of the Football League Cup in 1962 before losing 3–0 and 1–0 to Norwich City in the two-legged final. To put that feat in context I once, in the seventies, estimated that the income that Manchester United produced on the sale of meat pies in their kiosks during one match equalled Rochdale's total gate receipts for an entire season.

Tony went on to help produce some of the most successful years in Bristol City's history when assistant to Alan Dicks at Ashton Gate, taking them to the old First Division, from the bottom of the Second Division, at the end of the 1974–75 season, achieving top League ranking for the first time in 65 years. His standing in the game had not gone unnoticed by Big Ron, who always kept a firm finger on the pulse of the citizens of the footballing community, and had earmarked Tony as a man with a computer-like brain when it came to assessing current players and potential stars. So Ron soon made Tony Collins his chief scout after arriving at Old Trafford from the Hawthorns, and quickly built up a productive and trusting relationship with him.

Recalls Tony: 'I quickly found that here was a man who had no trouble stepping up into the hot seat at Old Trafford. He certainly could handle a big club, and despite his modest playing career he loved the big time. It didn't put any stress on him.

'He could really get a team going, and for my money he ranks as United's unluckiest manager. He put together a midfield that nobody could live with, and that ranks as good as any Manchester United have ever fielded. And he was always brave enough to play an outstanding youngster in the first team. He put Norman Whiteside in at seventeen, and then paid £25,000 to St Patrick's for Paul McGrath, signed at the age of 21 and put straight into the action.

'In a season that would certainly have seen the championship coming back to Old Trafford if the money had been there to provide the kind of squad system Sir Alex has since been able to build up, there would have been no catching United.

'They won the first ten games, and it was no fluke. No team had a chance against them. Then Moses and Robbo both had severe injury absences from the team. The club wasn't able to sign the players Ron wanted as backup, the thread was lost, and one of the most exciting and brilliant runs in the history of the club fizzled out.'

But Tony points out that the setback only served to underline Ron Atkinson's qualities: 'He handled situations so well, and would never let anything get him down. He would get on with the job. While United were never out of the top four in the championship until his last season, he had plenty of tough situations to handle, but he never let the pressure get to his players. He would happily take it on his own shoulders, and I don't think any of his players ever heard a negative word from him.

'He had a highly successful time at Old Trafford with continuity in European competition as well, but I still maintain he wasn't there long enough to build everything he wanted. He'd built a fine side at West Bromwich Albion, and despite his playboy image he was recognised throughout the game as a good pro with a sharp mind, and incidentally a tremendous memory for facts.

'It used to be said in football that you couldn't buy success. The arrival of the Premiership disproved that. Blackburn's title win when they had Jack Walker's millions at their back soon showed that the championship could be bought. But Manchester United balanced things out again: they spent big but also went against the trend by having a bigger home nucleus in the first team than any other club. So in terms of talking about greatest teams and greatest managers it's really only a level playing field if you call them the greatest in their own era. As managers get millions of pounds salary a year it's interesting to recall that when Arthur Rowe won the old Second Division and the First Division in successive years, a director said wearily to him: "I expect we'll have to pay you another £500 bonus now."'

Tony Collins feels it is impossible to answer the question of whether Busby or Ferguson was the greatest ever Old Trafford manager. He points to the days before the Premiership and the influx of foreign players, days when a contract meant something and it was possible to achieve continuity, whereas now a club will just tell a rival they are going to take their best player away from them. These days, if a player wants to move and is prepared to dig his heels in, there's no percentage fighting it. Paying a player £30,000 a week is no fun if he refuses to pull his weight for you on a Saturday afternoon.

Said Collins: 'Arthur Rowe at Spurs and Bill Nicholson after him, Stan Cullis at Wolverhampton Wanderers, Brian Clough at Derby County and Forest, Don Revie at Leeds United, Bill Shankly at Liverpool, as well as Matt Busby, all built great teams based on players prepared to stay with their clubs for a decade, but you can't hope for that today. Great players can keep you in a job; but when you discover one today you're unlikely to be able to keep him long enough to benefit unless you're managing one of the top four or five clubs. The Bosman ruling, made by a judge who knew nothing about the unique nature of football in comparison with other businesses, has been a terrible thing for the clubs, and has taken the balance too far in favour of players.

'But good managers can still make a difference. Tommy Docherty wasn't the greatest diplomat in the world, and sometimes he couldn't contain himself when directors got on his nerves. But he certainly signed some good players, and was prepared for a fight with one of his players if they upset him. He always wanted bright, exciting football, and that fitted in with the Manchester United ideals, even though he had a self-destruct button.

'Football, however, can take up so much of your time. I remember the old Spurs boss Bill Nicholson crying when his daughter got married and saying: "I never saw her grow up." Kids can't understand, and can't be expected to understand, when you can't go to watch them in a school play or running in the school sports, because you're working. The game isn't all champagne and roses by a long chalk.'

He continued: 'Tommy Docherty was a bit like Ron Atkinson in that he didn't let problems get to him. He was certainly not a worrier, and he always had a bright and breezy manner. Jimmy Murphy once told me that he was a funnier man than Jimmy Tarbuck.' (Author's note: not difficult – almost anybody is funnier than Jimmy Tarbuck.)

Thumbing down the list of Manchester United managers, Tony said: 'Frank O'Farrell was always a decent bloke who would never let anybody down. He was as straight as a die, and played everything by the book, while Dave Sexton was a similar type, a thorough football man.

'Wilf McGuinness was in a no-win situation following Matt: he'll always look back and think he could have done better. But he had a difficult job handling a team that had done it all, but included some players who were getting on in years. He would have known in his own mind it was time to call it a day with certain players, but he couldn't hope to wield the same authority that Matt had for 25 years in charge of the club.

'People will always ask if Alex could have dealt any better with George Best than Matt did. But it's worth remembering someone like Lee Sharpe. Although he wasn't in the same class as George, he was still a terrific young talent who earned international honours at a tender age. Then things went wrong with him – as they did with Norman Whiteside and Paul McGrath. The solution with these lads was to sell them, which was some compensation. But no amount of money would have been compensation for losing George Best.'

Finally, Collins reflected once more on Big Ron's contribution to the United adventure: 'The stars who have come through the youth policy at the club are innumerable: Duncan Edwards, Eddie Colman, Liam Whelan, Mark Hughes, Dennis Viollet, Best, Nobby Stiles, Bobby Charlton plus the present crop. But of the players bought in the transfer market I reckon Bryan Robson and Arnold Muhren were United's best signings.

'With great ball-winners such as Robson, Moses and Albiston there was never a better player to bring to United than Arnold Muhren. When the ball went to him you need have no fear, you could be sure something significant would be done with it. It was no surprise to me that Arnold was still playing international football for Holland at the age of 35.

'Of course in the nineties many more overseas stars became available, such as Cantona and Schmeichel, the catalysts for championship success at last. Ruud van Nistelrooy looks like being right up there among the best, but for my money he isn't yet comparable with a man United never had, that great striker Marco van Basten. He had the lot, and I've never seen his like. I can't understand why United never tried to sign him.

'Ron Atkinson loved good players. He had no problem in handling even the greatest, and he was totally in control of his teams. He could be a laugh a minute, but he was always totally professional in his job and he was certainly the guv'nor. The only people who criticised him were those who didn't know him. He was a terrific Cup fighter, and had built a team that if they had won the championship could have gone on to win the Champions' League at the first time of asking.

'He should have been kept on.'

Big Ron Wins by a (S)mile

Bryan Robson, without doubt Ron Atkinson's most influential buy for Manchester United, famously made the following prediction in May 1994 about the date of Alex Ferguson's retirement: 'Alex Ferguson, perhaps, sees me as a future manager of United, but he loves his football so much it could be ten years before he packs in.'

The quote from Old Trafford's own Captain Marvel looks spot on now, and there is no doubt that Bryan was as loth to quit playing as Sir Alex has proved loth to quit managing. Robbo eventually moved up to Middlesbrough as player-manager after he decided to take on the onerous task of transforming a struggling First Division club into a potent Premiership force.

He took Middlesbrough to areas of football they have never travelled before in their history, notably Wembley, after leaving Old Trafford following 440 appearances plus 24 sub outings, during which time he scored 99 goals and captained United to the Premiership and FA Cup in 1994, only the fourth team in the twentieth century to do the English double.

Despite disappointment when it finally ended in tears at the end of his seventh year in charge down by the Riverside, he had left a tremendous legacy of success to a club that had been deprived of top-class football for many years. In fact I cannot find anybody, since Matt Busby managed United from 1945 to 1969, who lasted so long with a top club in their first English managerial job. For instance Bobby Robson, one of the greatest and most durable

126

English managers, lasted only a year in his first job at Fulham. Time may indeed prove Bryan Robson to be a great manager.

He had signed for Manchester United in 1981 for a then British record of £1.8 million – and few supporters would disagree that his worth to the club was twenty times that. In 1982 he captained England for the first time, and in 1983, 1985 and 1990 he took United to FA Cup final wins over Brighton, Everton and Crystal Palace, before victory over Barcelona in 1991 in that magnificent European Cup Winners' Cup final in Rotterdam.

The following year he retired from international football with 90 caps, 65 as captain, having played in three World Cups and scored 26 goals for his country, but the greatest glory was yet to come with his title victories in the Premiership.

Whatever is the final result of his career, he will always give credit to the men he says he learned most from, his three gurus Alex Ferguson, Ron Atkinson and Terry Venables. He was, of course, managed by Atkinson and Sir Alex at Old Trafford; he worked with Venables for England, and also had Terry beside him in his last season at Middlesbrough. He told me: 'When I went into management I always spoke regularly to Ron, Alex and Terry, and welcomed their advice and experience.'

Bryan's all-time favourite player was Michel Platini, and he could easily have joined the French star at Juventus. United were prepared to sell him when the Italians came shopping with their cheque book, only to withdraw when the Old Trafford moguls wanted over £3 million, at the time more than the world record fee paid for Maradona.

He admits: 'I would have liked to have gone and sampled Italian football,' but look what he would have missed...apart from all those trophies, a ringside dressing-room seat to witness Sir Alex's verbal blitzkriegs.

The one dressing-room secret he likes to tell is one of those rare occasions when Sir Alex changed his mind. With that deceptive, lazy smile, Bryan told me: 'We were losing 1–0 at half-time to Norwich City. Alex hammered Gary Pallister. "You're useless," was one of the politer phrases he used to him, telling Pally to get changed as he was going to be substituted. Gary threw his shirt down and hurled his boots away before storming into the showers. But Archie Knox followed Gary into the showers to calm him down, and then came back and spoke quietly to Alex.

'A few minutes elapsed and the half-time inquest continued before Gary Pallister came back into the dressing room and started to pull his trousers on. But Alex looked at him, and said: "What do you think you're doing? Don't think I'm going to let you off so easily. Get your boots and shirt back on, and get out there."'

Robson continued: 'Alex was calmer after the early years. There were times early on when flying teacups, with or without hot tea in them, sandwiches, hair dryers and anything that came to hand punctuated the dressing-room talk, although the extent of all this was exaggerated. Fortunately I can't remember ever being used as target practice. He had a real go at me once at Newcastle United, but he quietened down when I replied: "Do you think I want to play badly here of all places when all my family have come to watch me play?"

'But I never thought it was a question of Alex losing control. He just used the fury to get the reaction he wanted from his players, and he went in stronger against the younger players. I do think, however, he was pleased if they stood up to him in the right way, and weren't completely cowed.'

Robbo had Alan Ashman, Don Howe, Ronnie Allen, Johnny Giles and John Wile as his successive managers at The Hawthorns before Ron Atkinson, and he admits that he learned something from most of them. He especially admired the coaching of Don Howe, 'who was so good at instilling good habits into defenders, and telling them how to react no matter what area of the pitch they were in'. But it was Big Ron and Sir Alex who really provided him with a soccer management teach-in.

He says: 'Ron's man management was superb. He was a football man through and through, but he underlined everything by saying he wanted us to enjoy our football, play with flair, and give spectators something to get excited about. He instilled terrific spirit in our dressing room, and there was an aura about him.'

The first three years of Ron Atkinson's reign at Old Trafford saw Liverpool complete a hat-trick of championship wins, and then in the next four years it was turn and turn about between Everton and Liverpool, the Anfield club winning the title from Alex Ferguson's Manchester United in the 1987–88 season by nine points. As Bryan points out, 'He came along in a period of great Merseyside teams. It would certainly not be true to say that he just couldn't go the last mile. In the end time was of the essence for Ron. I can go along with those who argue that Ron would probably have won the championship if he had been given more time.'

Bryan told me: 'Ron was as enthusiastic on the training ground as in a League match, totally committed, very knowledgeable. With his big-money signings there were terrific expectations placed upon him, but despite the fact that he had never had the top-flight playing experience of the players he was coaching (neither did Sven-Goran Eriksson), there was no question about Ron's ability to take us in the right direction. He was certainly never overawed by the job, and had no need to be after the great success he had in previously lifting the status of West Bromwich Albion.

'In fact he was desperately unlucky in the season when we won the first ten games and built up a massive lead at the top of the table only to get a rash of serious injuries. It was wonderful playing in a midfield that had Arnold Muhren, a marvellous player, Remi Moses, who came with me from The Hawthorns, and was so unlucky to have such a short career through injury, Gordon Strachan and Jesper Olsen.

'Although his big achievement was often seen as pulling us to that Cup final defeat of Everton when we were down to ten men after Kevin Moran was sent off, I think Ron was seen at his greatest in the Cup final replay against Brighton which we won 4–0 after a 2–2 draw. The replay was a game that we could have so easily have made a mess of, and it could have been as big a banana skin as the 1976 defeat by Southampton. We could easily have gone into the replay mentally tight and strained, knowing that everybody expected us to win; but he relaxed us, kept the preparation light-hearted without being carefree or careless about any of the details. It was a great triumph for him.'

Bryan was also eager to confirm that Ron's playboy image was nothing but that: an image. 'For every five times he filled up somebody else's glass he'd have only half a glass himself. He loved his football, and was thrilled at managing Manchester United. That was his priority.'

What, then, did Sir Alex Ferguson have that Ron Atkinson did not?

Answered Robson: 'Although Ron made some great signings that pushed Manchester United a bit further up the ladder, the overall quality of Sir Alex's buying and selling was that vital bit better. And an essential factor in Alex's make-up is his ruthlessness. He's been ruthless in every way he has run the team. If anybody lets him down he's out. It's not easy to do that, and perhaps Ron, like many good managers, was just a bit too sentimental when it came to clearing players out. He would stick to players when they should have been moved on, but not Alex. If he decided they should go that was that, no matter what anybody else thought about the matter.

'In my opinion there was no chance of Alex being moved out if we hadn't won the FA Cup final against Crystal Palace, the game that many say saved Alex his job. Everybody inside the club could see what a great job he was doing in putting everything in place, especially the way he was building up the youth policy. Talk of Alex being moved on was just paper talk, and there were no thoughts about it in the quarters where it mattered.

'The board appreciated the way he was turning things round, and the way youngsters were coming along, and once he won the first Premiership trophy when Eric Cantona provided that extra touch, then confidence just grew and grew.

'Ron Atkinson had taken the team that stretch further on towards success, and Alex picked up the pace. Two very different men, but despite having different personalities on the outside, there were plenty of similarities inside. They were both bad losers. I remember Ron going mental when we lost 2–0 at Bournemouth in the Cup. He brought us in on Sunday morning after the match for extra training and ran us for forty-five minutes nonstop, answering when we said that it wasn't doing us any good: "No, but it made me feel better."'

Robson's injury record alone shows what he was prepared to suffer in the cause of his team. And what a record – 1976: broken leg; 1977: fractured finger, another broken leg; 1978: third broken leg; 1983: severely torn ligament; 1984: broken nose, severely bruised foot, dislocated shoulder, torn hamstring (twice); 1986: dislocated shoulder (twice); 1987: broken nose; 1988: concussion; 1989: concussion and swallowed tongue, rib damage, hairline fracture of leg, hernia op; 1990: Achilles tendon strain, damaged toe, bruised heel.

Not surprising, then, to hear him talking about Sir Alex Ferguson's ruthless approach. When checking the records one finds that his sackings in his first year at Middlesbrough were in double figures. A man who has been through the pain barrier so many times, and so successfully, in the quest for points, is unlikely to be content with less than a hundred per cent from his players.

Like Bryan Robson, both Ferguson and Atkinson were totally committed to the cause. And who is to say that Robbo, a man Alex himself said could one day be Manchester United's manager, will not eventually follow in their footsteps?

The trials and tribulations of being a soccer boss have never wiped the smile off the face of Ron Atkinson. Early in his career he suffered the disappointment of seeing his West Bromwich Albion side miss out on Wembley when they lost an FA Cup semi-final to the eventual winners, Ipswich Town. But he still said afterwards: 'I've not known anything but enjoyment and pleasure from my years in management.'

As we talked close to the Hawthorns ground where it all started to take off so long ago, his message was still the same even though he is now in calmer waters, away from the furore of the chase for points and titles and the tension of the dressing room: 'All those years, the highs and the lows. They were sheer magic, and what wonderful times we had.'

His philosophy through his career has remained constant: a highly professional approach allied to a character that shows he is having a 'terrific time' even when the going is tough.

He insists that even includes the trauma of being sacked at Old Trafford to make way for Alex Ferguson, and the bitterness of Sheffield Wednesday fans when he left after taking them back to heights they had not reached in fifty years. And there was also the controversy of his sacking at Aston Villa only months after becoming the first manager to win Wembley Cup finals with three different clubs.

I told him of my interview earlier with Aston Villa chairman Doug Ellis, when I had put the same facts before him, facts that Atkinson himself had not realised qualified him as a record-breaker. I had said to Deadly Doug: 'It had never been achieved in history, an English manager winning three major Cup finals at Wembley with three different clubs, Manchester United, Sheffield Wednesday and Aston Villa. He seemed to do well for you. Why did you sack him?'

The irrepressible doyen of Villa Park hammed it up, hesitating dramatically between words as he replied: 'Well, the trouble with Mr Atkinson was that he'd been three years at Villa Park, and he still didn't seem to know that I was the chairman!'

He added: 'Ron was a great character, but he made the mistake of not accepting that I was his boss. He had so many good points. Great strength of character and a strong personality. But his big failing was that eventually he created disharmony in the dressing room by treating some players differently to others.

'It wasn't an entirely harmonious parting when Ron had to leave Villa Park, and he is the only former manager I don't still have a good relationship with.'

Of course it is worth remembering that another of chairman Ellis's former managers was Tommy Docherty, and it is about Ellis that the Doc spoke his most frequently quoted throwaway line. Ellis once told Docherty that whatever he did he would always be right behind him. To which Tommy replied, 'I would rather have you in front of me, Mr Chairman, where I can see you.'

And history tells that even Doug Ellis could be wrong. For it was on 9 January 1994 that he said of Ron Atkinson: 'I want him here for life,' after Ron's inspired Villa team booted Inter Milan, at the time one of the world's best teams, out of the UEFA Cup. Only months later, on 10 November 1994 to be precise, chairman Ellis was indicating, 'I want you out of my life,' when he gave Atkinson the sack.

Said Ron, now of course a highly successful TV match summariser: 'When Doug complained about me going off for TV work in my spare time I asked him if he'd rather me go off playing golf as most other managers did in what spare time they had. And when he complained that he could never get hold of me in my office I said he had better make up his mind whether he wanted me sitting on my chair in the office or being on the training ground with the players.

'Martin Edwards adopted a rather more logical viewpoint when I asked him permission to go to Mexico to work for TV in the World Cup. He said that he would much rather have the television people paying my fare to Rio than Manchester United.'

In terms of having the right attitude to football, the headline on one of my articles in the *Manchester Evening News* in 1996 tells it all: 'Big Ron wins by a (s)mile'.

He revitalised a host of different teams over the years and has always insisted that football is a game to be played with a smile, saying: 'I think football is the best way of life there is. I've always considered myself privileged to be involved in it.

'After twenty-five years as a manager it still gives me a thrill. Financially I've done well out of the game, but I believe I've always given value for money.'

He admitted to me that his worst moment in football was when he was relegated with Sheffield Wednesday. Every club he has managed have been in a better position when he left than when he joined, however, and he took them straight back up the following season. And he put another notch on his Cup belt – and what a notch! – when Wednesday won the 1991 Rumbelows Cup final with a 1–0 defeat of Sir Alex and Manchester United.

He commented: 'Even that didn't wipe out the memory of that previous end-of-season fight against the drop at Hillsborough.' Nevertheless he completed an outstanding double against the redoubtable Sir Alex when, with players clearly inferior on paper to their illustrious opponents, he again won the League Cup by beating Manchester United 3–1 at Wembley in an exhilarating 1994 Coca-Cola Cup final. It was further proof of his tactical acumen.

But he told me: 'In terms of achievement perhaps what gave me most satisfaction was the fact that after fifteen years, when United had only been rarely in European competition, I re-established the club as regulars in UEFA tournaments, and it brought back some great and very special nights to Old Trafford.'

Perhaps surprisingly, in considering whether he would change anything in his career, he talks about his predecessor Dave Sexton, says how he admired his coaching talents, and wishes that he had tried to re-employ him at Old Trafford on his coaching staff: 'I'm certainly not alone in admiring Dave's work in football, and when looking back that's one of the things I wish I'd done in my time as United's manager.'

Less surprisingly, Ron did not hesitate when answering my question about the most important player at Old Trafford during the Atkinson years. 'It was no contest,' he said. 'Bryan Robson is the best player I've ever worked with anywhere. Paying the British record fee for him was never even a gamble. In terms of his work ethic, his skill, enthusiasm and overall inspiration to everybody else in the team he was in a class of his own. When we went into the market for Bryan we were bidding for solid gold. He was always so competitive, and his skill factor was miles higher than anybody outside the game could recognise, while he could defend magnificently. Bryan always had great mental strength, and United have been very lucky to have a man like Roy Keane to fill his shoes.'

But there were plenty of world-class players breathing down Robbo's neck for accolades in the Atkinson years at Old Trafford, and none more so than Paul McGrath. Ron described Paul, whom he signed from Irish football, as his 'Rolls-Royce'. McGrath was a top-of-the-range player even though he had a knack of getting into trouble off the pitch. He was voted PFA Player of the Year in the early nineties, despite enduring recurrent knee injury problems that would have ended the career of many players years sooner.

Admitted Atkinson, who took McGrath on to continue his career at Villa Park after Sir Alex included the Irish World Cup star in an Old Trafford clear-out: 'Big Paul does get himself into a skirmish or two off the field, and things like that can get a bit irritating. But there has got to be a balance about it all. Remember Paul played forty-two League games for Villa, dicky knee and all, in that fantastic scrap for the first Premiership championship when only Manchester United finished above us.

'In thirty-five of those games he was probably the outstanding man on the field. Apart from that he truthfully does not deserve this reputation for causing loads of hassle. The fact is for most of the time when I had him at Old Trafford and Villa Park he was the quietest and most unassuming guy we had around. The simple fact is that his play gave so much pleasure to many thousands of fans, and he was without doubt the hardest defender in this country to get past. For my money he was, for much of his career, the best central defender in the world.'

In asking what was the greatest team performance against him Ron still could not keep Manchester United off the winner's podium, reminiscing: 'I needn't look any further than United's 8–1 win when I was manager of Nottingham Forest. Taking over the team when they were ten points clear at the bottom of the division was Mission Impossible, but I managed seventeen points from sixteen games, and one thing is certain: none of those points were gift-wrapped by Manchester United. I remember thinking that perhaps we'd weathered the storm, and the defeat wouldn't be too embarrassing, when Alex took off Andy Cole and Dwight Yorke. At that time they were on fire, and they were by far the best attacking pair in Britain. But Ole Gunnar Solskjaer came on and scored four more. "Super sub" doesn't do him justice. That man is something again.'

It was perhaps United's retribution at last for their old boss's temerity in beating them twice at Wembley after leaving Old Trafford.

It had been so near, yet so far, for the man who brought Old Trafford the most beautiful football for years, with a dream midfield. There had been those great Cup successes, with the team that lined up for the 1985 FA Cup final at Wembley still rated by many as at least equal in quality to Alex Ferguson's greatest teams. Even after Kevin Moran had become the first man ever to be sent off in an FA Cup final, United went on to beat Everton 1–0 through a goal from Whiteside.

It is worth recalling that line-up. The team that started that day (substitute in brackets) was: Gary Bailey; John Gidman, Kevin Moran, Paul McGrath, Arthur Albiston (Mike Duxbury); Jesper Olsen, Norman Whiteside, Bryan Robson, Gordon Strachan; Mark Hughes, Frank Stapleton. Not a team you would bet against on any occasion, and in the United tradition they produced their greatest moments with two wingers.

Then there was the fateful 1985–86 season when, after United won thirteen and drew two of their first fifteen matches, the Holy Grail of the League championship had looked like returning to Old Trafford. But it was not to be in the Atkinson era, and we had to wait a little longer.

As we shattered another illusion during the interview for this book by sharing a pot of tea, with not a champagne cork in view, Ron looked back over the electric start to the season that could have been 'it': 'We didn't have a massive squad then, perhaps four players above the first eleven who were top quality. If we'd had a squad system like today's, and the vast economic resources the club has nowadays, we wouldn't have lost that lead. But crucially we lost Moses, Wilkins and Robson and other key players through injury, and we just ran out of bodies. Liverpool also had started the season well, with only one defeat in the first ten games, and they limped past us on the run-in as we dropped to a disappointing fourth.

'That Liverpool team, in my opinion, were the best club side ever in European football. What a nucleus they had. Hansen and Lawrenson were probably the best central defensive pairing ever to turn out in English football, and Ian Rush the best centre-forward – although he may eventually have to give up that mantle to Ruud van Nistelrooy – and, of course, there was the phenomenal Kenny Dalglish. Ironically, at that time we had better results in our clashes with Liverpool than any other team.

'It was disappointing that I didn't get more time for the massive injury backlog to clear, because we'd been playing beautifully before, and a couple of wins would have soon had us moving up the table again.'

He certainly has no hang-ups about the success of the man who followed him into the Old Trafford hot seat: 'I always got on well with Alex Ferguson, and saw quite a bit of him on my trips up to Scotland looking at players; but I felt something was in the wind in the month before I was dismissed by United because unusually he didn't seem comfortable with me. Looking back I realised that even then the moves were being put in place for him to take over at Old Trafford.'

He continued with a grin: 'But history will tell that it wasn't a bad move by Manchester United to appoint Alex, and I'm the first to say what a brilliant job he did. He's produced teams that I just love to watch. One of the vital factors is that they play at such a fast tempo, and their football is always exciting. I know when I go to watch United I'm always going to enjoy myself.

'The player I most enjoy watching is Paul Scholes, absolutely my favourite player. It's a delight to see him in action. I always feel I'm watching a street footballer playing, and that's said with admiration. You know, the kind of lad you always see with the ball when you're watching a street game, seeing this kid dribbling through the field. He's such a natural footballer – there aren't many players who you'd look for if you came late into the ground, knowing that was where the ball was going to be. Any time in a game, drop your head for a few minutes and then look up and you'll expect to see Paul on the ball and on the move.'

In conclusion, Ron singled out once more the man who so many others have seen as the true catalyst of United's recent success: 'Mind you, none of the present team, or any of Alex's teams, or my teams, including Bryan Robson, were the best signing United have made in the last twenty years, and it's always heart-warming to get the chance to give an unsung hero his dues.

'The best signing for the club in the era of Ron Atkinson and Alex Ferguson was youth coach Eric Harrison.'

In many ways Ron Atkinson was perhaps the most misunderstood of all the Masters of Old Trafford. Right to the death he played up to the sceptics who sang from the same song sheet about his lifestyle. Even when commenting on his dismissal he couldn't resist a wind-up: 'I've had to swop my Mercedes Benz for a BMW, I'm down to my last thirty-seven suits, and I'm now having to drink non-vintage champagne.'

But he'd shown the true feeling behind the smile and the wisecrack, when thanking chairman Edwards for the chance to manage the club. And when at the final press conference I reminded him, 'There've been plenty of good times,' he replied quietly: 'I'll be happy if there are a few people who remember that.'

The Ron Atkinson Fact File

1939:   15 March, born in Liverpool.

1959:   Failed to make the grade as youth-team player at Aston Villa.

1960:   Joined Oxford United.

1965:   Promoted to Third Division with Oxford.

1968:   Won Third Division championship and promotion with Oxford.

1971:   Moved to non-league Kettering.

1971–74: Player-manager of Kettering Town, first promoted club to win Southern League in 1973.

1974:   Appointed manager of Cambridge United.

1977:   Cambridge promoted to Third Division.

1978:   Cambridge promoted to Second Division.
Appointed manager of West Bromwich Albion.
WBA reach FA Cup semi-finals.

1979:   WBA reach fourth round of UEFA Cup and qualify again following season.

1981:   Appointed manager of Manchester United.

1982:   United finish third in First Division.

1983:   United win FA Cup after replay with Brighton; runners-up in Milk Cup; third in First Division.

1985:   United win FA Cup, beating Everton.

1986:   November, leaves Manchester United.

1987–88: Returns for eleven months to West Bromwich Albion.

1988:   Manager for three months of Spanish League side Atletico Madrid.

1989:   Appointed manager of Sheffield Wednesday.

1991:   Sheffield Wednesday win Littlewoods Cup and promotion to First Division.
Leaves Wednesday to manage Aston Villa.

1992:   Villa finish second in Premiership.

1994:   Villa win Coca-Cola Cup and beat holders Inter Milan in quarter-finals of UEFA Cup, but Atkinson sacked in November.

1995:   Appointed manager of Coventry City.

1996:   Appointed general manager of Coventry.

1997–98: Manager of Sheffield Wednesday for a second time.

1999:   Manager of Nottingham Forest.

Rich and Poor Relations

Despite Ron Atkinson's Cup success, and the superb football his teams produced, the famine since the club's last championship success in 1967 was eating at the supporters' patience, and the longer it went on the greater expectations became.

There were so many ifs and buts. Would the Doc have ended the famine, as so many people thought he would, had not falling in love cost him his job? Would the coaching and expertise of Frank O'Farrell or Dave Sexton have done the trick had they been allowed more time?

Was Ron Atkinson nearly there? If he had been allowed his way and been given the go-ahead to sign England defender Terry Butcher in the final year of his management reign at Old Trafford – a request that caused a wholesale row at a board meeting not long before his dismissal, with chairman Edwards having to step into the confrontation between Ron and a director – could that have been the last piece in the jigsaw of success for United?

Or what if another League championship for Matt Busby or the Wilf McGuinness combination had maintained the continuity of success after the 1968 European Champions' Cup triumph?

Francis Lee hardly knew how to lose against Manchester United. He played fifteen League and Cup derby games for Manchester City and was on the losing side just twice: a 1970 FA Cup tie, and a League game on 5 May 1971. He remains the joint highest scorer in derby games, and in December 1970 became only the fifth player in history to score a Manchester derby hat-trick when City won 4–1.

He certainly knew how to win trophies. Manchester City were in the bottom half of the First Division table when he joined them in the 1967–68 season, but thanks to Franny's goals they went on to win the championship within six months by two points from Manchester United. And the same thing happened when he went to Derby County in the 1974–75 season and immediately fired County to the title.

And he would have joined Tommy Docherty's Old Trafford line-up if City chairman Peter Swales hadn't stuck his heels in, saying Francis Lee was available for transfer – but not to Manchester United.

Now a multi-millionaire self-made businessman who has also enjoyed a highly successful career as a racehorse trainer and owner, Lee told me: 'My last appearance for City was against Manchester United at the end of the 1973–74 season. The players of both clubs have always had a good rapport despite going on to the field determined to kick lumps out of each other.

'It must have been my record against United that made Tommy Docherty come in to sign me. We met at the home of Paddy McGrath, the nightclub owner, who was a close friend of Sir Matt Busby. Tommy Doc knew that City needed money; but when he said they'd heard I was available I told them it was the first I'd heard of it.

'So I went to chairman Swales via Tony Book, and Mr Swales told me that a move to Old Trafford wasn't on. Then he told me that there had been an offer from Derby County, and although I tried to get our chairman to change his mind about letting me go to Manchester United – a nine-mile journey to United for training was much better than a 120-mile trip to Derby – Peter Swales was adamant.'

So the Baseball Ground it was for Franny, where he showed what a difference he could have made to an ailing Manchester United team by proceeding to shoot Derby to the title a point ahead of Leeds United and Liverpool. And even when Lee later scored twice in a 4–2 Derby County victory over Manchester United in Alan Hinton's testimonial game the Doc tried again, asking: 'Will you just play one last season for United?'

But Franny's business was growing at a massive rate. He admitted: 'I just didn't have the enthusiasm to go on any longer; and all the travelling, and running my business, had taken it out of me. In fact, even after my talk with Tommy, Matt Busby came back to me and told me that he couldn't believe how Manchester United had missed signing me right back in his management days when I was available for £60,000 from Bolton Wanderers.'

It was an appropriate moment in the conversation for Francis to remind me that I had spoken on several occasions to the Old Trafford hierarchy when he was playing for Bolton, recommending him to the club, and even going down to Old Trafford with copies of the *News of the World Football Guide* to show them how consistently he had appeared on the score sheet for Wanderers, even when played mostly out of position on the wings.

Now they wanted him it was too late, and even the combined might of Tommy Docherty and Sir Matt could not make him change his mind. 'If they had been interested in signing me earlier I couldn't have thought of a better club to join, but I could hardly have won more trophies than I collected under Malcolm Allison and Joe Mercer at Maine Road.

'I had nothing against the Doc, and would have liked to play for him or Matt Busby earlier in my career, even though there was never anybody in my footballing experience to match Malcolm Allison as a man to lead you into a game of football.

'The Doc was always a hail-fellow-well-met character with quick words and one-liners, and apparently a great knack of saying the right things in the dressing room to calm players down or gee them up.

'Wilf McGuinness had the same ebullience as Tommy, but he just had no chance in following Matt Busby. It didn't help having great stars like Best, Law and Charlton when the club was on the wane; but in any case City had become so dominant at that time that it presented an enormous problem for Wilf and Frank O'Farrell, who had the additional handicap of the directors always turning to Matt Busby and asking his advice if things weren't going well.

'Nowhere in the world would you expect a team to become European champions only for the poor relations in the city to dominate the next fifteen derby games. And of course the expectation level at Old Trafford was immense. There are only one or two clubs in the country where the fans won't accept being out of the top three placings, and that was Ron Atkinson's problem later on.'

Lee, a living legend at Maine Road as a player, was eventually persuaded to take over as chairman of the club, and reveals that he actually shook hands on a deal with Brian Kidd for him to take over as manager at Maine Road after the departure of Brian Horton. Kidd, who earned so much praise from Sir Alex as his assistant, and then so much vitriol from the same man when he decided to go into management on his own account with Blackburn Rovers, was one of a distinguished group who wore both the red of Manchester United and the blue of Manchester City as a player. And he was close to being manager at Maine Road as well as coach and right-hand man to the boss at Old Trafford.

Lee emphasised that Kidd's part in Manchester United's glory in the nineties should not be forgotten: 'In the early days of Alex Ferguson's reign at Old Trafford, when it looked as though he might lose his job, nobody knew what good work he and Brian Kidd were doing in laying the foundations of what was to be fantastic success later on. There should be no mistake about Kidd's input. He was responsible for nicking Ryan Giggs and Nicky Butt from Manchester City when we had them as juniors.

'Kidd had been out of work in the eighties, and Steve Fleet gave him a job at our Platt Lane training ground with the youngsters. But in the end, when he moved to Old Trafford, he took two of our brightest young hopes with him. It was a bitter blow.'

What was never publicised, however, was that later, when Kidd, despite all the success his partnership with Sir Alex was producing, was having no joy in attempts to get the salary deal he wanted, he applied for the managerial post at Maine Road that Horton had vacated.

Lee told me: 'While Alex Ferguson was on holiday Brian applied for the job and had talks with me. It was all agreed for him to take over as manager. Remember, he'd played for both clubs so he would have been welcomed by our supporters, and at the time it seemed a good move for Brian and our club.

'As chairman I remember shaking hands on the deal with him. Then everything was quiet for five or six days until Brian came back to me, saying he didn't have the heart to tell chairman Martin Edwards that he was going to leave. My immediate comment, after getting over the surprise about a deal we thought had been settled, was that if he couldn't make a binding decision over something like this how could he manage a football club? It was a view that was probably underlined when he took over at Blackburn Rovers but didn't make the grade.'

But that was the end of Kidd for Maine Road. Lee had to put an urgent call in to Royal Ascot in order to track down Alan Ball and install him as manager with time running out before the start of the new season.

Which, with the story of the emergence of embryo racehorse owner Sir Alex Ferguson as successor to Ron Atkinson about to unfold, seems the right moment to digress again and tell the Bookmaker's Tale.

In anybody's book Selwyn Demmy is a pretty cute cookie. Son of the late and legendary Gus Demmy, boxing promoter and bookmaker, Selwyn followed in his father's footsteps. He not only built the Demmy empire of betting shops and on-course pitches at the greatest racecourses in the land, but surprised the racing world in the eighties and nineties by selling his betting empire three times in eighteen years for escalating sums of £5.5 million, £6 million and £10 million... and he is still in business!

A friend and confidant of George Best, through his support and care he saved Britain's greatest ever footballer from doing even more damage to himself in his early days, and he knows more of the secrets of Britain's top sporting and showbiz personalities than MI5. He is also the man to know if you want to be told how to make a fortune.

He is a good man to make comparisons between Sir Matt Busby and Sir Alex Ferguson, especially when the question comes up: Would Fergie have been able to handle George Best better than Sir Matt, and extend his career so that his world-class talent shone well into his thirties rather than starting to fade, through his social excesses, in his mid-twenties?

Admitted Selwyn: 'It's an argument I've heard, that Sir Alex's more abrasive nature and his iron-hard discipline would have controlled

Best's lifestyle outside football from the start, when he was a teenager staying in digs with Mrs Fullaway in Chorlton-cum-Hardy.'

He reasoned: 'Matt Busby would be as successful now as he was through his long and distinguished career. He had the Midas touch, and his groundwork made it possible for Sir Alex to take the club on to the situation where, from being worth £20 million, they've become the most successful, wealthiest, and most influential club in the world. You only have to look at the people who now want to buy into the club to understand its status. The message has clearly gone out to the Stock Exchange, to the really big men of the world of finance, that you now have to be a serious big-hitter to get a piece of Old Trafford.

'The George Best era provided the first hint that a British football club might become as big as MGM. It was the first marriage of sport and showbiz – Best became number one at the box office, and he was hailed worldwide as "El Beatle" after his sensational performance in Spain in European competition. He was a teenager of unbelievable charisma and talent but, unfortunately, socially naïve as well as *personality plus* both on and off the field.'

Selwyn Demmy continued: 'He was a phenomenon that no football manager had previously had to deal with, and certainly if anybody in the game was capable of dealing with Best then Matt Busby was the man.

'The simple answer to the Best conundrum is that if he was around in the modern game as a youngster coming from school into professional football there would be more answers already in place to solve some of his problems. With the massive finance in the game nowadays, and the amount of backup for youth schemes, it would have been unthinkable that the greatest young talent, apart from Duncan Edwards, ever to blossom in British football would have been allowed to go astray. The mega money of twenty-first-century football would have found an answer.

'But at that time football and football administration was in a different dimension. My view is that Matt Busby, operating in the nineties, would have been just as successful in every aspect of running a football club as Sir Alex Ferguson has been. The club has been lucky to have two such great managers in forty years.'

Certainly Selwyn Demmy will never forget the authority of Sir Matt, or the awe and respect in which he was held. He believes: 'His persona was very different from that of Sir Alex, but in the final analysis they both had that special quality of producing a winning football team that not only scored goals, but provided great entertainment value along the way.

'I remember being in Sir Matt's company at a Variety Club lunch in London, and when the Duke of Edinburgh came in the room he made a beeline straight for Matt. He was the first person he wanted to meet, and believe it or not he was clearly in awe of the United manager. When Sir Matt came into a room all conversation stopped. But he was a perfect gentleman. He had time for everybody, and he really was a man of the people.'

Both Manchester United's manager-knights came from salt-of-the-earth, hard-working family backgrounds, and yet, the higher they climbed in the world, the more certain it seemed that neither would ever forget their roots or their old friends. Selwyn pointed out: 'Both men gave freely of their time for charitable causes, and their giving was non-sectarian...they supported every good cause they could. George Best wouldn't have been so generous with his time for other people if he hadn't been set a good example by the man who was the leader of every activity at Old Trafford.'

Not being able to say no was, of course, one of George's problems. He couldn't say no to a string of dolly birds, models and a succession of Miss Worlds. But he also never said no to his fans, and he would always take on too much in terms of turning out at charity events, presenting prizes to local junior teams – whatever was demanded of him. The truth was that, just as none of the players worked harder on the training ground than George, so none worked harder in supporting good causes off the field.

The bottom line was that nobody played harder in the nightclubs, and at entertaining young ladies. But in view of the skulduggery of certain young professionals in the twenty-first century on a drunken night out that ended up in the High Court, and many other indisciplined revelations that have reached the front pages of the newspapers in the last decade, it must be pointed out that the only person who was hurt by his excesses, some 35 years earlier, was George Best himself.

Said Demmy: 'He would always admit that the man he was most upset about disappointing when he had fallen off the straight and narrow was Sir Matt Busby. In retrospect it would have been better if the club had managed to persuade George's family to come over and set up house for him in Manchester; but in those times Best as a teenager was the biggest fish in the pond of sport and entertainment, up there with the Beatles, and he simply had too much too soon.

'Best, in fact, was infinitely better natured than Gazza or Maradona, and a better player, sublimely better. For a man of his tremendous talents it was a tragedy that he didn't extend his career at Old Trafford, which really was his home.'

Said Selwyn: 'But looking back at Matt I don't know anybody who ever saw a dark side of him. The Master clearly commanded respect, and he gave respect as well, while Sir Alex doesn't have the same image. But both produce the same reaction in so many ways, because the world loves a winner. And if either of them in their careers were guests of honour at an event it was immediately guaranteed to be a success.

'Both have delivered trophies and championships for Manchester United in the best possible way, while their standing in the football community could not have been higher.'

Admits Demmy: 'Nobody can deny the existence of rumours over the years that major success was short for some time because Sir Matt interfered; but I know nothing of that. I must admit that in my own empire I've retired three times, and I will not let go, so I can understand a man wanting to make a point if he sees something that has been his baby, that he has built up to unimaginable heights, not making progress.

'But I can't see Arsène Wenger or Sven-Goran Eriksson being put in a position where they aren't their own man, completely in control of every facet of the football affairs of the club, if either of them eventually get the job when Alex does retire. I would feel that Alex is too intelligent a man not to see the dangers, and would be too astute to interfere unless he's asked.'

But then what if he is not asked, and feels he should be asked?

'The board is now professional enough, and sufficiently strong, surely, to have all this thrashed out before any problems arise. And I should really hope to see Martin Edwards given the chance of a casting vote on any judgements, because but for him Sir Alex would never have been appointed manager of Manchester United, and but for him would never have been allowed long enough to win anything.'

Another man who was in close contact with all the seven ages of Manchester United management, because of his long-time service as a Manchester City director, was Chris Muir, now a director of Blackpool Football Club and, like Sir Alex and Sir Matt, a Scot.

He came south to Manchester just after Munich, joining the City board in 1967. He says: 'Matt was the greatest. If he'd decided to make his life away from football he could have ended up chairman of a big company or been a great success in politics. What a prime minister he would have made! He had great vision and a knack of remembering the name of anybody he met. But he was a humble man who never forgot his Belleshill upbringing. In the 1970 general election the *Daily Mirror* made a feature of his socialist connections, one of many similarities with Sir Alex.'

Chris was at close quarters with all the United managers, but said: 'There was an extra burden for all the managers between Sir Matt and Sir Alex. And it was the hardest, I'm sure, for Wilf McGuinness. Matt had been in charge for so long and all the players knew that he was smarter than them and they gave him their complete respect. But Wilf only started off level with them as one of the boys, and I'm sure that whoever had been upgraded from within the club at that time would have evoked the feeling from a large percentage of the established players that they thought they knew better what was needed.

'Wilf never had a chance; but he had all the right qualities. I'll never forget the occasion at a fundraising dinner for some sporting venture when a former Lord Mayor of Manchester pilloried Manchester City in front of me, and Wilf stood up and saved my embarrassment by telling the diners lots of good things about Manchester City. I used to see Wilf watching his son Paul play junior football in the park. He always had a kind word for everybody, and was never too busy to help anyone. His feedback to me about the job was: "I took it ten years too early."

'Frank O'Farrell, who followed him, was a quiet, kind, good family man but he was let down by his players, who took advantage of his good-living, slightly naïve nature. But he was always an interesting man to listen to when talking about football, and he had an exceptional reputation as a coach. His football experience was second to none, coming as he did from the West Ham United football school. But when he came into Manchester United, which was a family club, he was treated as an outsider and badly let down.

'Dave Sexton had similar problems although they weren't so marked. But he's an outstanding coach, and I've been very happy to serve on the England Youth Committee at the level he was coaching at into his seventies. His great forte was getting all his knowledge through to the young players, and teaching them and moulding them into good habits.

'The youth coach is one of the most important jobs in any club, with development in those formative years so vital. Dave always liked to reminisce with me, especially about Malcolm Allison; even though they couldn't have been more different in personality he looked upon him as one of the most outstanding gurus in post-war football thinking.'

Added Muir: 'Talking about personalities, you couldn't get a greater contrast between Sexton and the man who preceded him, Tommy Docherty. He was a gold-medal extrovert in an era in Manchester that was a golden era for the sports writers, because the City manager at the time was Malcolm Allison. There weren't enough sports pages in the newspapers to cover their escapades and their views.

'I remember watching Tommy play for Celtic and Preston, and there was certainly no greater battler in a Scotland shirt than Tom. And right back to his playing days he always had a crack that made sure nobody was ever allowed to be pompous in his company. One day I met him at Maine Road as we were both getting out of our cars. I was with my new wife, and he introduced himself to her, saying: "We Scots aren't beauties, but we're brilliant in bed" – a comment he naturally keeps reminding me of every time we meet, especially if my wife is with me. Even so, when it comes to charisma Ron Atkinson takes some beating, and again he would talk about football all night.

'I remember a reserve match during which he was goading Doug Ellis, even at a time when he looked to be heading for the sack. There was certainly no kowtowing to Mr Ellis for Big Ron. His way was that he was a players' manager, rather than an Establishment manager, and he made sure his players had the gold-nugget treatment, and they responded to him in kind. Robson was probably the making of the modern Manchester United team; he was an outstanding captain who ran the team on the field while Ron ran it in all other departments. And, of course, Muhren was the predecessor of all the wonderfully skilled players who arrived in England from the Continent.'

Heavily concerned with youth football at Maine Road as he had been, it was no surprise to hear Chris reminiscing about the time when City had the whip hand over United in that respect. And he confirms Franny Lee's claim that United snatched some of City's best youngsters: 'While United were making such great signings in the transfer market Manchester City were winning the battle hands down with their youth system until Brian Kidd and Alex Ferguson outflanked us. We even had a youngster called Ryan Wilson, better known now to football as Ryan Giggs, whose father had agreed he would sign for us; but United were stoking up a more aggressive approach to signing youngsters, and they stole him from under our noses.

Chris Muir has seen a rich tapestry of diverse personalities, methods and characters in the managerial hot seat during his own time in top football, but he reckons: 'There has never been such a mixture of personalities as that man called Alex Ferguson. I'm a great admirer of his achievements.

'He has to be *the* manager of the late twentieth century. I can't see anybody surpassing his feats. He's a football man from top to bottom. He's had the same appetite from his early days as a Queen's Park player through to his most successful days as manager of Aberdeen and Manchester United, and his enthusiasm has always been absolutely undiminished. He must rank as the strongest, most single-minded personality ever in British football, and when you look down the list at people like Brian Clough, Herbert Chapman, Bill Shankly, Bob Paisley, Don Revie, Matt Busby, Harry Catterick, Jock Stein, Bill Nicholson and Bobby Robson that's some list to head.

'Of course, it's some feat for Sir Alex that there's even such an argument as to who is the greatest in Manchester United's history. It seemed impossible that anybody would come along to rival Matt; he had everything to make him an icon for the game, never mind Manchester United. He was a very good family man, and part of his success was in making Manchester United a family. He was an idol in Scotland all the time he was living and working in England, and he'll also be remembered as a player of great vision and a wonderful passer of the ball, an attribute that made up for his lack of pace.

'He was the greatest because he led the way in being the first to start a youth policy and develop it, when no club had even thought of such a move. Busby was a crafty man when he needed to be, but he charmed everybody. Alex is the proverbial hot-headed Scotsman, but because of his fanaticism he's been a magnificent successor to the man who was the greatest manager in Britain for a quarter of a century after the Second World War. The fall of Manchester City coincided with the arrival of Fergie across the town and the gradual erosion of our monopoly of young talent in the area.

'He was always destined to be one of the greats from his country alongside Shankly, Stein, George Graham and Busby; but what worries me now is that we have no world-class managers or players in Scotland.

'It wasn't so long ago when our country beat England three times out of four games in the seventies, crowned by that 1977 2–1 win at Wembley through goals from Kenny Dalglish and Gordon McQueen. Now Alex has taken Manchester United light years ahead of the rest of their rivals in Britain, it would be wonderful if, when he does finish, he could devote the rest of his footballing life to taking Scottish football back to the standards of the Good Old Days.'

Watched by chairman Louis Edwards, manager Frank O'Farrell (right) congratulates Sir Matt Busby after he is elected a director of Manchester United in 1971.

Top: No doubt about Tommy Docherty being a tracksuit manager here.

Bottom: Happy days together for physiotherapist Lawrie Brown (left) and the Doc as they celebrate beating Liverpool in the 1977 FA Cup final at Wembley. Later they were to be divided for the love of Mary.

Triumph on the balcony of Manchester Town Hall. Watched by player Martin Buchan, Docherty shows the 1977 FA Cup to the thousands of supporters who packed Manchester's Albert Square.

The Thinker. Quiet man Dave Sexton came so close to producing a team to win that elusive championship, but in the end he did not bring a single trophy and had to go. However, he left immensely respected by his players, with dignity and the determination to carry on. Sexton was still coaching at the highest level in his seventies.

Opposite page
Top: A delighted Ron Atkinson hugs Gordon Strachan after Norman Whiteside's goal at Wembley produced a 1–0 1985 FA Cup final victory over Howard Kendall's Everton.

Bottom: The start of a first ever Wembley 'Cup' hat-trick. Big Ron went on to win the League Cup at Wembley with Sheffield Wednesday and Aston Villa.

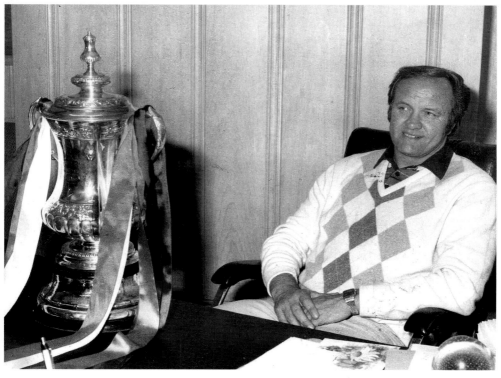

'Go on my son!' Ron Atkinson is an enthusiast from the tips of his toes to the top of his head. Says Eric Harrison: 'There wasn't a morning before starting a day's training when he did not come up the stairs to his office whistling and singing.'

Top: Ooh aah Cantona. Eric's match-winning goal was enough to beat Liverpool 1–0 in the 1996 FA Cup final. Sir Alex Ferguson and his asistant Brian Kidd help him celebrate with the trophy.

Bottom: An almost surreal picture of Sir Alex, never more in the spotlight than when his team scored that dramatic 1999 Champions' League final victory over Bayern Munich.

Top: Another trophy – another Manager of the Month award for Sir Alex in 1994. He said: 'I have been very lucky to have two great captains in Steve Bruce [left] and Bryan Robson.'

Below: Facing the press in the 1990s. Sir Alex reads a newspaper while David Beckham answers questions before another key European game.

Half a Crown from Uncle Matt

Martin Edwards, multi-millionaire chairman of Manchester United from 1980 through into the twenty-first century, has some wonderful memories of the great success story of Old Trafford. In turn, the club owe him an enormous debt: he was the man who singled out Alex Ferguson as a future manager of the Reds, and who then stood shoulder to shoulder with him against a massive campaign by supporters and people within the club for the manager to be sacked. It was Edwards's determination and courage that kept Ferguson at the club when everybody else, inside and outside Manchester United, was calling for his head and demanding he be put on the next train back to Glasgow.

Taking on executive responsibilities years before as a director when his father Louis was chairman, he shared in the glory of United's achievement in becoming the first English club to win the European Champions' Cup in 1968. And later, by now in charge of the club, he was able to enjoy years of success under the inspired management of Sir Alex.

But like most of us, some of his most vivid memories are from his childhood. Edwards recalls: 'Matt Busby was "Uncle Matt" to me as a child because as chairman and manager my father and Matt had a close relationship. I was certainly in awe of him, but not frightened. I still have such a clear memory of Christmas 1957 when, at a cocktail party my father was giving, "Uncle Matt" came up to my sister Catherine and me to give us half a crown each.

'What a treasure that Christmas present was. I don't remember ever spending it, and I felt as though I owned the crown jewels.'

But there were turbulent times, as well as wonderful, exhilarating times ahead. At the age of 24, Martin was brought on to the board in 1970, after Wilf McGuinness had taken over from Sir Matt.

He says: 'Wilf had been groomed by Matt, but he came in at a difficult time. Having been a player himself it was difficult to get the right relationship with the senior players. He had to change things round and get the club to move on, but he didn't adopt the right approach. Even the experience of being on Alf Ramsey's backroom staff wasn't enough.'

Martin Edwards later found out himself how important experience can be. Already a director for ten years when he was made chairman, he had the solid background of working on the board, learning from his father on the business side, and watching at close quarters the way policy was formed by his father and Matt Busby. By 1974 he was also managing director of the retail side of the Edwards family meat business, with 1,000 staff and a £10 million turnover.

Martin's respect for Matt Busby was a vital part of his formation as a football man, and he said as we talked in his office in the executive suite of the grandstand: 'The fact that Matt lived into his eighties after the injuries he received at Munich showed his spirit and courage. And the way he came back to manage United towards that pinnacle performance against Benfica ten years later was like a film script: almost too much of a fairytale to be true.

'Everybody respected him. He had been a very good player for Manchester City, Liverpool and Scotland and he built up his reputation by getting on the training ground and showing his players what to do. Being a great passer of the ball in his day as a player – he was apparently a bit like Paddy Crerand in his style – he always wanted to produce a side that was a bit special in terms of quality and entertainment.

'But it's important to point out that, despite the fact that by the sixties he had achieved so much and survived so much, he was a humble man, never boastful or arrogant.

'He was clever with the press. He was prepared to talk to the media as long as they wanted to talk to him, but he never gave anything away, never told them more than was expedient. He was a master of manipulation.

'Older players would tell of him calling them into his office, and asking them how they thought they were playing. There would be no confrontations over him dropping a star player; he would get them to volunteer the information that they were not playing well before he said: "Well, I think you're right, son. Maybe it would be good for you to have a wee rest." He would drop a player and they would practically leave the room thanking him for leaving them out of the team.'

Any weaknesses Edwards could detect in Matt Busby were, as he admits, only hearsay, although he told me: 'I'm not sure whether Matt was a tactical genius. He relied on his astute judgement of a player, and after Munich he bought players of great ability, motivated them and gave them their head. He certainly couldn't have survived had he not been absolutely on top of the job, but he wasn't a Don Revie who spent hours on tactics, and he always emphasised to his players that he wanted them to go out and enjoy their football.

'Jimmy and Matt were a great team, and Jimmy always had a little motto for every situation. Bobby Charlton claims to remember to this day the Murphyisms that used to run constantly through his head to cover situations as they developed in a game.

'I don't think there was any doubt that Matt's greatest moment was winning the European Cup final in '68 after being the first English club manager to take a team into European competition in the 1956–57 season against the wishes of the Football Association. I know there were times when he felt partly responsible for Munich because he insisted on playing in Europe, and he was heard to say that if he hadn't done so the disaster wouldn't have happened. It was no secret that he wanted to give up after Munich and only his wife Jean and family plus his players kept him going, and saved him retreating into a shell.'

It was an understandable feeling, but nobody can control their destiny. It is always a mistake to look back in regret, but it is a mistake many of us make. So it was a natural question to ask if Busby ever spoke to Martin Edwards about feeling he'd failed in his recommendations over his successors, and if he would have done anything different if he'd had the chance over again.

'The appointments of Wilf and Frank O'Farrell were Matt's recommendations to my father, and he had a say in Tommy Docherty's appointment, and was disappointed that things hadn't worked out.'

But no club in history can look back without finding their story littered with controversies, problems and mistakes, and Manchester United have been no exception. Said chairman Edwards: 'There's no doubt that George Best was Matt's crowning glory and perhaps his only failure, but could anybody have handled him better? I don't know the answer. Certainly Wilf McGuinness, Frank O'Farrell and Tommy Docherty couldn't.

'Wilf had so much enthusiasm, and was and is an extremely likeable person, but in terms of being a football manager one has to say clinically that if you look at his career he didn't make a big success of management anywhere else. There's no doubt that Matt would have to carry the can for that: he was very confident in his recommendation to the board that Wilf was ready to do the job.'

He added: 'In a way it shattered Wilf's life when he found he hadn't made the success he hoped of managing Manchester United, but his spirit enabled him to rise above it all eventually. Just look at him now. He's a contented man, and he's found his niche as an entertainer. He was very upset at the time, but never bitter, and he's always been a Manchester United man through and through. I have great admiration for the way he's gone through adversity and come out the other side so successfully. It's true to say that his appointment, without much experience under his belt, was something of an experiment, a learning curve for the club, which actually could be said to have trodden water for the three years that covered the management of Wilf and then Frank O'Farrell.

'Even though he took the club down into the Second Division there was no doubt that Tommy Docherty started the upward curve. For after going down with an average gate of 44,000 he brought us straight back up with an average 48,000 at the turnstiles, and brought together a team of players with the added confidence to go on and finish third in the old First Division on their first season back. With that plus an FA Cup final appearance at Wembley, we'd moved a few rungs back up the ladder.

'It was the kind of step up in form that we thought was on the cards when Frank O'Farrell came and started so well. But although Frank courted the press and got good reviews, the players thought he was a bit aloof, and Bobby Charlton, as captain, approached the manager and the chairman to tell them how the players felt. Frank hadn't spent a lot of time on the training ground – he let Malcolm Musgrove do most of the coaching – and the players complained that they never really got to know him. It was all falling apart and we had to do something.'

'Looking back, it's obvious we hadn't fully recovered from the mistakes made at the end of Matt Busby's reign. Against his better judgement he'd been persuaded to stay on after winning the Champions' Cup, and when he did leave the players coming through weren't as prominent. It might even have been that our peak was the year before we won the European title. The 1966 side was probably the best of the sixties teams, and perhaps it was beginning to wane even towards the end of 1968.

'John Connelly was tremendous in 1966, David Herd was still in the side but broke his leg in '67. After the Champions' Cup win, Munich survivors Bill Foulkes and Bobby Charlton, along with Shay Brennan, had perhaps hit their peak, even though some of them carried on to win more international caps after losing the '69 European semi-final. Then Nobby Stiles and Denis Law, such important players for us, started to pick up injuries, and the replacements were just not there.'

And until sex reared its head the Doc was regarded by the supporters as the Messiah, the man who was going to bring the championship back at last to Old Trafford. Revealed Edwards: 'Tommy wasn't the first choice. We had approached Dave Sexton, but he turned the job down. But it looked for a long time as though our second choice was going to be an inspired one, and that Tommy was going to be the man to take the club back to past glories.

'He was a likeable rascal who was getting great results, and doing it with sweeping, entertaining football. He got success to some extent with the younger players through fear. For despite his wise-cracking he could also crack the whip, and it helped that he didn't have the legacy of the older players who had seen and done everything, to question his authority.

'But even at his peak there would have been signs, if we'd been able to read them, that Tommy wasn't perfect. He certainly couldn't bully the senior players or pull the wool over their eyes. And afterwards it came to light that there were severe problems even when we were doing well.

'Even so, he was still proving to be a manager capable of winning things, especially in Cup football. And who knows, if the Mary Brown situation hadn't surfaced just after that great Cup final win then he might have become the first manager since Busby to win the League title.

'Dave Sexton came along with a reputation as a fine coach, and he also nearly won an FA Cup final in 1979 when we lost that marvellous game with Arsenal. After the Doc era, I remember when we were thinking about the next manager my father said: "Get a gentleman", and Dave Sexton was certainly that, a very nice man. But although he was respected throughout the club, he never quite made it.

'I don't know if he improved what Tommy built. He certainly maintained it, but the problem was the style of play. He was more cautious and defensive, and the supporters weren't as happy. They didn't really warm to him, even though some of the players were genuinely upset when he was sacked. He was a bit of a philosopher, and on tour he would often sit in a deck chair and find a peaceful spot to read some highbrow stuff. But all that didn't hide the fact that he was a terrific football enthusiast, and an interesting person.

'What did he lack? He didn't improve on what the previous manager had done, and his team wasn't as entertaining as it had been in the previous four seasons. There was a lack of flair, although I'm sure he would answer by saying that the time for flair is after you've got results. It comes back to Manchester United teams being required to play a certain style, although we know that times have moved on, and we would never go back to the total philosophy of Matt Busby of playing off the cuff.

'But there was Ron Atkinson to come, and that provided a change of pace and plenty of entertaining football. It was a big difference after Dave. Although Ron had come up the ladder from a modest playing career with lower-division clubs, there was no doubt that he didn't mind travelling executive class.

'I feel he was very close to producing a team to bring the championship back, and made some great signings. He finished third in the League in his first two seasons, and was never out of the top four until the season he parted company with the club, when we were lying in thirteenth place in November 1986. He had had some tremendous winning runs, but things had started to slacken off. Quite simply he hadn't done what every Manchester United manager is appointed to do: win the championship.

'I know his sacking was a savage disappointment to him, but he took it well, never ever criticised the decision, said how he had enjoyed managing the team and thanked me when he left. He was never the type to wallow in misery, and was prepared to get on with the next stage of his life when a door closed on him.'

Just as any manager needs to keep ahead of the game in the transfer market, Martin Edwards was always aware that one of the most important facets of his job as chairman was keeping an eye on prospective managerial talent, and Aberdeen boss Alex Ferguson intrigued him. Here was a man who seemed capable of breaking the mould, a man who had worked miracles at Pittodrie in prising loose the iron grip the Old Firm, Rangers and Celtic, seemed to have on Scottish football, and who had proved that no hurdle was too difficult for him to leap by producing one of the great European shocks of modern times.

Aberdeen's 1983 Cup Winners' Cup final defeat of odds-on favourites Real Madrid in Gothenburg had shocked the world of football, and with their Scottish League championship wins in 1980, 1984 and 1985 plus four Scottish Cup final victories in five years in the eighties, Martin Edwards, having done his homework, knew there was just one question mark beside the name of Alex Ferguson.

Could he cross the border and still be successful? English football had produced plenty of successful Scottish managers, but from within its own system. No Scot had played, managed and coached in Scotland and then gone to England and found success. Even Jock Stein, a man many consider the greatest ever British manager, found the going too tough. And one of Scotland's canniest management forces, Jim McLean, a man who turned water into wine with Dundee

United and drove himself to the limits in bringing glory to his beloved club, turned down several offers to prove himself in England because he felt the culture gap was too wide.

Martin Edwards knew his man. Before anybody else at Old Trafford had even thought of the possibility of hiring a man who was known to be a bit wild, had been involved in fights with pressmen in Scotland, had some hairy confrontations on and off the field, Edwards recognised that here was someone clearly born to be a winner.

That was what United needed so desperately now, and the United chairman had another ace up his sleeve. He knew that this abrasive Scot, who some people painted as a cross between Desperate Dan and Attila the Hun, had it written in his contract that if the Manchester United job became available he would be released by Aberdeen.

Ironically, even before Sir Alex came to Old Trafford, Martin had to unravel Aberdeen's transfer saga with Gordon Strachan, who had been at loggerheads with Fergie at Pittodrie and had, in a tangled contractual web, actually signed for both Cologne and Verona before it became known that Ron Atkinson wanted to take him to Old Trafford. The negotiations were part of Martin Edwards getting to know Sir Alex, seeing how he operated, and helping build a dossier that made him confident this was the man to finally bring the English championship back to fill that empty gap in the boardroom trophy cabinet.

Having wanted to put daylight and even a border or two between himself and Alex Ferguson, the flame-haired Strachan must have felt he was living a nightmare when his old Aberdeen manager followed him to Old Trafford; but it did not do his career or his trophy collection any harm, although hostilities continued between them even when they were opposing managers. But it was a further irony that it was Strachan's agent, who had played in the same team in Scotland as Sir Alex, who initially reported to the United chairman much of the detail of Ferguson's career and character.

Martin Edwards recalls the day he signed Ferguson: 'Dick Donald, the Aberdeen chairman, wasn't surprised. He'd already persuaded Alex to turn down Spurs, telling him: "The only job for you, Alex, is Manchester United."

'The day after Ron Atkinson left I flew up to Aberdeen with fellow director Maurice Watkins, and we went straight to Dick Donald's house, having already established that Alex was interested. We were talking with the Aberdeen chairman to reach a settlement figure over compensation for the club – £60,000 was the fee we agreed on – when Alex arrived at the house, and it was clear that there was a great deal of affection between the Aberdeen chairman and his manager. They'd been together for nine years, and Dick was like a father, giving his son his big opportunity, although it did upset him when he found Alex taking his assistant Archie Knox with him.

'Clearly, however, Alex hadn't needed much time to make up his mind.' And on this occasion, unlike January 2002, Ferguson was to have no second thoughts.

As we talked about Alex Ferguson's glittering career, Edwards made it clear that the United boss, despite repeated claims in the media, is not now his enemy. He smiles at stories that the man he brought to England has worked tirelessly to weaken his position at Old Trafford, and that when his managing days are over he will try to usurp his position as chairman of the football club.

He told me: 'Alex wrote in his book that he always gets on with Martin Edwards except where it comes to money. I certainly didn't see that as a criticism. No employee gets everything he wants. I had my job to do, which was looking after the best interests of the club by keeping wages to levels the club could afford, and playing my part in making decisions about how much money was available in the transfer market.

'I've had one up-and-downer in sixteen years with Alex, and the situation between us has been blown up out of all proportion by people who don't know the facts. I stepped down, as I'd always planned to do, from my position as chief executive on my fifty-fifth birthday in July 2000, and if there had been anything wrong in the relationship between Alex Ferguson and myself there was no way this club could ever have been as successful as it has been over all these years.'

In fact it took a Liverpool icon, former secretary and chief executive Peter Robinson, who was the quiet inspiration behind much of the Anfield success in his support to Bill Shankly, Bob

Paisley and the other managers of his extensive period at the club, to reveal a previous secret that underlines the humanity and team spirit that existed, at least at one time, between Martin Edwards and Alex Ferguson. It concerns the Hillsborough disaster of April 1989, when 96 Liverpool supporters died, crushed to death at the Sheffield stadium.

Peter told me: 'There are many sides to public figures other than the recognised profile. Another side to Alex and his chairman was shown to me when they travelled to Anfield after the Hillsborough disaster, the first people outside the club to come over personally and show their grief and support. They insisted on arriving quietly to pay their respects, making it clear they didn't want any publicity, that it must be kept under wraps, and brought with them an outstanding cheque for the disaster fund. The private way it was all done, and the care they showed towards us, underlined that the friendship between the people at Liverpool Football Club and Manchester United is as intense as our rivalry on the field, and that should never be forgotten.'

Ferguson's short fuse, especially in the earlier days of his success at Old Trafford, was no secret, and very public rows, such as the tunnel turmoil at Anfield between himself and Kenny Dalglish, were seized with delight by the media who are never slow to turn a spat into a 'cauldron of hate'. But in fact, behind the confrontations, the apparent tantrums and vendettas, few of his decisions concerning the running of his team and the organisation of his club have been anything other than clinical.

He has flaws; so did Brian Clough, but they didn't stop him being one of the greatest managers ever. And Sir Alex has always had a knack of making even his faults work for him. My observation has been that he parades his flaws like a badge of honour.

Martin Edwards, while admitting that he would not disagree with most of those sentiments, pointed out: 'At the end of the day he doesn't show favouritism, and goes out simply to win games with what he thinks will be the best team at his disposal for the task in hand, even if it means dropping a club icon. He dropped David Beckham when he felt he wasn't doing it, and stifled his own emotions when knowing how much it would hurt Jim Leighton when he dropped him for the FA Cup final replay against Crystal Palace. I know it must have caused Alex inner turmoil to make the decision, but he felt certain it was the right decision for his team, and that in the circumstances it gave us a better chance of winning the Cup.

'Quite simply Alex's gift is his ability to run a football club brilliantly, to select the right players and mould a team through his tactical skill in fielding that team, and preparing them both physically and mentally.

'And it has helped that he's had a club the size of Manchester United with the resources capable of fulfilling his dreams, resources that many of his rivals don't possess. Had the club not been organised to create more money for expansion and further investment in the team on the top of his victories, it's doubtful if the success story would have been so marked, with the club finding money to buy Yorke, Stam and Blomqvist for £28 million the year after Arsenal did the double, and more recently spending £50 million on Van Nistelrooy, Veron and Carroll.'

Who else in British football has that kind of financial clout?

But it would be no surprise to find that Sir Alex had thought through all these factors when he was deciding his future. Probably it was the reason why he had far-sightedly inserted the clause in his Aberdeen contract that he should be freed if the job as Manchester United's manager became available. What, though, has been the secret of his success?

Answered Martin Edwards: 'Obviously he's a man absolutely driven to find success, a man whose inner forces drive him on and on. No sooner has he won one trophy than it's dismissed, and the next triumph is being planned. Alex certainly isn't a man to dwell on his triumphs. There's always another winning post beyond the one he has just passed. One success is the stepping stone to the next.

'Manchester United and our supporters want success all the time. If seven titles are won not winning the eighth is just as desperate for everybody at Old Trafford. It's an affront to lose. The more success you have the more you hurt when you lose.

'Even for Alex the learning curve took a bit longer than he expected. He cites as one of his early mistakes keeping Jesper Olsen and not signing John Barnes from Watford when he could have done. He was really distressed in 1992 when we lost to Liverpool and Leeds United went on to win the League.'

The following year, though, that 26-year famine was finally ended. United won the first ever Premier League title with 84 points, leaving Aston Villa ten points behind them and third-placed Norwich a further two points back. 'Alex had waited six full seasons to achieve the goal that he had been pointed at when he took the job, and there's no doubt that Eric Cantona was the catalyst for that success.'

There is no doubt, either, that the Sir Alex Ferguson who has won everything there is to win as a manager, is a very different man to the one Martin Edwards brought down from Aberdeen in November 1986. Edwards says: 'He's a great manager and will stand alongside Matt Busby in the history of the club.'

But he adds: 'Arguments will rage forever about who was the greatest and clearly Sir Alex has won more trophies than Sir Matt. But while Alex clearly had a lot of rebuilding to do when he took over, the club was powerful with massive assets, whereas in 1945 we didn't even have a ground to play on and had to ground-share, and, of course, Matt had to start all over again after the tragedy of Munich.

'Putting the two men in their position in the United hall of fame is a difficult one, but there's no doubting the greatness of them both. Alex certainly took longer to come to terms with the English game than he expected, but once he did – after a twenty-year period during which Liverpool were pre-eminent – he virtually turned the ranking list on its head.'

Born Leader

Can you think of anything more ludicrous than comparing a former trade union official who loves a fight, whether mental or physical, who reduces grown men to tears, and who is the most hated man in half of two of Britain's greatest cities, with Queen Elizabeth II?

How about trying on Sir Alex Ferguson for size?

Reading an article about our Queen in her Jubilee year I came across her words to the country at her coronation: 'My whole life, whether it be long or short, will be dedicated to your service.' As I said, it sounds ludicrous at first glance – and to most people I suppose it will still sound the same after twenty glances – but on reading it the first thing that came to mind was: Sir Alex.

Somehow that suddenly seemed exactly how I imagined the Manchester United manager, setting out on a lifetime of dedication to the great god of football success.

Somehow also, and – dare one say it – perhaps more successfully than the Queen, he has juggled the keeping of that vow with also having a successful, happy and dedicated family life.

His life has been full of controversy, packed with success, and from ordinary but loving roots he has grown into a quite extraordinary man. Football has been his life, and in his management career first Aberdeen and then Manchester United have consumed that life.

He has wrought amazing success at both clubs, but Manchester United was already a legend when he arrived in the 1986–87 season to produce modest first-season success, finishing in eleventh place in the old First Division with a third-round League Cup defeat and an FA Cup exit in the fourth round. Statistically, it was the tidiest possible start to his Old Trafford career: wins 14, draws 14, defeats 14. No hint of the turbulence, hysteria, anger, tantrums, vendettas, bloody-mindedness, confrontation, ecstasy and excitement to come.

There is no doubt that from humble beginnings Alex reached for the stars and found them. That fact was appropriately emphasised the first time he found real confirmation that his management style was going to make something special of his life, when he was honoured with the freedom of Aberdeen in 1999.

It was the year of his fantastic Manchester United treble, culminating in the Champions' League injury-time defeat of mighty Bayern Munich; but he was with his 'ain folk' when he followed in the footsteps of the Queen Mother, Winston Churchill, Nelson Mandela and Mikhail Gorbachev and, wearing the traditional blue hat with a ticket in it, proudly accepted the honour presented to him by the people of Aberdeen.

His life had started on 31 December 1941 in Govan, Glasgow, a joyous 'first footing' for his parents. His climb to football fame started calmly enough in 1957 as an amateur with Queen's Park while an apprentice toolmaker in a Glasgow factory, and three years later he joined St Johnstone as a part-timer. He quit his job to join Dunfermline in 1964, and after three years as a full-time pro the big breakthrough came when he joined Glasgow Rangers in a £65,000 move. His warriorlike style – all elbows and knees, and generally the fittest man on the park – earned him a lot of enemies but also plenty of goals; leading scorer one season with 23, he told me around the time of his U-turn at Old Trafford that in his best season he hit the net 45 times, when playing for Dunfermline.

His opponents certainly always knew they'd been in a game after facing Alex, but he was as aggressive with his club directors as he was with his opponents on the field, and after two years with Rangers he left Ibrox amid considerable controversy to go to Falkirk in a £20,000 move. In 1973 he became a part-timer again with Ayr United, when he also became a pub landlord near Glasgow Rangers' home. Within a year he had started his long climb to managerial distinction: he spent three months as manager of East Stirling before joining St Mirren. After four years and all manner of infighting with officials at the club, he blew his top once too often and was sacked.

But that messy farewell to Love Street was the making of his incredible managerial career. Appointed manager at Aberdeen in succession to Billy McNeill, within two years he had earned his first managerial honour, ending fifteen years of Old Firm dominance in winning the Scottish Premier Division by a single point from Celtic. The pinnacle of his 'wonder years' at Pittodrie came with victory in the Cup Winners' Cup in Gothenburg, where Aberdeen defeated Real Madrid 2–1. In all he had eight great years there before the call came from Old Trafford, by which time the football world lay at his feet waiting to be conquered.

But climbing new peaks was never a problem, certainly not in the mind of Sir Alex, even though in the aftermath of his Champions' League success and the treble in 1999 he dropped his guard enough to say: 'I was never a great player, but I wanted to be great.' But then he added, with his customary bravado: 'I thought I could climb Mount Everest in my carpet slippers. That's why I have to have players around me who mirror that same desire, drive and need.'

In his quieter moments he will, surprisingly, admit that he could have done certain things differently; but in truth that only mirrors his remorseless drive for perfection. And the painstaking way he analyses his own approach and his players' attitudes, ability and outlook on every match, and refuses to be satisfied, is the foundation for his success, rather than the abrasive exterior of confrontation that catches the newspaper headlines.

Ruthless is perhaps the word used most frequently in describing his approach to football, even to life. Perhaps occasionally even he may look back not with regret, but merely wondering if he could have done things differently. A classic example is the way he off-loaded the man credited by many with saving his managerial career.

It was said at the time that a goal scored by Mark Robins saved Ferguson from the sack which loomed if United had lost their FA Cup third-round tie at Nottingham Forest in 1989–90. The Old Trafford boss admitted later: 'It seemed I might become yet another statistic in the pursuit of success. But the FA Cup came to my rescue, starting with a morale-boosting victory over Forest – we got a 1–0 win with a goal scored by Mark Robins, bless him.'

Robins's goals enabled Manchester United to get to Wembley for the 1990 FA Cup final against Crystal Palace, but he was not on the starting list for either the first game at Wembley or the replay, a game in which Lee Martin scored United's winner. Mark and his family were more inclined over the years after that Cup run to remember Sir Alex by saying 'Alex Ferguson, blast him,' as Mark – in my opinion an Ole Gunnar Solskjaer years before his time – never got the chance he yearned for when at the age of fourteen he left home to join the new residential school at Lilleshall, with a dream of becoming an England star of the 1990s.

He admitted that all he ever wanted to do was play for Manchester United, and had a scoring record almost on the Ole Gunnar scale, hitting 11 goals in 19 starts plus 29 sub appearances. His third goal in the Cup run was the semi-final winner that took United to Wembley and everything seemed to be coming up roses for him.

But instead it turned out to be one of football's many hard-luck stories, even though Mark still had a fruitful career, playing into his thirties and enjoying an Indian summer in two successive promotion-winning teams with Rotherham United.

Rolling with the punches is part of the life of a professional sportsman, and that applies especially to football managers. Even Sir Alex had his share of doubts before his final championship breakthrough. After one particularly disastrous match at Old Trafford against Leeds United near the end of the 1991–92 season, a friend opened the door of one of the rooms at the club to find Alex alone, berating the result, crying: 'That's the end, I'm finished!' as yet another hope of title glory slipped away.

Few people know the man better than Archie Knox, the first of Sir Alex's three long-term assistants during his time at Old Trafford and perhaps the most important, as he was at the master's shoulder during his most difficult opening years at Manchester United. One of Sir Alex's most valued foot soldiers in his rise to the top of the tree in management, he was his most important aide for the best part of a decade at Pittodrie, during their Aberdeen days, as well as down in Manchester.

Archie had interrupted the partnership once before to take on the management of Dundee between 1983 and the summer of 1986. Sir Alex was sorry to lose him again, this time for good, when the lure of returning to Scotland – and for more money than United were prepared to pay him – proved too much. He left Old Trafford in 1991 to rejoin another old pal, Walter Smith, as the assistant at Glasgow Rangers.

Having been at Alex's right hand during the wonderful years at Aberdeen, a club largely regarded as merely provincial and dismissed as second-raters by the aristocrats of Celtic and Rangers, he had helped oversee that sensational Cup-final defeat of Real Madrid, as well as sharing in outstanding domestic triumphs. When he decided to return to Scotland and join Smith, his teammate at Dundee United when they lost 3–0 to Celtic in the 1974 Scottish Cup final, he had only a few days previously helped Fergie move a step nearer his first international trophy by eliminating Legia of Warsaw from the Cup Winners' Cup to earn a final tilt at Barcelona, who United were to go on and beat 2–1 in Rotterdam.

Said Sir Alex, who at the time was not strong enough to take on his own board and insist they pay his number two a rate matching Rangers' offer of £90,000 a year: 'We are very disappointed that he is going because he has done a great job for United; but there are no hard feelings. We wish him well.'

There was no immediate announcement of a replacement, although eventually Brian Kidd was to take over. Fergie added: 'We'll take our time about a successor here, so we can be sure we come up with the right person. Archie has been a big influence. With the Barcelona game so near the timing is not good; but he had to look after his family, and his own interests. No one at United will blame him for going from one huge club to another.'

Archie's trophy cabinet was not to be depleted through his move to Rangers. The Ibrox Park club were in the middle of a run of nine consecutive Scottish Premiership titles, concluding with a five-point winning margin over Celtic in the 1996–97 season, so the £150,000 compensation they paid to Manchester United to secure him was small potatoes.

And, six years younger than Sir Alex, he said: 'There are still a few years left in me in the game; but football generally will miss Sir Alex when he does eventually decide to retire. He's been an enormous influence on Manchester United, and who knows, he might still appear again somewhere as a national team manager when he does eventually decide to call it a day, if he gets bored with his horse-racing.

'What he's achieved at Old Trafford so far has been fantastic, and however long he remains he will never give less than 110 per cent to any job he takes in hand.

'It's a credit to his determination and desire that each season he's come out fresh and hungry to prove he and his team are the best once again. There's no doubt that it's difficult for any man in any sport to go out at the top. Muhammad Ali was just one sporting great who couldn't resist the temptation of one more fight, and even the greatest stars generally have to feel the pain of having slipped off the pinnacle before they get the message.

'With Alex, the horse-racing interest is there now to sustain him as well as his family life, plus whatever less stressful job he decides to take up when he does finally quit Old Trafford. Even so, his affinity with racing has surprised me. During our association he never showed the slightest interest, and in fact in the dressing room at Pittodrie if ever racing came on the radio he would switch it off. Footballers generally want to know the racing results, whatever club they're with, so perhaps that was just one of his ways of keeping the players in their place.'

Archie has some great memories of their times together, and a ready analysis of Sir Alex's success. He told me, as we spoke looking out on Everton's training ground: 'He would always build correctly: getting a youth scheme up and running at Aberdeen, and going on to unbelievable success, while that was again his priority at Old Trafford, as apparently Matt Busby had done all those years before. Giggs was just starting to come through – although he wasn't in the team – when we won the FA Cup replay against Palace.'

It was ironic that former United hero Steve Coppell was the Palace manager, and may well have been offered the United job if the board had not stuck firmly behind Ferguson.

Continued Archie Knox: 'I don't know if the sack was ever close. We didn't get any hint that it was likely, and I think the people that counted were conscious that reorganisation had been necessary and that the club was going forward in the right direction.

'But Alex was never short of confidence and the desire to win, and wanting to be the best. The intensity of his belief that what he is doing is right is something that people can't copy, only take a lead from. We talk about players who were born with the ball at their feet. Well, Alex was born with leadership qualities, and he's cultivated those qualities throughout his life. He's perhaps calmer now with success, and nobody can make a point now from a greater position of strength than he can.'

The strengths and qualities of his former boss come out in conversation without prompting. It is significant, in view of the highly promising managers who have failed right at the top when they have had to deal with big star players, that Archie says: 'He's always managed to deal well with bigger-name players, headliners and internationals, because of his total belief that what he's saying is right for them. He has a terrific talent for man management.

'All the top people in management have to have that fear factor on their side; their staff must always have some degree of apprehension about what's going to happen next. And nobody keeps his players on their toes and uncertain which way he's going to jump like Alex Ferguson.'

But did Archie expect him to make such a fantastic success of the job at Old Trafford?

'It was heading that way. A lot of groundwork had to be done when we went, and he quickly decided that Manchester United had to be rebuilt from the bottom up. People tell me that the similarity in the long-term aims of the two longest-reigning Old Trafford managers, Busby and Ferguson, was amazing. But that was how he did it at Aberdeen – he was dedicated to putting a youth policy in place, and having a vision for the future.

'Certainly in those early times there weren't many days when there was a calm sea and a following breeze. While Alex was putting the structure in place it perhaps wasn't fully appreciated by some of the fans what he was doing, and soon after there were all kind of controversies involving the sale of the club and the sideshow provided by Michael Knighton. But Alex was steadily getting on with his job, not only with the team, but with every aspect of the club, having his finger on the pulse in every corner of Old Trafford.

'He took so much care to ensure that everybody in the club, the landladies, laundry people, the office staff, all felt part of the family; but while all the flak was flying I saw no sign of him ever wilting or his desire and enthusiasm lessening. In fact we never had the feeling, even when newspaper talk was at its height, that we were on the brink. There was never a suggestion he was going to be out of a job; but then he was a man for keeping his own counsel.

'And he would certainly have been able to deal with anything because he's never been a man to shy away from a difficult situation. I believe he did have the strength to know that the board realised, and appreciated, that he was putting the club on the right lines.

'He's always been happy to take on everybody. His tremendous desire meant that he knew inside him that the world would never beat him, and that he would succeed. He never had any self-doubt. Analyse himself? Oh, yes. He would analyse deeply when things went wrong; but he was never a man for telling the results of his analysis. He would just get on with the job, and I've certainly never seen anybody impose themselves on him in a direct challenge.'

Plenty of people – not only erring media people, but those who worked with him, played against him or schemed against him as a manager – would concur that he has an aggressive nature. Having said that, I must admit it is like saying that a dog chases cats: not exactly a statement of Freudian perception.

But he has used it magnificently, winding up even the thoughtful and poised Arsène Wenger, and in Kevin Keegan's days at Newcastle reducing the former England manager to tears. Perhaps the unusual thing about the Ferguson–Knox partnership was that they never played the usual dressing-room role of manager and assistant manager.

Reflected Archie Knox: 'No, there was never the good cop, bad cop scenario in our behaviour. I never, not ever, calmed him down. If he was having a rant I'd go right in at the back of him, and perhaps even raise the decibels. In any case, in that situation with Alex nothing is up for discussion.'

Not *Any Questions?* More like a Hitler Youth rally.

On the face of it some of Sir Alex Ferguson's comments about other people have seemed, to outsiders, unnecessarily cruel and abrasive. But Archie pointed out: 'I think it's a significant point about Alex's nature that he looked after the little people in the club. That was part of his efforts to ensure that the smallest details were looked after so that the club became one entity, a family with everybody pulling in the same direction. It was certainly an important part of his success.

'His philosophy was that if you leave things to other people without taking an interest in what they do, something will be lacking. Let everybody know how important their job is and you get everybody working for one purpose. Certainly at both Aberdeen and Manchester United that philosophy had everybody pulling for him.

'I never had any doubts about his success as a manager. He made terrific signings, not only people like Schmeichel and Cantona, but his first signings like Denis Irwin, Steve Bruce and Gary Pallister. He's had a great track record in the transfer market, in getting the right players to make that little bit extra difference. And he's never been afraid to put his judgement on the line. Many managers, for instance, would have written off Ruud van Nistelrooy after his medical and his injury problems; but just look at his potential now.'

He revealed: 'It seemed as though everything was in place for Gazza to sign for us from Newcastle United, and Alex was excited about it. All the talking had been done, but then we heard he'd signed for Spurs. I suppose they offered more money; but it was a shock, and a shame for Paul Gascoigne, because having got to know the lad since he joined Everton I know from his character that Alex would have got the best out of him at that stage of his career. He would have made such a difference. Just look at his man management with Cantona, a man nobody had been able to handle. Gazza doesn't know what he missed.'

Which led to the inevitable question: Does that mean that Alex would have handled George Best better than Matt Busby, ensuring that he had a longer and even greater career?

'Not necessarily. They were in totally different eras. Football is more aware of the problems now, and prepared to keep a tighter rein on situations that are potentially career-threatening; but Best was a phenomenon, something new at the time. I don't think it's possible to compare the way Best was handled in the sixties to the way Beckham was handled in the nineties, any more than you can say that Stanley Matthews was a better winger than Ryan Giggs or vice versa.

'One thing I do know is that Alex Ferguson's track record will take some beating. He had to get the monkey off the club's back of having gone so long without winning the championship; but his signings were vital, and his assessment of players spot-on.

'He looked at their temperament and character as well as their skills, and if people didn't measure up there was no shillyshallying. They were out in the quickest possible time.'

What now for the man whose record of seven title wins in ten Premierships may never be matched, but who ended the season scowling to himself about being the first Manchester United manager to lose five successive games to Liverpool?

'Nobody can take away from him that his reign at Old Trafford has been special, and there's still enough mileage for great success in his remaining two years. After all, what major world club will have kept its manager for around twenty years? And he's given continued success, and – despite all the dressing-room stories – he's been a father figure to his players at Aberdeen and now Manchester United.'

Archie Knox also knocks down, surprisingly, my question about Sir Alex as a confrontational manager. He admits that there would be arguments, as in any team, because in football there is confrontation around every corner. But it is the way the situation is handled that counts, and according to him such situations were meat and drink to the Old Trafford boss.

Even the alleged bust-ups with Gordon Strachan weren't life and death. 'We had two fiery characters there, and they had their ups and downs, but there was nothing more sinister, never any continuity to their rows.'

Perhaps it is Archie Knox who should be a diplomat, not Sir Alex.

The Demon Barber

At heart few managers really enjoy press conferences. Although Sir Matt Busby always dealt easily with the press, and the Doc and Ron Atkinson seemed to revel in the attention, Sir Alex Ferguson started by wanting to leave his chair as quickly as possible, and ended by booting the scribes out of their chairs, usually in even quicker time.

Press conferences in the later years of his career were always a roller-coaster ride. In what was originally scheduled to be his swansong season, the press meeting held the day before a match against Newcastle United at St James's Park that Ferguson's team were to lose 4–3 was one of the shortest on record. Just one question had been asked, and one sentence written down, when he exploded. Citing bad publicity over Dwight Yorke and Jaap Stam, he launched into an outburst littered with more expletives than a politician's broken promises, before saying: 'That's the end. Get out! I've had enough from you.' He then amiably called to Diana Law, his press secretary: 'Get the Sunday papers in now.'

It was like the Demon Barber calling, 'Next please,' with his apron covered in blood and his last customer still in the chair with a cut throat.

A week later it was as though nothing had happened. Ferguson conducted the press meeting impeccably, answering every question with a smile. Jekyll, Hyde or the Demon Barber – it was never easy to guess the face that Sir Alex was going to put on.

He rarely failed to surprise. The first time Neil Custis of the *Sun* asked a question at one press call he was laced into by Fergie for

173

having written a story that displeased the Master. Alex was only halted in his tracks after five minutes of raving and ranting when Neil pointed out that the article he was complaining about had been written in the *Express* by his brother Shaun Custis.

The same year I returned from three weeks in Cyprus to take my Friday press conference seat, only for Sir Alex to order me outside with him, saying he wanted to speak to me. As we moved into the reception area at the Carrington training ground he pointed to the toilets and said: 'In there.'

Bewildered, but with a clean conscience, I walked trembling through the door, fully expecting a 'Glasgow kiss'. I envisaged lying slumped unconscious, with my head in a urinal, until the cleaners came in at the end of the day. But it was merely to be a verbal assault. He accused me of writing a story the previous week that upset him – and worse, for a paper he had banned from the club.

He had been deliberately misinformed by some treacherous pressman. Not having written a line for three weeks, I was nevertheless too astonished to be coherent, apologised for whatever it was I hadn't done and wondered whether to call in a stress counsellor.

In his relations with the press Sir Alex certainly blows cold, cold and very occasionally hot, though even the friends of the press occasionally turn against the purveyors of the printed word. None other than Tommy Docherty, a wizard of the one-liner and a joy to interview, has occasionally had a go, as witness one of his after-dinner speech lines: 'I've always said there is a place for the press, but they've not dug the hole yet.'

Sir Alex should certainly adopt a more philosophical approach. The late Liberace is famously quoted as answering a bad review of one of his shows with: 'The criticism hurt me so much that I cried all the way to the bank.' The maestro of Old Trafford, when he buttons his glittering smoking jacket in the evenings, might do well to follow Liberace's laid-back example.

It is unfortunate that so talented a man should have such an attitude about attempts by the newspapers to give all the news on sport that the man in the street wants, and weigh each ton of praise and even adulation he gets in the media as nothing beside a hundredweight of criticism. Quite simply it has always come with the territory – and especially with the Manchester United territory, because the public want to know everything about the club.

In the second year of Alex Ferguson's management at Old Trafford, when almost to a man the supporters were calling for him to be sacked, I wrote a piece in the *Sunday Express* totally opposing the view expressed in every other national paper. I said that Alex would do for Manchester United what he had done for Aberdeen, in other words bring them back to the top and end the famine of championships, and that the board and Martin Edwards were totally supportive of him and knew he was doing a good job.

At a difficult time, when most chairmen would have succumbed to the 'sack the manager' cries of the crowd and the backstabbing behind the scenes at Old Trafford, Martin Edwards thanked me for that article. But sometimes Sir Alex apparently forgets what he owes to his chairman. Edwards stood by him resolutely against a barrage of hate thrown towards the directors' box by a section of the supporters, at a time when, apart from Bobby Charlton, Ferguson did not have many backers. Edwards was responsible for bringing him to the club, and it is a shame that Sir Alex's Achilles heel takes some of the gloss off his great achievements.

In comparison with Sir Matt this is where Sir Alex lets himself down. Len Noad, before his retirement one of the most respected writers in the game during a long career with the old *Topical Times*, the *Weekly News*, *Daily Mail*, *Sun* and *People*, has said: 'Matt never made a fool of himself as Sir Alex does with his rages with the press, and the way he conducts his vendettas.' Although he was quick to add: 'Nobody can deny that a manager who has done what he has done in the last sixteen or so years at Old Trafford must be something special.'

Len does admit that not all the fault is on one side: 'Matt Busby was certainly approachable, and was a first-class diplomat, and no journalist ever had any trouble getting to see him. But, of course, we didn't ask stupid questions in those days. There was no need to fall out with a manager. We were all pals together and there was much more openness in the game.'

But Len admits also that he might well fall out with some of the present cognoscenti of the game if he placed all his views in front of them, just one of his comments being: 'In my day you'd never see a goalkeeper daft enough to be chipped because he was standing off his line. Now you see it every week, and that's with a goalkeeper coach now for every club.'

One man who has had more genuine bust-ups with Sir Alex than anybody is *Daily Express* sports writer John Bean. He had a particularly classic encounter with the man when his office received a tip that Mark Hughes was going to re-sign for United from Barcelona. On his way back from a trip to Wembley John phoned Alex's house several times, but received no reply until midnight. Said John: 'I told him we'd had a tip that Hughes was returning.'

There was a menacing silence and then the reply came staccato: 'Do you mean to say you're plaguing me at this time of night with such rubbish? I'll tell you this, Bean, you're finished with me and finished with this club.' Yet, the next day, when John went to face the music, and sought Alex out at the club to apologise and try and recover the situation, he was astonished to find the manager grinning at him and saying, 'Forget it. I know you've got a job to do.'

And Sir Alex had the last laugh, because four months later he signed Mark Hughes. There was no apology from him. That was just one of a series of what John picturesquely describes as 'volcanic overtures with Fergie'. But the other side of the fiery Scot came later in 1995 when John had a heart attack. The first contact he had from the outside world when he was lying in his hospital bed was when a nurse came down the ward with a massive bouquet of flowers and the message: 'What have you been doing to yourself, you silly old tap dancer?' signed by Alex Ferguson.

All part of Sir Alex's mixed-up psyche. You can have the best of times and the worst of times with him. He is the most caring and sentimental of men, and at other times the most illogical, ruthless and dictatorial. But when you are one of his foot soldiers there is nobody better to stand by you in the trenches when the muck and bullets are flying.

And for all their rows, when John Bean decided to retire on doctor's orders from the demanding job of covering Manchester and national football for the *Daily Express*, one of the first to phone him was Sir Alex, saying: 'Any time you want to come to Old Trafford, give me a ring, and there will be a seat in the directors' box.'

One of the most volcanic episodes witnessed by 'Beano' concerned another of Sir Alex's regular sparring partners, Ken Lawrence, formerly a writer for the *News of the World*, *Daily Mirror* and *Daily Mail*. Said John: 'We were flying back from a European match in Athens, and it was proving impossible to do any after-match interviews because Alex was hemmed in by reporters from all over the world, and the British media just could not get a word in.

'So Ken Lawrence was delegated to tell one of the directors that we had been unable to talk to Alex, and could he arrange for us to speak to him on the plane going back. The English newspapers had spent lots of money in covering the match but had been unable to get a word with the manager.'

The plane took off in a quick getaway after the match, only for Alex – who had obviously been given the tale that the English press were complaining about not having heard any quotes from him – to come charging aggressively down the aisle straight at Ken Lawrence. Being a pretty fiery Scotsman himself, Ken stood up to Fergie as United's manager let fly at him with a torrent of abuse.

Added Bean: 'They were standing face to face with Alex's veins pumping and Ken staring back at the manager. It looked as though Alex was going to swing at him when Brian Kidd came down the corridor, took hold of his shoulders to restrain him and pushed him back down the plane.

'The following day Lawrence had a call from Alex saying, "Come and see me," and he made his peace over the misunderstanding. We weren't complaining about Alex, just trying to ensure we had him to ourselves for a few minutes on the plane to get the quotes we couldn't get in the pitchside scrum after the game.'

Early in Sir Alex's career, John suggested that, when making some pointed comments about Mirandinha, Ferguson was motivated by jealousy since he had not been able to sign the Newcastle player himself. Again Bean was summoned to the holy of holies, Alex telling him forcibly: 'I'd like you to know I've never been professionally jealous of anybody in my life. We knew about

Mirandinha. He was touted round the country.' And, of course, Alex's judgement in not signing him was totally vindicated.

Although his reputation overshadows all others in terms of cruelty to us shrinking violets of the media, Alex is not the only manager ever to blow his top. Even that most amenable of men, Ron Atkinson, gave Peter Johnson of the *Daily Mail* a spine-chilling moment when Johnners uncovered a story of a training-ground battle between Remi Moses and Jesper Olsen, an incident that had led to Remi being given the cold shoulder.

Incandescent with fury that the sanctuary of the training ground had been breached, Ron issued a royal summons for Peter to report to The Cliff to explain himself the following morning. The *Mail* man knocked on his office door, and was astonished to find not only manager Atkinson but every member of the United playing staff cramped in his room, squirming under the oxyacetylene gaze of their boss.

Peter Johnson didn't feel much more comfortable than the players looked, but when Ron said: 'Right, now tell me which one of these gave you the story?' Peter stood firm. Later that day the player rang him to thank him for not revealing his source. Finally, after repeated denials by Ron that the incident had ever happened, the photograph, taken through a telephoto lens, proved that the battle between Moses and Olsen really had taken place.

Nobody had made the mistake a player made several years before at another club when I was placed in a similar situation. I had been given a headline story and a team meeting was called by the manager to find out who the villain was. But my mole failed with his attempted double bluff, blurting out: 'Who's Peter Keeling?' and was immediately put on the transfer list.

When Sir Alex announced that he was no longer going to conduct press conferences apart from the mandatory ones for UEFA matches and MUTV, there was soon a logical response from Tommy Docherty in his newspaper column:

He should think twice about boycotting the press because it will be the fans who suffer in the long run. By refusing to speak to the media he is cutting himself off from United fans. Even speaking to Manchester United TV puts the wrong message across because the club's TV channel is for people who pay for it, and a 'pay up or forget it' policy does not do the United image any good.

Never slow at putting the boot in, Tommy concluded: 'He was pretty keen to speak to the press when he was selling his book.'

But ex-United keeper Harry Gregg pointed to the priorities when discussing a number of errors made by his successor, flamboyant Frenchman Fabien Barthez, in 2001–02, with a recall that underlines there was not such a big gap in philosophy between Sir Alex and Sir Matt as there appears to be through a superficial analysis of their characters.

Gregg, perhaps second in the all-time list of great United goal-keepers behind Peter Schmeichel, has said: 'I was similar to Barthez in being a keeper who never played on his line, it was never my style. But in one of my first matches after signing from Doncaster Rovers I played in the big derby game against Manchester City, and I was caught off my line, chipped for one of City's goals.

'Even so, I was still pleased at my overall performance until I picked up an evening sports paper on my way home that told all about the chipped goal, and had a cartoon showing me strapped to a totem pole and with my teammates dancing around me with tomahawks. The story was questioning whether I was a goalkeeper or an attacking centre-half.'

On reading the article his first thought was, 'What will Matt Busby think?' To set his mind at rest he went to see the manager when he reported back for training on Monday, but Matt told him: 'If I think there is anything wrong I'll let you know. I'll call you into my office. There's no need to come and see me unless I call you. I know what I've bought.'

Gregg feels that likewise, while Sir Alex has perhaps told Barthez to cut out some of the fancy stuff, he will not try to get him to change his instincts or his natural goalkeeping style simply because of a few articles in the Sunday papers. He too knows what he has bought.

Perhaps Sir Alex's attitude is more an extension of the general attitude of people in pro football towards anybody, no matter how knowledgeable, who hasn't played the game professionally: 'Who did you play for then?' or 'How dare you question me on tactics, or think you have as much right to be fanatical about the game as I am?' I wonder if his racehorse trainers feel the same about him when he makes a suggestion about the training of his horses.

It is a paranoia, perhaps, on an equal footing with that of newspapers and media people, myself included, that the freedom of the press is absolute; but that if anybody criticises the press it is a disgrace, an abomination, an assault on civil liberties. But it has been said more than once of a journalist writing a supposedly factual report that he deserves the Pulitzer Prize for fiction. Perhaps there is still some truth in the old, cynical description of newspapermen – that they 'never let the truth spoil a good story'.

A Poor Man's Vinnie Jones

One of the oldest clichés in newspapers is to describe somebody as a 'poacher turned gamekeeper' or vice versa. The phrase can certainly be applied to many football managers, who not only feel it is in the best interests of their club to be 'economical with the truth' on many occasions, but also conveniently forget their own past.

Who can blame managers pontificating occasionally, as though their words are preceded by a papal puff of white smoke, when we in the media so often print even their most mundane outpourings as though they have just been discovered inscribed on tablets of stone in a Dead Sea cave?

Even so, in what was supposed to be his last season as manager of Manchester United, until he did his U-turn, it was amazing that none of us challenged Sir Alex Ferguson at a routine Friday press conference when he angrily denounced the use of the elbow in football.

No tongue could be discerned in our old friend's cheek as he said, his face reddening to emphasise his sincerity, that the biggest blight in football was the use of the elbow. He went on to aver that he would never allow any of his players to adopt such tactics, and said it was the most vicious and unpardonable foul in the book.

I understand that throughout the glens of the Highlands, the tenements of Glasgow, the mansions of Edinburgh, wherever old footballers and discerning supporters gathered in Scotland there were, apparently, when the newspapers were read the following day, shouts of disbelief, roars of amazement, and the sound of muffled choking as players and fans from the Fergie era digested his latest words along with their bacon and eggs.

His words had particularly jolted my memory because only a week before I had been interviewing Tommy Docherty and, with no prompting on the subject of elbows, I asked him what kind of a player Sir Alex was. The Doc replied firmly: 'He was a poor man's Vinnie Jones, playing with a number nine on his back. He wrote the manual on how to use your elbows on the football field.'

He added: 'He was a one-hundred-per-cent battler and very fit, and would chase a piece of paper on a windy day; but he was a good pro who lacked one thing: ability. He used his arms and his elbows so rigorously that they used to say he should have worn his boots on his elbows, or at least strapped pads on to his arms.'

Now, to put the argument in context, it must be reported that the Doc and Sir Alex fell out early in the Ferguson reign at Old Trafford because of comments made by Tommy in the press, and on radio, about the way Ferguson was handling the job as manager, and there is no love lost between the two. So you can disregard as a trifle exaggerated some of Tommy Docherty's comments to me; but the expertise with the elbows should not be disregarded, according to absolutely anybody who played on the same field as Sir Alex.

In fact Sir Alex so revelled in his roughhouse reputation that when he was 'mine host' at a pub on the Paisley Road Toll in Glasgow, near to Ibrox Park and virtually across the road from Jim Baxter's pub, he named his lounge the Elbow Room.

Top boxing promoter and businessman Alex Morrison spent some time with Alex in their younger years, so much so that one night when they were out with their pals he was responsible for a typical laddish prank. Noticing Fergie engaged in conversation at the bar by two girls, he went into the toilets and came out with a couple of condoms which he proceeded to slip unnoticed into Ferguson's pocket.

Next morning there was a furious phone call from Alex, who said tersely: 'Did you do it?'

Morrison admitted he'd pulled the trick that so many young men have done to their married pals before. As he told me: 'Alex was ready for a fight, but I apologised to his wife who had discovered the condoms the following morning when straightening out her husband's suit, and we eventually made it up.'

Alex Morrison, being a useful boxer and bigger and taller than Fergie, would probably not have been a wise match for his football pal to make; but even so he admits that Sir Alex could well look after himself, and recalled that as a landlord he stood no nonsense. He remembered: 'In the pub one night I saw a punter going at Alex with a broken bottle, but there was no backing down. He just ran straight at his assailant, nutted him with all the force of a charging hippopotamus, and the guy hit the floor with the blood flowing before he even had time to think about raising his arm with the bottle.'

The pub itself, rechristened 'Fergies' when Alex moved in, was what might be called a lively place, already notorious for the illicit dealing that went on behind the landlord's back. An amazing amount of stuff fell off the back of lorries in that area before the Road Safety Act came into force.

Alex Morrison admits: 'A lot of things went off there, and Alex could not be expected to clamp down on everything or know everything that was going on, things that had been going on for ages in that area. I was involved in quite a classic sting for those days when learning that a local gang were going to "snatch" a container off the docks from a shipment going to South Africa. The gang did the work, took the container with 1,750 cases of whisky inside, and then I helped rob the robbers, and naturally started distributing the whisky to the poor.

'It was a long time before the shock waves from that action died down, and the original thieves came looking for me in Fergies, showing the barman a shotgun, and asking where I was. Eventually they caught up with me in my car, and put the gun to my head. Fortunately as the gunman pulled the trigger I pulled his gun down, and the shot went into my stomach instead of my head. Before he had time to have a second shot I got up and ran at him, and his pal sliced at my legs with a meat cleaver. I was lucky that I only needed three days' treatment in hospital. The villains were never caught, but of the people who bought some of the whisky three were jailed for six months.'

He admitted: 'Those were hairy days thirty years ago, but everybody in the area has been delighted to see the success Alex has had, although there are plenty of Rangers supporters who have no time for him because they see Manchester United as an English Glasgow Celtic.

'But despite the controversy around Alex (he was always called Alec by his pals because his dad was Alex as well), he's always been regarded as a decent man, and prolific in his work for charity. He will always support any local charity that's going, even if he really hasn't got time to fix it in his diary. He'll try and answer every call from organisations asking him to help with a charitable effort, and I should think few public figures give as much or find as much time to help.

'It's an amazing contradiction of his character that he should be so caring this way, and yet he'll trample over anybody to meet the targets he sets himself in football. In this he's totally focused, just as Frank Warren and Mickey Duff have been in my own sport.'

He added: 'It was a shock when he changed his mind about retiring, and it was a disappointment to Rangers supporters, because we were hoping that Celtic would lose Martin O'Neill to Manchester United and give us a chance to start winning a few matches again. But for anybody who's had so much success as he has had in the last twelve years it must be hard to leave the stage.

'Obviously it will be hard for whoever eventually follows him, but knowing him over the years I'm convinced that he won't interfere with team matters when he does retire as manager and perhaps takes another job in the Manchester United organisation. There's no doubt that he is a man who would have succeeded in most walks of life, and with his teenage background learning a trade as a toolmaker, and even at that tender age being a very involved trade union organiser, he would clearly have become an important politician if his ambitions had taken him in that direction instead of into football management.

'I'm sure he would have relished giving the Tories the elbow.'

Bernard Manning, the abrasive comedian who numbers singer Madonna and George Best among his greatest fans, is a lifelong, dyed-in-the-wool Manchester City supporter. But he bows to nobody in his admiration for Manchester United's two great icons, Sir Matt Busby and Sir Alex Ferguson, and says: 'When Alex finally does retire I hope Manchester United build a lasting monument to their two greatest trophy hunters of modern football.'

Sitting in the easy chair that Madonna was to occupy only a few days later for a photo-shoot with Bernard, I was speaking to the controversial funnyman not in a quest for one-liners, but because through a long association with him over the years I know there is nobody who follows Manchester football more closely, and that for all his politically incorrect instincts, his act and his mind are full of a great deal of philosophy, insight and common sense.

And with his massive contributions to charity he has worked hand in hand with the celebrities of British sport and show business for half a century, not the least of his fellow fundraisers being the two Manchester United knights of the realm.

Not that his close affinity to the big names has ever absolved them from being a target for his act if he has spotted them in his audiences. Arriving late for a dinner at the height of the controversy over his split with Brian Kidd, and trying to slip unobtrusively into his seat, Sir Alex was greeted by Bernard in full flow: 'Alex, Brian Kidd's been on the phone. He says you can eff off.'

Nobody, but nobody, gets off lightly once Manning has spotted them; but even he was treading on dangerous ground when he followed up with, 'Alex, I saw your documentary on TV the other night. Your wife was on it. No wonder you're out every night at these charity dinners.'

Alex's wife, of course, is a charming woman, and the United manager is devoted to his family. It was fortunate that, knowing Bernard's script by heart, and having heard the same joke directed at a string of the great and the good – including Prince Philip – at Variety Club dinners, he refrained from what would have been his natural reaction, to bury Bernard's face in a cauldron of hot soup.

In fact, Manning feels that he and Sir Alex in some ways share a similar character. He told me, as he relaxed in the normal daywear of vest and pants that he usually dons to greet visitors: 'He's like myself, and he makes a lot of enemies because he doesn't bow down to people or tell white lies just to please them. He's straight talking, one of the most special people I've ever met, even though it hurts me as a Manchester City supporter to say so. I only wish he'd taken the wrong turning when he arrived in Manchester all those years ago and gone to Maine Road instead of Old Trafford.

'His media image is totally at odds with the type of person he is. He has a heart of gold, and he'll turn out at as many charity events as he can cram into his crowded diary.

'In that respect, as in so many other things, Alex and Matt are like twins, even though their public profile often comes out different. Both were always good family men, and Alex has always been typically Scottish, calling a spade a spade, and not beating about the bush. If something was wrong you'd get it with both barrels.'

But has his ranting and raving been in any way a sign of his insecurity?

'Quite simply he's proved his way is best. If anybody could do the job better I'd like to see him come to Maine Road and do it for City. He must get lasting recognition for what he's done or there's no justice in the world. He's given United a full house every week, more trophies than any other club, and operated brilliantly in the transfer market.

'But I was glad for his own sake when he originally said he was stepping down at the end of the 2001–02 season, because I thought he couldn't, for his health's sake, go on like he was. In that respect he was in some ways his own worst enemy, and not selfish enough about his own time. I know how difficult it is to turn down a good cause, and with such a massive operation to carry as Manchester United, even his great fitness and resilience would surely crumble eventually. He's had constant demands everywhere, and yet shown such great strength both mentally and physically.

'And I hope, for the sake of a man I respect so much, that he doesn't regret changing his mind. His upfront, confrontational way of managing has worked for him and Manchester United in amazing fashion, and I would be the last man to knock that style.'

What is his greatest strength? It was a question I could just as easily have asked Sir Alex about Bernard Manning, and would probably have received the same answer.

He said: 'Just being himself, with no airs and graces.'

But the Prince of the Put Down, the King of the Knock Back, His Imperial Highness of Insult, revealed a secret side to Sir Alex. Although the man himself would scoff if you compared him to an Eastern mystic, or one of those Indian gurus the Beatles made fashionable in the seventies, he has an innate ability to nurture his inner strength.

Bernard told me of the time he arrived early at a function where he was performing and Sir Alex was guest of honour. Looking for the VIP room where the top table were to gather before the 'do', Bernard peeped round the door, and saw the United boss sitting straight-backed in a chair, as though in a trance, completely quiet and initially hardly aware that anybody had approached the room.

'Seeing him there, isolated for a few moments, and clearly at ease with himself, you can understand that he doesn't waste a moment of his time. On that occasion he was clearly using the few minutes of quiet to harbour his resources and refresh himself mentally.

'Not that he was brooding, because within minutes he was chatting away to me, and as the room filled he was the centre of attention as usual. When you work too hard, and are out half the night trying to please everybody, and fulfil nearly impossible demands, somehow you just love to have a few moments to yourself. If, like Alex, you can utilise those moments to recharge your batteries it's a massive help to your lifestyle.

'He's such a successful, and seemingly fit man, despite all the demands, that he can probably even harness his own temper to act as a safety net by exploding now and again when he needs to shake up his players – or the media.'

Manning continued: 'He puts himself out in the open. He even makes no secret of his politics, and as a former trade union official I suppose that's no surprise. Many people who get on in life try to submerge their views and even their roots. There's none of that nonsense with Alex.'

He sees no dark side to the manager's nature, despite apparently compelling evidence, in Sir Alex's unnecessary criticism of and hostility to former colleagues, of a weakness that some would prefer to term 'openness'.

On the contrary, Bernard says, when asked about any weakness in his friend: 'Perhaps his biggest fault is in being too kind. I see a different side of him to the newspaper headlines. Having so often seen him signing autographs until midnight, and talking with anybody who comes up to him when he's probably had a real pig of a day at the Carrington training ground, I can say that no guest at a dinner ever gives more value for money than Alex. He stays at fund-raising dinners and mingles with everybody long after the rest of the top table have gone home, and he can't do enough for people if he thinks he is supporting a good cause.'

When he eventually does quit, will he be able to handle stepping down from management?

'Yes, because he has other interests. He loves his racing, he owns racehorses, he likes a game of golf. And if he started shaking hands tomorrow with all the people who love and respect him he would still be shaking hands at the age of 190. I hope all the Manchester United supporters, and football in general, give him the lasting credit he so richly deserves when finally he does decide it's time to call it a day.'

But if he stays at Old Trafford in some other capacity when he does finally retire as manager, will he be a handicap to the new manager?

He replied: 'Ideally, when a new man takes over Alex will be at either York or Newmarket watching Rock of Gibraltar [one of his horses] winning a big race; but in the end nobody can tell until the time comes. It's up to the man himself to handle the situation correctly and resist the temptation to make his views known unless he's asked.

'But how can you criticise him for something that hasn't happened yet? It's like telling Pavarotti he's not allowed to sing. There were players who would die for Matt Busby and Manchester United, and there are players now who would die for Alex Ferguson and Manchester United. The new man will have to be patient, show great man-management skills, and get on with the job.'

There is no doubt that history will be repeating itself when Sir Alex does finally call it a day, and the job description will undoubtedly be: An impossible act to follow. Even after the 1999 Champions' League final win, one of the main memories of past glories was not that Matt's team won it in 1968, but that six years later Manchester United were relegated.

But Bernard recalls: 'Matt was a role model for football and footballers everywhere. Everybody looked up to him. He was a great manager, twice built the club from ashes in twenty-five great years, and he was certainly a better diplomat than Alex. He'd been brought up in Scotland's "skint members" club, his family never having a lot of money, and he always realised the worth of good friends and the value of getting on in life, whatever the problems.'

But a man who nearly lost his life in his service for the club, became manager when the club did not even have a ground, and then thirteen years later had to rebuild the team again, probably had every right to feel that his job was harder than the one presented to Alex.

Said Bernard: 'Matt was perhaps entitled to interfere unless somebody said it was against the rules, and perhaps the 21st-century board of directors, with all the power of the plc as well as the football club, will be better able than the board of thirty years ago to make sure themselves that the new man, in two years or whatever, has no interference. There certainly was going to have to be a change eventually, even for such a period as the Busby era, and if Bobby Charlton was past his best then OK, but if the engine wasn't broke, why change it?

'It's all, I fear, an argument close to my own heart. I've had my pianist at the Embassy Club for forty years. All the other clubs around in the sixties and seventies alongside me have gone by the wayside, and I know the feeling of any man who doesn't want to let go, because I want to go on for ever. I want to die on stage, and I don't mean the kind of death comedians used to get at the Sunderland Empire.'

He first met Matt Busby when they were kneeling next to one another at the funeral of a bookmaker named Johnny Foy. Bernard told Matt that it was Johnny who first paved the way for him to audition as a vocalist with the Oscar Rabin band in London, his first job.

The Old Trafford manager and the nightclub singer, soon to become a comedian and compere to the band, became firm friends after the meeting. Over the years, as they met at various functions in the bustling nightlife of Manchester, the Manchester United icon, who had an entire kingdom praying for him after being read the last rites in a Munich hospital, admitted that he only really knew he had got over the worst when Manning started to insult him again.

'Matt Busby here again tonight, gentlemen. Matt, you'll never live to be as old as you look.' And here's another: 'I went to a party at Matt's house the other night. The whisky flowed like glue.' Or, 'Talk about a mean Scotsman. Matt was a window cleaner as a teenager in Scotland, and he was at the top of a ladder when he dropped half a crown. He was down the ladder so fast that the half crown hit him on the head.'

Said Bernard, as we reminisced over those jokes: 'He would always have time for anybody, and would be at ease with dukes or dustbinmen. It didn't matter how many important people were in the room, the wealthiest or most famous people in the land; when Matt walked in it went quiet. The respect for him throughout the country was incredible.

'But the man who followed him, Wilf McGuinness, had a rough time. I've always had enormous respect for him. I think, like me, he's a great believer that your life is mapped out for you the day you are born, and he's made a good life, always enjoying himself, making a laugh out of any situation good or bad. He's never felt sorry for himself; he's made more people laugh than anybody I know and had a ton of laughs himself.'

Bernard Manning always likes to stir things up for his pals. His opinion is that Tommy Docherty never got on with Lou Macari, and he always makes a point when in the Doc's company of saying that Lou must be one of the greatest players Manchester United have ever had. He just loves to see Tommy grinding his teeth in fury. While admitting that 'Tommy was a great manager for United', he also admits admiration for Ron Atkinson: 'Ron was another who would never need a charisma bypass, and he produced some terrific United teams.

'Ron ran his teams brilliantly, was a great communicator, and seemed to be especially suited to producing great Cup-fighting teams. He wore more medallions and gold rings than Goldfinger, but he could certainly manage a football team, and his teams were never boring. And when he needed to gee his teams up from the touchline he didn't need to shout at them. He just jangled his jewellery.'

A Caring Manager

Henning Berg was one of the first of the gathering torrent of foreign star players to join the Alex Ferguson revolution when in 1988, with the master motivator still finding his feet, the Norwegian first went for a trial at Old Trafford as a starry-eyed eighteen-year-old.

Initially he could not obtain a work permit, but he eventually signed for Alex in 1997 having spent five years with Blackburn Rovers, to whom he was to return and end his career in England after a great spell of trophy hunting at Old Trafford.

As we spoke at Blackburn Rovers' remote training camp in Lancashire, he told me: 'When I first came to Old Trafford people would be surprised to find how caring the manager was, his first promise being that "you will really enjoy yourself with us". And when I signed from Blackburn after Jack Walker had spoken with Martin Edwards he again emphasised the enjoyment I would get out of playing for Manchester United. We recalled that I had been on the losing side for Rovers against Manchester United when we won the Premiership in the 1994–95 season and on the winning side for Rovers when United won the title the following year. I had also been sent off in a game against United when the referee thought I made a dangerous tackle on Lee Sharpe, so my life seemed to be interconnected with them even when I wasn't on their books.'

Henning, like his compatriot Ronny Johnsen, was unlucky with injuries at Old Trafford – although not nearly as unlucky as Ronny was – and missed the 1999 Champions' League winning final after being carried off with damaged knee ligaments in the semi-final. He remembered: 'That was the worst blow of my life; but Sir Alex was always most caring of his players, and he isn't the demon he is made out to be. He made sure I received a medal, telling me that I had earned it by playing my part in the earlier rounds. And he ensured that Roy Keane and Paul Scholes, who were suspended for the final, were similarly rewarded.'

Contrary to the accepted view, the boss allowed his players to disagree with him. Said Henning: 'It was a side of him that isn't shown by the majority of managers, in that he would always pick you out and explain why you weren't in the team if you had been left out. He would be honest with you, and you didn't have to agree. He would certainly accept somebody disagreeing with him if they did it in the right way, privately. And believe me, it can't be any fun juggling with team selection with the massive list of stars that he has under his wing. Probably his greatest feat over the years has been keeping so many people happy most of the time, and getting players who would be in any other first team in Europe to sit on the United bench. In this he has set a precedent for other clubs, and his methods have made sure that his players are always fit and sharp.

'I've heard people say that you should always field your strongest team, and that the rotation system means you never get a settled team; but that isn't a logical argument with the present structure of club and international programmes. If the rotation system wasn't in use by the top teams it could well lead to failure. Players wouldn't be at their peak for the vital last two months of the season, when the titles are decided.'

He pointed out that there was criticism of United for using the rotation system even in early October when, after only six weeks' play, surely the players were not stale. But he explained: 'There were a lot of players, such as David Beckham, who needed a rest after playing right through the summer, and it did them the world of good to have a breather. Sir Alex is probably supreme in his manipulation of the team; it's one of many factors in his success, and he has obviously thought deeply about it.'

The Norwegian World Cup star made it crystal clear how thorough the manager's routine is for running one of Europe's most high-profile sports teams. His search for perfection is tireless, and clearly the moment one trophy is won is the start of rehearsals and practice, planning and scheming for winning the next one. 'Nothing is left to chance, especially in the psychology of his man management. He is hard and strong in the dressing room with the players, but he doesn't say bad things about them outside, and he cares a lot about every detail of his players, from their work on the field to their personal and family lives. He always stands up for his players; for example, he has spoken up well for Veron against criticism from outside in his first season, when he has only been good some of the time because it has been such a big culture change for him playing in the Premiership. But I expect him to really blossom in the Manchester United team next season.'

Looking at Sir Alex's great success story, he went on: 'During the hard early years at Old Trafford he must have felt at times that he was close to losing his job, but I feel sure that the fact he was determined to learn everything he could from those hard times has been one of the reasons why he has done so well. And the abrasive part of his image is only a part because, believe me, there is no happier man in football than Alex when things are going well.

'One thing to emphasise is that he most certainly does not take it out on his players when things aren't going well. But he will be very analytical and say what he thinks, and what has gone wrong, and the players can accept the logic of that, because they know he is the first to defend his players if the flak is flying.'

Mention of flak flying would make the ears of any reporter prick up, and the question came out as though shot from a gun: Is the action in the United dressing room as fiery as we hear?

Apparently Henning Berg, used to those Arctic winters in Norway, must have always worn one of those extra-thick woolly hats over his ears and eyes in his days at Old Trafford, for he answered: 'In three years at Manchester United I never once saw Alex throw anything.'

So apparently Henning's secret is out. He had a dressing room to himself!

He added: 'I've seen him angry and annoyed. If he didn't show any emotion it would show that he didn't care. If he thinks the players aren't doing what they are capable of he will tell them, and he has told me in some matches that he thought I could have done better.'

I consider this reply, and wonder if I've been hallucinating on the many occasions I've seen Sir Alex in furious action against the press. Perhaps next time he has twelve or so hardened sports writers cowering against the back wall of the press room with their heads between their knees, his desk a tortured mess of twisted metal at his feet, someone will have the courage to ask: 'Do you think we could have done better with that report of the 5–1 defeat by Halifax Town?'

However, as Berg continued, with the masterly understatement characteristic of most Norwegians: 'Sir Alex's aggressive nature isn't part of his success. No, it is his nature of being desperate for success that is important, which is a different thing. He wants to win so much, and his determination is total.

'But his motivational ability is simply tremendous. He wants the most talented players in his team, but he won't accept even the greatest talent in the world if he doesn't give a hundred per cent to his team. He works so hard in giving his players the right attitude in football and in life.

'He is a talented manager who is prepared to take something positive from anybody in the game who he can learn from. I feel that he did this when he signed Steve McClaren from Derby County as his assistant. He was the best coach I've ever worked with, apart from Ray Harford at Blackburn, and while he took a lot of knowledge from Alex, the manager learned a lot from Steve as well. They both gained great benefit from their partnership.

'Sir Alex is very strong tactically. He is great at listing the strengths and weaknesses of the opposition, and especially in working with individual players to tell them how to play against opponents. For all his fierce reputation, I'm certain that it is respect of him rather than fear that drives his teams on.'

The United boss is not slow to admit the debt he owes to Jim Smith for recommending Steve McClaren to him. I spoke to Jim at his villa in Spain, and he told me: 'Alex had obviously done his homework on Steve, and he rang me for my view, warning me that he would like to take him to Old Trafford. I've been good pals with Alex, working with him on the League Managers Committee.

'I told him that I didn't want Steve to leave, but that I wouldn't stand in his way, as the move would be a marvellous step up for a coach I spotted at Oxford before bringing him to Derby. I regarded him as the tops, and joked with Alex, "He'll cost you a million."

'But I wanted the best for Steve, and it had long been obvious to me that he would move up to that level eventually. As we were to play at Old Trafford that night the deal was virtually done after the match, and Fergie went on to show that even at his age and experience he was still prepared to learn more about the job. Steve took modern sports psychology with him and initiated at Old Trafford the method that we had been using at Derby of filing every aspect and statistic from matches, and I'm sure the fresh outlook played a part in driving United to the treble for the first time.'

Smith, who has won twice with Derby County at Old Trafford, could not be more vehement in saying that Sir Alex Ferguson's public image of being a bit of a bully and a poor sport is totally false. 'Let's face it. He isn't used to losing. But he was magnanimous in defeat against Derby, although it's fair to say that he is nice to people he gets on well with. But I've never found him anything but helpful and kind. A good example was when I signed Danny Higginbotham from United. Alex had told me that he would do well for me, but he didn't have a good first season. So Alex went out of his way to ring up and assure me that Danny would do better and that I must persist with him. Not bad advice, because this year he was voted our Player of the Year.'

Jim added a final word: 'If you ask me what is Alex's greatest strength I'd say it's his courage. He'll drop or fine the best player in his team if he thinks that is the right decision, and from the moment he came to Old Trafford he was never intimidated by the job he had to do.'

No matter how much of a roughhouser he was in his own playing career, there is no doubt that Alex Ferguson has – apart from their attitude to referees – instilled good habits into the players under his care. It is significant that, in a year when the image of the game's young millionaire Premiership professionals has been denigrated off the field by loutish behaviour from household names, there has not been a breath of trouble off the field involving Manchester United players – apart from the sideshow that Roy Keane has provided with his book revelations and his withdrawal from the World Cup.

Most of his players regard him as something of a surrogate father, although sometimes a twinkle in Roy Keane's eye, if Sir Alex is acting to excess at a press conference, makes one wonder if Roy is Alex's uncle. There is no doubt that the relationship between them is special, and Sir Alex probably sees in Keane a lot of the pride and the passion that made him go overboard as a young man. He has said: 'You need to find somebody who is like you when you are looking to choose a captain, somebody who has the same outlook. And I have been fortunate in having Keane and Bryan Robson as my captains because they have similar attitudes to me. You need a captain who is prepared to give everything for his club.'

There's nothing so controversial as a top football team – supporters have hundreds of differing views on any given subject concerning their favourites. But one question to which Manchester United supporters would provide an almost unanimous answer would be which player is most like Sir Alex.

It would be no contest, with 99.5 per cent answering in chorus: 'Keano, Keano'. Roy Keane has been called 'The Beastie Boy' and many other more uncomplimentary names by his opponents, who generally also are his grudging admirers. It has been written that, 'He is a man who could lose his temper with Mother Teresa, and has the petulance of someone who would knock off a policeman's helmet just for the hell of it.' Which sounds about right for a Sir Alex Ferguson Mark Two.

He is said to be a possible to join the Manchester United coaching staff in the next year or two or even become Sir Alex's assistant. But after his histrionics in the World Cup, which displayed an appalling attitude to Mick McCarthy, Roy may have to first learn the Army mantra of being 'able to *take* orders and not rock the boat before you can become an officer and *give* orders'.

But there is no denying Roy's wonderful contribution to the Manchester United success story, and the admirable job he has done

as a captain, showing as much driven intensity as his manager. He
has admitted: 'I'm no angel. I've got a temper.' Even so, his views
of his Old Trafford manager are valid ones, and he said in a heartfelt
tribute: 'Winning is what Manchester United should be all about. So
long as Sir Alex Ferguson is manager, we know we will be geared
to that.'

He makes no bones about the influence Sir Alex has had on his
career: 'When I first talked football with Alex Ferguson, that was
when I decided I would sign for United rather than for Blackburn
Rovers who were offering me more money.' And just as he criticised
the Irish football establishment in the contretemps that saw him
leave the World Cup for home before a ball had been kicked in
Japan, he claimed in April 2001, after United's Champions' League
failure: 'There are a lot of areas in the side where we aren't good
enough; but that's for the manager to look at.'

Here are just a few other viewpoints by Keane's teammates, and
others, about their manager:

Ole Gunnar Solskjaer, on 10 February 2002, after United had
beaten Charlton Athletic 2–0 at The Valley following that week's
announcement that Sir Alex was staying on as manager: 'It means a
lot to us that the manager is staying on, and it gives us a great boost.
Now we know what is required of us and what is expected over the
next few years. This club could not be in better hands.'

Denis Irwin, Alex Ferguson's first signing for Manchester
United: 'I've only had two managers in sixteen years as a player,
and it was a bit of a shock to hear that Sir Alex was staying, but it's
great news for the players and the fans. There will be a bit more
stability at the club than seemed likely, and it might have a
favourable effect on the contract negotiations within the squad. One
or two players have been hanging on to see who the next manager
was going to be. Now they can't use that as an excuse.'

Gary Neville: 'The best thing in football is continuity. The
manager has had a lot of players with him for a long time, and this
news of his decision to stay on can only give us a boost.'

Ruud van Nistelrooy, who reacted to Sir Alex's news of a U-turn
by shouting and clenching his fists in salute: 'I feel a debt to the
manager who stood by me throughout my knee injury and

breakdown before I signed for the club, when other clubs would have written me off.'

Ryan Giggs, whose entire professional career has been spent under one manager: 'I always felt Sir Alex would stay. There was a thing in the back of my mind that thought he just could not go, because whenever I was asked if I felt he still had the hunger I always replied that he had. It's just the same as it was ten years ago. I think that's now been proved. He still wants the pressure and excitement of managing Manchester United. His appetite is still the same. He's still there at 7.30 every morning. He's still the same. Now we've got the continuity of the next three years, and know what the expectations are again.

'I respect him because of the way he has handled me personally, and because of what he has achieved in the game. I have played under him for eleven years in the first team and we both know each other very well. Apart from international managers I've never played for anyone else.'

Dwight Yorke: 'I never worked harder to please the manager, but sometimes I ask myself, "Do I need to do this?" My football has been such a success, and now I've been a bit of a failure. I realise I've done wrong in some ways in the past year because for six or seven years I've never scored less than twenty goals a season. Things looked really well in pre-season but it hasn't quite worked out.'

David Beckham: 'People have made a lot of the rifts I've had with the manager. Obviously we've had our ups and downs, but then I think it's common with most players and their managers. The only difference with me is the fact that mine attract so much publicity. But I'd like to think there is mutual respect, and I certainly respected his decision to drop me from the side.

'He always called me in to explain why I was being left out. If he hadn't done this I might have felt differently, but he said he would protect me and tell everyone why I was being rested. I wasn't playing the kind of football I had been the month before, so I understood what was going on. I respect him as a manager and a person.'

Beckham said, when Sir Alex revealed he was staying on: 'We are closer than we were six months ago, and it's good to know now who the manager will be for the next three years. It has also made it easier for me to make a decision about my future. But we were surprised when he told us about his own decision to stay. A few clapped and a few tutted; but obviously we were pleased to hear that his wife Cathy had had a chat with him about staying on.'

Added David, with a grin: 'You know about wives. They always make the important decisions.'

Paolo Di Canio, on learning that Manchester United were interested in signing him: 'As a professional, knowing that the greatest manager ever wants you in his team is the ultimate honour. Knowing he wanted me to fill the Cantona role, partnering one of the best strikers in the world, and having the best midfield in the world behind me, it doesn't get much better than that. Not to mention the honours I would win playing for United, the satisfaction of playing in the Champions' League.

'And it would be great to knock out Roma or Juventus in Europe, once again shutting up all the people in Italy who look down on me and English football. Playing for the best club in the world may even help me to reach one of my unfulfilled dreams of playing for my country.'

Steve Bruce, member of Sir Alex's championship breakthrough team, shocked at criticism in February 2002 of Sir Alex's tactical acumen: 'With his record, how dare they even question him? I learned so much from him. The hard thing is to try and emulate him because he had his own way, and I don't think anybody will ever do again what he has done – his work ethic, his dedication to winning, his eye for a player, and the way he handles players, particularly young players. It can't be bettered. When I joined up at Old Trafford I was a carthorse among thoroughbreds. But look at the medals I won with Sir Alex.'

It needed Sir Alex's very good friend Gerard Houllier, the Liverpool manager, to sum up the importance and the passion of being a manager of one of the world's top teams. When asked if he intended retiring, he replied: 'Do I look as though I want to stop breathing?' Football still provided the oxygen of life, and was the driving force for Sir Alex in his 61st year.

But let an avid Manchester United supporter have a word during the closing stages of the book. I might also add that the reader must make the final decision about who is the greatest, Busby or Ferguson, on the evidence produced. After all, if Buckingham Palace could not separate them, but knighted them both, who am I to say otherwise? But the following quote from fan Jack Trickett, an old pal of mine and manager of many British pro boxing champions over the years, neatly illustrates the affection as well as the awe felt for Sir Alex. It came when I told him that when Sir Alex retires he is going to be an ambassador for Manchester United.

He replied like a shot: 'If Alex Ferguson becomes an ambassador we'll be at war with Switzerland within an hour.'

The Sir Alex Ferguson Fact File

1941:   31 December, born in Govan, Glasgow.

1957–73: Played for Queen's Park, St Johnstone, Dunfermline, Rangers, Falkirk and Ayr United.

1974:   Appointed manager of East Stirling in September, moves to St Mirren three months later.

1978:   Sacked by St Mirren, appointed manager at Aberdeen.

1980:   Aberdeen win Scottish League championship, his first honour as manager.

1982:   Aberdeen win Scottish Cup, beating Rangers 4–1.

1983:   Aberdeen retain Scottish Cup and beat Real Madrid to win European Cup Winners' Cup.

1984:   Aberdeen win League and Cup double. Ferguson awarded OBE.

1985:   Appointed caretaker manager of Scotland following death of Jock Stein.

1986:   Leaves Aberdeen to take over Manchester United.

1990:   First trophy at Old Trafford, winning FA Cup final after replay with Crystal Palace.

1991:   United beat Barcelona in European Cup Winners' Cup final.

1992:   United win European Super Cup and Football League Cup.

1993:   United win English League championship at last after 26-year wait.

1994:   United become fourth team in the century to achieve League and FA Cup double.

1995:   United runners-up in both League and Cup.

1996:   United become first club ever to complete the championship and FA Cup double twice.

1997:   United win championship for the fourth time in five seasons.

1998:   No trophies, and United go out to outsiders Monaco in the Champions' League quarter-finals.

1999:   Sir Alex leads United to the treble, Champions' League, Premiership and FA Cup, and completes a four-timer by being knighted in June in the Queen's birthday honours.

2000:   United beat Arsenal by eighteen points to win the Premiership.

2001:   United win Premiership for the seventh time in nine seasons, by a margin of ten points.

2002:   Decides to stay for an extra two seasons after the first half of the season is wrecked by speculation.

Epilogue: The Long Goodbye

Sir Alex Ferguson had vowed that 2001–02 was to be his final year as manager of Manchester United. As far back as 8 May 2000, Ferguson had announced that he would step down when his contract ended in 2002. But the season billed as the longest soccer swan song in history turned out to be a roller coaster of predictions, promises, U-turns, arguments, rows, controversy, anger and turbulence, calm professionalism and sweet nothings.

Who better to make a pre-season prediction than Ron Atkinson? 'Don't believe what you read in the newspapers,' was his highly original opening gambit. And the punch line: 'Sir Alex will change his mind at the end of the season, or even before the end of the season, and decide to carry on for a few more years.'

The only answer to that was: Watch this space.

Before the main action started, Sir Alex and his Premiership champions were off on an exhausting tour of the Far East, not to win trophies but to spread the gospel, let all the girls in Asia grab at the hem of David Beckham's red jersey, and remind the world that every good retail outlet in Bangkok, Deadwood City and Death Valley, Cairo, New Delhi and all points east, south, west and north would soon be stocking Manchester United merchandise.

Just what has that to do with running a championship-winning football team? Well, for a start it allowed Sir Alex to spend nearly £50 million pre-season on Ruud van Nistelrooy and Juan Sebastian Veron; but it was no help in fielding a fresh and winning side shortly afterwards at Old Trafford in Ryan Giggs's testimonial. For Martin

O'Neill was to send his Celtic side into action with fire in their bellies. They outclassed United in a brilliant first half, and even after bringing on five youth players as subs in the second half they still went on to win 4–3. Was that another line on O'Neill's CV that will ultimately find its way into chief executive Peter Kenyon's office as he decides on a successor for Sir Alex?

Former Arsenal striker Alan Smith, now a newspaper pundit, nevertheless claimed in the *Daily Telegraph*: 'Manchester United are as close to unbeatable over a distance as any side in English history.' Keeling's analysis: 'Perhaps United will become beatable once they start thinking they are unbeatable – or when Glasgow Celtic join the Premiership.'

Meanwhile Sir Alex himself was showing he still intended to be wicked in the 2001–02 season when claiming that Manchester United should have had two penalties after losing 2–1 in the Charity Shield to old enemies Liverpool. It seemed only yesterday that Roy Keane had led his United teammates like a pack of snarling dogs at Billericay referee Andy d'Urso when they disagreed with a decision at Middlesbrough in January 2000. This time canny Sir Alex used a different tactic: killing him with kindness. Or was it damning him with faint praise?

His assessment was clever and pointed: 'I felt sorry for the ref today. It doesn't matter how much training you have in any job. It's about temperament, and I just think the lad was too nervous for that today. I wonder if he still had the Middlesbrough game in his mind? What happened that day was wrong. But today the lad was nervous, which was a shame because he's a decent referee, and a good person.' What a lovely way to say a man is not up to the job!

And after all, being beaten in the Charity Shield had been the ideal way to warm up for their previous two Premiership-winning seasons. Nobody can fail to admire the way Sir Alex has consistently brought his side to the boil at exactly the right time for the really big challenges. Charity can begin away from home as far as Manchester United are concerned.

As the countdown to Sir Alex Ferguson's final season approached ever nearer to liftoff, he could have done without his minions making extravagant predictions. But that did not stop 'golden boots'

David Beckham halting just short of predicting a Boat Race and Grand National win for United as he said: 'We've set ourselves the target of remaining unbeaten all season as a sendoff to the boss.' (That target lasted for less than a month, until Newcastle beat them on 15 September.) England's captain had made it clear that nobody would be allowed to relax in this Apocalypse of a season. He said: 'To win every trophy we play in would be a fitting last season. The Premiership, the European Cup, the FA Cup and the Worthington Cup, and then to not lose a game all season.'

That, felt Becks, would be a perfect farewell gesture from the players. 'It might be his last year,' he added, 'but I don't think he's mellowed one bit, and he won't be taking his foot off the pedal.'

But he also had to keep a steady hand on the tiller – duck while you can: the metaphors are coming thick and fast – especially when, with only a few days to go to the start of the season, one of his favourite players, Jaap Stam, revealed in his life story that illegal approaches had been made to him by Manchester United when he was still employed by PSV Eindhoven. In his book Stam admitted that an unofficial approach was made in a secret meeting with Ferguson, set up by agent Ton val Dalen, although he ended his revelations with the comment: 'I guess he just wanted to meet me and see what kind of guy I was.'

All the clubs who have rushed into the transfer market in recent years without doing their homework would certainly be collectively a few billion pounds better off if every manager found out exactly what 'kind of guy' their new prospective signing was before they signed on the dotted line. But that was not the kind of lateral thinking the Premier League were considering when they said: 'We cannot comment because we have not received any complaint from PSV Eindhoven.'

Any such moves by PSV would in any case have to be put on hold. Fulham were preparing to open the season at Old Trafford, and Beckham, Cole and their mates were playing their final warm-up for the Premiership, an incidental trip to White Hart Lane to play for England against Holland. Meanwhile, Manchester United were shown in a published review of the 1999–2000 season to have become the highest income earners in world football with

£117 million, a figure that was expected to top £200 million per annum by the end of Sir Alex Ferguson's last season as Master of Old Trafford.

But there was to be no golden start to that last season. In fact, knowing the average football manager's enjoyment of old gangster movies, it flashed through my mind as early-season results went from bad to worse that Sir Alex might have taken a leaf from Jimmy Cagney's script when starring in that old classic, *Angels with Dirty Faces*.

Remember the story: a hoodlum from the meanest streets of America, who is idolised by the local youngsters, faces the death penalty, and the kids are waiting to hear him go bravely to the electric chair. But a priest pleads with Jimmy to play the coward, so that the youngsters will not have a hero and vow to follow in his footsteps. Of course Cagney screams and shouts and cries for mercy, deciding to be the good guy as they strap him down. Exit right the gang of kids muttering, 'He's yellow,' and we all know they will grow up to be fine upstanding citizens.

Now, with Fergie's retirement announced, we knew he was going to be a hard act to follow, and it would be harder if he went out with another treble. Was he going to deliberately go out on a low to give the next man a chance?

Perhaps not; at least, two goals by Ruud van Nistelrooy and a strike by England captain Becks got them off to a closely fought 3–2 win against Fulham. Then, however, came the first wobble, the earth-shattering sale of Jaap Stam to Lazio after defensive frailties appeared. Despite repeated protests by the boss that the sale was nothing to do with the revelations and criticisms by Stam in his new book, few people believed initially anything but that it was Fergie's kneejerk reaction to Stam's 'behind the scenes' stories. In fact it was beginning to look as though the priest had made a visit to Sir Alex's cell already.

Stam was hustled out of Old Trafford by 27 August. The following day, wearing a Lazio shirt that was too tight for him, and looking bewildered at the turn of events, he was introduced to the Italian press by Lazio general manager Massimo Cragnotti, who said that Stam had been put up for sale by Sir Alex

Ferguson. In reply Sir Alex insisted that Lazio had made an offer of £16.4 million, 'too good to turn down', and United started to close ranks.

Just six months after signing a new five-year contract Stam was saying: 'I was astonished at being told by the manager I was no longer part of his plans, although other people were telling me it was the book that did the damage. I was desperately unhappy after playing so successfully for three years only in two weeks to be told that I wasn't wanted any more.'

Two games had been played, the narrow defeat of promoted Fulham and a 1–1 draw with Villa, and it was a question of 'The King defender is dead, long live Laurent Blanc.'

The 35-year-old Inter Milan defender arrived with indecent haste; but despite his world-class skill being eminently apparent, there were no blank sheets at the back for United as in September impressively easy wins over Everton and Ipswich were surrounded by a 4–3 defeat at St James's Park by Newcastle, a shattering late, late show by Deportivo la Coruña, who won the Champions' League clash 2–1, and then a first-half 3–0 losing scoreline at White Hart Lane.

But that really was a game of two halves. Sir Alex performed his half-time magic, and goals by Cole, Blanc, Van Nistelrooy, Veron and Beckham produced an amazing and historic 5–3 win. United's previous best recovery had been way back in 1910 when Welsh wizard Billy Meredith masterminded a 4–3 win over Newcastle United at St James's Park from a 3–0 deficit. Goals were raining in the United net, and there were murmurs on the terraces about the departure of Stam, but goals win matches, and entertainment has always been the catchword for United fans. Without a doubt the entertainment value of the defeat of Spurs will still be talked about when Sir Alex no longer has the strength to throw a teacup.

Whether it was in-house diplomacy or whatever, the 'family' were doing the best they could to wipe out the memory of Stam. Norman Whiteside claimed that the end of the Stam era had nothing to do with his thoughts in his autobiography, but that the decision was purely a professional judgement, while Manchester United icon Bill Foulkes agreed that on footballing grounds Sir Alex was justified in his decision.

But now it was October. The United boss clearly had some thinking to do about his priorities, and clearly all was not well in Europe.

A 1–0 home win against Lille had been far from impressive, the defence was slipshod as the points were lost in Coruña, and now, just like England, United must overcome the Greeks. United faced home and away clashes with the talented, ball-playing Olympiakos, and their away form in Europe over a three-season span was looking anything but champion. Sir Alex, however, still had his joker card in reserve, and he played it perfectly.

Yes, he produced Ole Gunnar Solskjaer from his pack, and the baby-faced striker provided his usual magical touch, sparking a 3–0 Old Trafford win against the Athenians. Eight days later Norway's 'magic dragon' had scored a vital goal in the 1–1 draw against Leeds in the Premiership and again produced the crucial points-saver just when things were going pear-shaped against Lille in France, to ensure another draw.

So every little thing was going OK. Was it heck!

Within days besieged Fergie was saying: 'I never want to see a Manchester United team go down as easily as that again.' Solskjaer had saved their bacon with three goals in three matches after a shattering 2–1 derby defeat by Bolton Wanderers at Old Trafford, but soon the Master of Old Trafford was doing a Victor Meldrew 'I don't believe it' dance of fury as he saw his millionaires capitulate against Liverpool at Anfield, and then faced a revolt the following day from Paul Scholes, the last person you would expect to defy his boss.

Scholes was the man who Sven-Goran Eriksson, when he took over the England job, publicly stated was 'the man I am most looking forward to managing'. Scholes, a player never known to even think about kicking over the traces, a model pro, is the man who has for several seasons earned the plaudit of 'the guy who makes United tick'. His central midfield partnership with Roy Keane had always seemed as if made in heaven. Irish captain Keane carried the piano and Scholes played it. They could run those central areas from penalty box to penalty box as though they were sole holders of the patent.

But Fergie, despite his liking for history, had apparently never heard the saying 'If it ain't broke, don't fix it'. He had shelled out

£28.1 million for Juan Sebastian Veron to get in the way of the Scholes–Keane double act. Instead the flame-haired Scholes was asked to play behind new striker Ruud van Nistelrooy, and ahead of his midfield teammates.

It was like asking a high jumper to equal the Olympic qualifying height from a standing start; loyally Paul tried, but he kept knocking the bar off. His frustration showed, his confidence and assurance was dented, and the balloon went up when he was asked after the Liverpool match to travel to Highbury with a virtual reserve team for a Worthington Cup tie that was to produce another walloping for United.

He did not turn up, upon which he was heavily fined by Ferguson. Eventually he was calmed down by his boss, and warned by his England captain and teammate David Beckham: 'There's only one winner in a clash with the manager: don't cross him.' Decoded, that was a warning: 'When Fergie's wrong he is convinced more than ever that he is right.'

Beckham knows better than most that his boss is a hard man to have an argument with. He had been sent to sit in the stands at Elland Road for a vital game the previous season after failing to turn up for training two days before. Alex did not tell his 'golden boy' until the bus arrived in Leeds that he was out of a match in which he dearly wanted to play.

Scholes would not have been the first to be shown the door if his manager had decided his face no longer fitted. Jaap Stam, of course, had only just been banished to Italy; midfielder Paul Ince had earlier been discarded, winger Andrei Kanchelskis, who had a problem with the Russian mafia and did not really need any more trouble with Sir Alex, was shown the door in double quick time, and so, ultimately, was Aussie goalkeeper Mark Bosnich.

Diplomat Beckham helped to pour oil on troubled waters by calming things down: 'There won't be a problem,' he said. 'Scholes is a strong character, and a strong player, a big-game player. He's proved that time and again over the years, and knowing his approach to football I'm sure there is no chance of him leaving Old Trafford.'

The Premiership champions had entered November having qualified for the next round of the Champions' League despite losing twice, and were now set for the final group stage against

Bayern Munich, Boavista and Nantes. But the media were in uproar: 'Has Fergie lost the plot?' they were beginning to ask.

Certainly the situation called for the gaffer to muster all his man-management skills, and not a little reappraisal of team formations and tactics. Sir Alex had been through it all before and his backers were confident he could handle it. Even so, since a period two years into his career at United there had never been such a crisis for him.

But November saw just one victory, a 2–0 defeat of struggling Leicester City thanks to goals by Ruud van Nistelrooy and Dwight Yorke, although a gritty 1–1 draw was achieved in Germany against Bayern Munich courtesy of another from Van Nistelrooy. Signs were ominous as December started with little sign of improvement, bogy team Chelsea crushing a bedraggled United 3–0 at a bemused Old Trafford.

Even a 3–0 European win against a Boavista side who would not have outclassed Carlisle United did not prove a confidence booster. The next match, a Paolo di Canio-inspired 1–0 win for West Ham, concluded a nightmare run including just that one Premiership victory against relegation-threatened Leicester.

Sir Alex once again turned to a familiar life-saver, introducing Ole Gunnar Solskjaer for his first start in seven games. And, with David Beckham left out of the starting line-up for eight of the next nine matches, United embarked on an incredible run of nine successive victories.

Ploughing a lone furrow up front, Van Nistelrooy had somehow still managed to evoke memories of Tommy Taylor with his skill, ability to hold the ball, and calm, clinical approach to scoring goals; but, with a partner of the quality of the Norwegian World Cup star, his true brilliance began to blossom, culminating in a Premiership record of scoring in eight successive League matches, rounded off by rocketing home a penalty against Blackburn Rovers in the mid-January 2–1 victory at Old Trafford. Van Nistelrooy's record-breaking run also equalled Billy Whelan's eight-match club record run of goals in consecutive matches, set in 1956.

The spin-off from the Viking's return was significant; it meant Paul Scholes's torment was over and he was able to play his natural game, even though pushed out wider than usual on the left, while the axing of Beckham, Quinton Fortune and Andy Cole, a great soldier in the Ferguson success story over the years, allowed the indomitable Nicky Butt to form a fiery partnership in central midfield with that gentle soul Roy Keane. And it also paved the way for the greatly anticipated return of Ryan Giggs, United's most important player in European competition but missing through injury for most of the season.

A month earlier, bookies had seemingly heralded the demise of United as a Premiership threat by pushing the Reds out to an incredible ten-to-one against successfully defending their Premiership title. But after a fantastic run of victories the Northwest was awash with pessimistic punters grinding their teeth in anger at not accepting those odds as a gift from the gods.

Even in the run of fabulous victories through December and January, however, Sir Alex was still tinkering with his side. When he fielded an unchanged eleven against Blackburn on 19 January, statisticians found that it was the first time a United side had remained unaltered in an amazing 77 Premiership matches.

After four winning games without the England captain, Sir Alex decided a return to Beckham's roots in London was the right time to return him to the starting line-up at Fulham; but the brilliant Giggs was the key figure, scoring twice in the 3–2 United victory. Said Sir Alex after the match: 'Giggs has great penetration, and he can beat opponents and hold the ball up for us. I thought he did very, very well for us.' And Van Nistelrooy hailed Giggs as 'the best player in the team: he has everything. He has pace, touch, he can score goals and supply them. What more do you want in a player?'

Raising his glass to celebrate his sixtieth birthday that weekend, Sir Alex was pouring cold water on revived talk of United winning the championship. He claimed that United were still outsiders in the title race: 'We've got an uphill struggle. You can see the way the League is now and we can't afford to make mistakes. Our opponents have still got the best chance of winning the League. They recognise that, and it's why it is such a fantastic League at the moment.'

Perhaps Sir Alex will take up Scrabble when he retires. He's a champion at word games!

It was now well into January, and the United punters were starting to enjoy their prawn sandwiches again. Victories over Newcastle United, Southampton and Blackburn were upstaged by a sensational FA Cup revival against Villa. Incredibly, United now led the Premiership by two points. It was reminiscent of that old *Dick Barton, Special Agent* radio serial of many decades ago: when the scriptwriter had written the detective into such a tight corner that he couldn't think of a way of getting him clear, he solved the problem by penning the immortal words, 'With one leap he was free.'

It was just like that with Manchester United. One minute supporters were in mourning, eleven points behind the field, and the next, so it seemed, suddenly with one leap they were two points clear.

But now they faced a crucial Old Trafford confrontation with Liverpool. Victory would leave them eight points ahead of Gerard Houllier's side if they avenged the previous season's defeat by a Danny Murphy goal. Here was United's chance to deliver the *coup de grâce*. The Solskjaer–Van Nistelrooy partnership was on fire: both had scored in the fantastic 3–2 Cup victory at Villa Park after being 2–0 down deep in the second half. Certainly record-breaker Ruud was enjoying his job as never before now he had teamed up with the Norwegian wizard, and United fans were looking forward to Roy Keane's men laying waste the old enemy.

But wait. What was that sound rising from the terraces? It was the Victor Meldrew syndrome once more as 60,000 throats moaned: 'I don't believe it!'

Ferguson had pressed the self-destruct button again. Ole Gunnar was on the bench, and not only that, United were doubly weakened when Giggs was paired in a central attacking position with Van Nistelrooy; the Welsh wizard is only seventy per cent as brilliant in that position as on his regular left-wing beat.

Eighty-seven minutes after the start, Solskjaer came on for David Beckham, the England captain once again a shadow of a man who was playing so vitally for Sven-Goran Eriksson; and this time even Norway's 'magic dragon' couldn't change the pattern in three minutes. For a second time Danny Murphy proved United's nemesis, with a beautifully delicate touch over Fabien Barthez from Steven Gerrard's piercing pass.

The title race was open again and Sir Alex had become the first manager in Manchester United's history to lose five successive games against Liverpool. And just to heap on the agony, another trophy chance disappeared within days. Steve McClaren was giving double thanks to his old club for a route to the fifth round of the FA Cup after Giggs and Van Nistelrooy were left out of the starting line-up, and Laurent Blanc again blanked out to let Noel Whelan score the vital first goal with five minutes remaining.

The FA Cup might have ranked only third among United's aspirations; but you just had to look at the faces of Roy Keane and his teammates as they lined up for the restart after Andy Campbell had scored the second Boro' goal to know the pain they were feeling. They were hurting and hurting bad, and so were the supporters on the Riverside terraces.

Tough for United. A bout of flu sweeping the Carrington dressing room had obviously not helped; but probably nobody was more bemused than new South American striker Diego Forlan, who had turned down a move to the Riverside Stadium to sign for Sir Alex; within the space of five days he had watched his new teammates lose to Liverpool and then in the Cup to Middlesbrough, the team he had spurned.

It did not help the United fans when their old favourite Andy Cole shot his new club Blackburn into the fifth round of the FA Cup – and he was also to score the winning goal playing at Cardiff's Millennium Stadium in the Worthington Cup final against Spurs.

There was another potential banana skin looming at the end of January as the United caravan hit the road to the Reebok Stadium to try and atone against Sam Allardyce's Bolton braves for that humiliating 2–1 defeat at Old Trafford in September. As they went into the game former Manchester United winger Johnny Giles, one of the few men to defy the maxim that when you leave Old Trafford the only way to go is down, was saying that previous defeats, including the loss at Anfield in November, should not hold any lasting terrors; it was the quality of performance that United players should be guided by. He recalled a phrase of Sir Matt Busby's from the sixties: 'Don't worry, lads. If you keep on playing like that you'll win a lot more than you lose.'

Giles summed up: 'Defeats should not fill Alex with despair but rather give him confidence that he is on his way to eight championships in ten years.' But the former Leeds United star might have added: '...if Sir Alex has the sense to field his best team in every match from now onwards.'

At least he did that at the Reebok Stadium, restoring Ole Gunnar Solskjaer to his front-running role with Ruud van Nistelrooy, and Ryan Giggs to his rightful position as Europe's most lethal winger. Ole Gunnar scored a hat-trick in the 4–0 win, and United kept their lead at the head of the Premiership even though Arsenal, Newcastle United and Chelsea all won in midweek.

The guessing game was still in full swing about Sir Alex's successor. It seemed to be mandatory, once a week at least, for the media to come up with a new name for the job, and the unlikeliest of candidates were queuing up to say they did not want to become the guv'nor at the Theatre of Dreams.

But one man who did, a man with a track record to compare favourably with the best in the world, was Italian national coach Giovanni Trapattoni. He became the first world-class manager to step forward and say he wanted to replace Sir Alex. Despite being 63 at the end of the season, three years older than the man he wanted to replace, he said: 'I do not think it is too late for me. United are a great club, and I'd love to work with them and fight in the Premier League.' He would also love to add to the twenty trophies he had won, which included the Champions' League, three UEFA Cups, a Cup Winners' Cup, a European Super Cup and a World Club Championship.

Nevertheless, on the morning of 23 January they were still reporting in the papers that Old Trafford chiefs were closing in on Louis van Gaal and had approved his youth coach, sacked Ajax boss Co Adriaanse. The tie-up seemed logical: chief executive Kenyon had previous links with the Dutchman during his time at the sportswear giant Umbro, while Sir Alex had previously named van Gaal as one of the three coaches he respected most alongside Marcelo Lippi and Bayern's Ottmar Hitzfeld.

Meanwhile a projected deal for Paolo di Canio to come to Old Trafford in time to beat the signing deadline for Europe had fallen through because Dwight Yorke refused to sign for Middlesbrough. Ferguson, however, still had his new South American star striker, Forlan, to add to his strength, and the player was given the Number 21 shirt last worn by Henning Berg.

At this critical stage of the season, Sir Alex Ferguson gave his state-of-the-nation address: 'This is the time of year we really have to step forward. There can be no more messing about. We need performances like the Bolton result, and the genuine quality shown by Ryan Giggs, Roy Keane and Fabien Barthez as well as Solskjaer, who played the role of the quiet executioner to perfection.'

Sir Alex waxing lyrical? That was really something! He added: 'We know there is a big challenge ahead of us; but it's good for the game to have five or six teams involved in the title race. It's good for Manchester United because we need the battles, and it will be a race right to the wire.'

It was clear that there was hunger in the camp again, and Solskjaer added to his master's words: 'One game doesn't make a difference. We need to go on another seven- or eight-game run of victories to make sure we are up there in April or May.'

Meanwhile the directors were intensifying their search for Fergie's successor. His new role, it had been announced, was to act as 'ambassador' for the club. Peter Kenyon stressed, as though potential candidates needed reassuring: 'The circumstances of Sir Alex's new job will not in any way conflict with the new manager's freedom to do the job.'

England manager Sven-Goran Eriksson and Celtic's Martin O'Neill were still favourites to take over from Sir Alex despite the fact that both had repeatedly said they had contracts still to fulfil and had no intention of breaking those contracts. But an old name in a new context was thrown into the maelstrom of conjecture as February dawned. Step forward former skipper and living legend Bryan Robson, who had been called in by Sir Alex to help coach the youngsters at the club. Until the closing months he had done well in his first managerial job with Middlesbrough. Most people, however, discounted him, despite the fact that Steve McClaren was finding life at the Riverside even tougher than Robbo had done, and even though few would deny Bryan's potential to eventually become manager at Old Trafford.

The board had made it clear that one of the specifications for the new manager would be that he speak good English, which was ironic; not too many English managers speak good English. When he arrived south of the border, Alex Ferguson would barely have qualified as an English speaker, while Matt Busby – and this is a true story that I uncovered delving in the vaults of Manchester City Library – would have had no chance.

When Busby first arrived in Manchester in the late 1920s a census was taking place. The clerk asked the young Manchester City player what his job was, but his accent was so broad that when he described himself as a footballer, 'fruit boiler' was painstakingly written down. And to this day, the occupation insert in the Manchester Registry describes the great Matt Busby as a 'fruit boiler'.

The board were still agonising over his successor when Manchester United players, board and supporters got the lift they wanted: a statement from Sir Alex saying that he wanted to stay at Old Trafford. The record-breaking Scot announced that he had agreed to reverse his decision to end his career. It was 5 February, after United had scored eight goals in two games with the defeats of Bolton and Sunderland. The red half of Manchester danced in delight.

It had been a close-run thing; there was talk that the board were close to clinching a deal for Sven-Goran Eriksson to take over at Old Trafford after coming back from the World Cup, and then there would have been no way back for Sir Alex. Of course the change of plan still meant that Eriksson could complete a smooth transition as successor to Sir Alex in 2005.

I shook hands with Sir Alex that night at an FA Youth Cup tie at Old Trafford, welcoming back the man who had not left, and the smile split his face ear to ear, a rare sight for media men approaching the Master.

There was no more time to be wasted as he set about sating his still unquenchable thirst for glory on behalf of Manchester United.

The spin-off was immediate. The following day David Beckham's father said that once Sir Alex's future at Old Trafford was extended his son would be convinced to stay at Old Trafford and sign a new contract, adding: 'David's known Sir Alex since he was eleven, and at the club he's been like a father figure to him. He has been David's inspiration. He has the utmost respect for him.' Mr Beckham was quoted claiming that David had never said anything about playing abroad, and that he certainly would not play for another English club.

A measure of Sir Alex's power was that the club's share price immediately rose by three pence when he announced his U-turn, and that meant that nearly £8 million was instantly added to United's market value.

It was revealed that Ferguson's wife Cathy and sons Mark, Jason and Darren, a player with Second Division Wrexham, had been instrumental in his change of heart. Sir Alex claimed that, after 28 years in football management, 'I don't feel any different, and I don't feel as though I'm stressed,' although he admitted that he would perhaps tailor the burden in the remaining years: 'I'll reduce the workload a bit.' Which would probably mean that he would get somebody to stir his cup of tea at lunch time.

It was the inspiration for an unbeaten run in February with three Premiership wins out of three, alongside a 1–1 draw in France against Nantes and a crushing 5–1 victory in the reverse tie at Old Trafford.

A goalless draw with Bayern Munich at Old Trafford and a 3–0 defeat of Boavista on the Continent put United into a European Champions' League quarter-final tie with Deportivo la Coruña, the Spanish champions who had already beaten them twice in that season's competition and were confident of a hat-trick. Despite United's revival, there were still no certainties at Old Trafford except that the defence was uncertain.

They just could not master the art of keeping a clean sheet regularly in a tight Premiership game. Former coach Steve McClaren brought his Middlesbrough side back to Old Trafford on 23 March to score a shock 1–0 victory and a second win in two months over United. Despite a quick follow-up victory by Gary Neville and his teammates in the next game, a thrilling 4–3 win at Elland Road, Arsenal were now in the driving seat of the Premiership, on top with a game in hand.

Unable since signing for the club to convince supporters that he was worth the £28.1 million paid for him, Juan Sebastian Veron was ending the season in the treatment room nursing an Achilles tendon injury. But ultracompetitive skipper Roy Keane, as driven and ruthless as his manager, was sounding the clarion call, admitting: 'We have got our purpose back now after slackening off in all aspects after winning the Champions' League in '99. This season's big-money signings have shown our intent, and we are capable of winning the European Cup.'

As soon as the draw was made bringing United and Deportivo together in the quarter-final, you can bet Fergie was scheming his tactics both on and off the field against coach Javier Irureta.

No spin doctors needed for Sir Alex! He can spin like a top when he needs to. His pre-match warning boomed out loud and clear as he set about putting the Spaniards on the back foot. The team between United and a semi-final place had already beaten them twice in the earlier rounds, to underline that the Champions' Cup is not a knockout competition any longer, and the Old Trafford boss immediately went on the offensive: 'We're playing a lot better than the first time we met, and we had chances to win both games. We haven't failed to score in Europe this season, and I want us to be in a strong position by the end of the night.

'We've shown great consistency over the last six years by qualifying for the last eight on consecutive occasions, and we had a fantastic year in 1999. But we are capable of better.'

Then he threw his verbal grenade, claiming that Deportivo had made a big mistake in underestimating United by suggesting that they were an easier quarter-final option than Liverpool or Bayern Munich. The Deportivo coach had made nine changes for his final group game against Bayer Leverkusen, allowing United to become champions of their group, and reportedly Sir Alex was furious that Deportivo were suggesting they thought Manchester United were easy meat. He said: 'We won't worry because we think we will qualify, and I'm sure Deportivo are in for a hard game.'

How right he was. In that electric first-leg game a magnificent goal by David Beckham, and then a clincher by Ruud van Nistelrooy from a perfect cross by the outstanding Mikael Silvestre, rocked the Spanish champions and left them with a mountain to climb in the second leg at Old Trafford.

The boss had plotted the route to the last eight perfectly, but he had reckoned without the shock 2–0 win in Spain ending in disaster as he lost his inspirational captain Keano through a second-half hamstring injury. And his central midfield plans for the second leg totally disintegrated when Paul Scholes was booked to earn a suspension for the next European game.

David Beckham was also stretchered off the field near the end with an ankle injury after a clash with Diego Tristan that even had his own coach admitting: 'There was no sense in what he did. Maybe he should have got the red card instead of yellow. It is always dangerous when a player comes across with his foot up like that.'

And before the second leg, the old trooper was again giving an impression of a sixteenth-century witch heating up a cauldron on a blasted heath. Talk about 'hubble, bubble, toil and trouble!' Before you could say 'Kenny Dalglish' he had incanted another spell against the wicked English media.

'There's a witch-hunt against Juan Sebastian Veron,' roared the Grand Vizier of Old Trafford. Apparently Alex had been aware of a media campaign against the man nicknamed the 'Little Witch' ever since England and Argentina were paired together in the World Cup. He claimed: 'Seba is a marvellous player, but I think since England drew Argentina the press have turned on him. I don't know what the agenda is, but I don't like it. He's had a lot to cope with since coming from Italy into the Premiership and into a new country and culture. I think he's done well, and we're very pleased with him.'

Beckham's injury was not as bad as feared; but it was only a temporary respite. The second leg against Deportivo at Old Trafford saw United claim a relatively comfortable 3–2 win for a 5–3 aggregate in Alex's 100th European match for United; but the game created the biggest case of sporting hysteria since the days half a century ago when even the subdued and relatively sober media of the time made a meal of Denis Compton's knee.

A two-footed tackle by Aldo Duscher left a small fracture in the metatarsal bone of Beckham's left foot, and Duscher the Destroyer was overwhelmed by the publicity: 'The reaction to this has been like I killed somebody, and all I did was go for the ball, just as I always do against any opponent. I feel bad for what happened to Beckham, but my conscience is clear.'

He added: 'It was a normal accident, a fifty-fifty ball, the type of which you see a dozen times in any match. But because of everything which Beckham represents in his country, and the fact that I am an Argentine and that we are playing each other in the World Cup, many have thought terrible and different things to what actually happened. When I play, I don't worry about who my opponent is, and it's crazy to think that anything was premeditated.'

Following on these comments, Deportivo president Augusto Cesar Lendoiro described Beckham's injury as 'a hazard of the trade'.

It was only natural that it should cause a stir on the sports pages, and even that it should be deemed front-page news: it would have caused him to miss the Champions' League final had United qualified, and put a question mark next to his availability for the World Cup. In fact there are hundreds of athletes who have been in full training three weeks after such an injury. But the press were following Sir Alex's prediction of eight weeks for the healing process.

Ever the populist, Tony Blair was making a fool of himself in Parliament. He made his own prognostications on the seriousness of the Beckham incident that left one wondering about its effect on global warming, the state of the National Health Service (was Beckham going private?), and the fate of Railtrack shareholders.

Almost forgotten was the fact that Beckham's injury was just the thin end of the wedge for United. In a single week they had lost their most inspirational player, captain Roy Keane, through a hamstring injury and seen Paul Scholes put out for a period of suspension – both men infinitely more important to United as players than Beckham. And in the same second-leg game in which Beckham was injured, Ronny Johnsen limped off with a recurrence of the hamstring problem that had plagued him all his career, and now brought to a premature end what would be his final season with Manchester United. In fact the loss of Johnsen, who had given the defence much-needed stability after returning from a previous injury, was probably the most significant in terms of the immediate future.

There was, however, some happier news. Sharpshooter Ruud van Nistelrooy was giving double thanks to his colleagues and the press for being voted the Professional Footballers' Player of the Year. The Dutch striker offered his generous appreciation to his supporters, saying: 'I am so grateful to the fans of United because they gave me a great welcome when I arrived. From the very first day they lifted my game so much. I owe them a big thank you.'

And, amid all the injury problems gathering in the medical room at Carrington, there was more good cheer: Wes Brown made a successful comeback against Deportivo after a knee problem and was now looking for a late-season surge into United's Champions' League semi-final against Bayer Leverkusen, and into Sven-Goran Eriksson's World Cup squad.

England Under-21 boss David Platt was delighted to see Wes back, even though the defender missed an Under-21 game through a training incident when he went up to head a ball: 'At the end of the day he's got some big games coming up for Manchester United, which Sven will be attending. So I don't think his chances of going to the World Cup have been hindered. In fact, if everything goes well now with his fitness he will go to Japan fresher than most players.'

But the boost of good news was just too much for Sir Alex. He started rattling his cage as chairman of the England Appreciation Society, saying that he doubted if England would even reach the semi-final stage of the World Cup, and that Sven's men were not even certain to progress from their group: 'I'd have to say the England group is very difficult. Apart from Argentina they have Nigeria who aren't easy to beat, while Sweden have a great record in matches with England.'

But the brittle bones of the United players, and their even more brittle defending, were quickly in the limelight again as Klaus Toppmoller brought Bayer Leverkusen to Old Trafford for the first leg of the semi-final. He left with United supporters in mourning at the loss of Gary Neville, with an identical broken metatarsal bone in his foot to that of his pal Becks. But sadly for Neville, there was now too little time to recover before England's opening World Cup game in June.

The disastrous 2–2 final score was a triumph for the Germans. It brought a quick riposte from Sir Alex, who reminded his opponents that United had gone to Italy to defeat Juventus in 1999 and were good enough to go now to Germany and beat brave Bayer.

But there was no quick fix for United at the home of the headache pill. Despite a magnificent captain's performance by Roy Keane, who put United ahead with a fine 28th-minute goal, his teammates were incapable of matching the blazing intensity of his own performance. Keane's efforts in Turin three years before had inspired his team to their winning final, but this time Bayer rallied. Oliver Neuville's equaliser just before half-time was enough to give his team victory on away goals and see them to a final in Sir Alex's home town of Glasgow against Real Madrid.

Afterwards Ferguson said trenchantly: 'We'll be back. It's been a great European campaign, and I don't think we're short of anything. We are as good as any of them. We've played the best football in the Premiership, and scored the most goals, and we've been a whisker away from the final of the Champions' League.'

But within 24 hours more sober thoughts had surfaced. There was talk that Fabien Barthez and Juan Sebastian Veron would be sold before the start of the following season, and it was being realised on closer analysis that apart from captain Keane it was hard to find a Manchester United man who on the night had played up to form. Bobby Charlton did not sound impressed when he said: 'It shouldn't be put down to luck. A result like that hurts everybody at the club. It would be nice to put our mark on the competition like Real Madrid have.'

Although not long afterwards he was to hear of the shock news that led to his club skipper's return from Ireland's World Cup bid before a ball had been kicked in anger, he added: 'Roy Keane was fantastic. I feel sorry for him more than any other player. He is a great, great captain, and should be on the big stage.' And Sir Alex agreed: 'I wish I had ten Roy Keanes. He was marvellous, and I am so disappointed for him. He put everything into the game.'

Ferguson must have felt equally disappointed for himself. He still had not beaten Sir Matt Busby's one European Champions' Cup gold medal, and he had lost his grip on the Premiership when Arsenal clinched the English championship – and, of all places, at Old Trafford.

The season that had started with tears at the thought of Sir Alex's imminent departure ended in tears of defeat; but the man who had brought glory and a lorryload of trophies back to Old Trafford had given himself another two years to bring more success and honours to the club. The Champions' League was still the target in Sir Alex's bid to overtake Sir Matt Busby, Jock Stein and the rather less renowned Aston Villa manager Tony Barton and become part of a triumphal triumvirate, with Bob Paisley and Brian Clough, of British managers who have won two or more Champions' Cups.

It is a brave man who would choose between Matt Busby and Alex Ferguson as the true Master of Old Trafford, but if Sir Alex were finally to succeed in his dream of winning that second Champions' Cup there are a few at least who would no longer deny him the accolade of greatest ever manager of Manchester United.

Index